Tropical agriculture; the climate, soils, cultural methods, crops, live stock, commercial importance and opportunities of the tropics

Earley Vernon Wilcox

BIBLIOLIFE

TROPICAL AGRICULTURE

THE CLIMATE, SOILS, CULTURAL METHODS, CROPS, LIVE STOCK, COMMERCIAL IMPORTANCE AND OPPORTUNITIES OF THE TROPICS

BY

EARLEY VERNON WILCOX, A.M., Ph.D.

STATES RELATIONS SERVICE, U. S. DEPARTMENT OF AGRICULTURE

ILLUSTRATED

NEW YORK AND LONDON
D. APPLETON AND COMPANY
1916

TO

MY PARENTS

ABRAM FRANK WILCOX
AND
SALLY MEAD WILCOX

PREFACE

The importance of tropical agriculture in the commerce of the world is increasing daily. Sugar, coconuts, coffee, tea, cacao, bananas, fibers, rubbers, gums, spices, tans, oils, tropical woods, silk, ostrich feathers, and the hundreds of other tropical products hold a large place in international trade. The United States imports tropical products to the value of more than $600,000,000 annually, $350,000,000 in sugar, coffee, and silk. Year by year new tropical products, previously unknown to most of us, are added to the list of the world's economic products. Year by year more tropical products pass from the class of luxuries to the necessities.

The English, French, Dutch, Belgians, and Italians are putting forth earnest efforts in the development of their tropical colonies, and the Latin Americans in the development of their own countries. Their great activity in scientific research and in the study of labor, transportation, marketing, and general economic conditions is sufficient evidence of their keen interest in the future of the Tropics. Experiment stations and departments of agriculture are being established everywhere. Studies of the technical utilization of tropical products are under way. Commercial possibilities are receiving expert attention.

We, as a nation, have reason to be more interested in these matters. The "splendid isolation" of our forefathers is a thing of the past. We are a part of the world. Tropical products are brought to every household. The humblest table bears food products from Brazil, Cuba, India, Java, Molucca Islands, Tahiti, Mauritius, Gold Coast, Jamaica, Hawaii, Porto Rico, and other parts of the Tropics. We are

vii

the largest users of tropical products among the nations of the earth.

The Philippines, American Samoa, Guam, Hawaii, the Canal Zone, and Porto Rico belong to the United States. The Philippines with their abaca, copra, tobacco, and kapok; Hawaii with its sugar, pineapples, coffee, and sisal; and Porto Rico with its sugar, coffee, tobacco, citrus fruit, and pineapples are important elements in the tropical world.

Much greater development, especially in the line of diversification of industries, is possible in all our tropical possessions. Our business men are doing their part. They are in the vanguard of tropical progress with their technical investigations and their studies of commercial conditions in the Tropics. But there is a lack of information on tropical agriculture among the general public. In fact, a woeful ignorance prevails as to the essential nature and features of tropical problems. I have been asked by otherwise intelligent persons if Spanish is the prevailing language in Honolulu, if pineapples grow on trees, and other equally significant questions. How can the serious business of properly developing our own part of the Tropics be accomplished without the intelligent interest of the general public?

The literature of tropical agriculture would in itself make a library of respectable size. In the appendix to this volume I have given some hints as to the extent of this literature. The chief contributors to this field of knowledge are English, French, Dutch, Italians, Belgians, Germans, and Latin Americans. Tropical agriculture has received only scant attention from our writers. A few journals devoted to tea, coffee, spice, fibers, and oils, occasional bulletins from the U. S. Department of Agriculture, publications of the Hawaii, Porto Rico, and Guam Experiment Stations, and of the Philippine Bureau of Agriculture, a volume on the banana trade and bulletins from the Florida and California experiment stations, constitute the most of our contribution to the literature of tropical agriculture. We have produced many handbooks and cyclopedias of horticulture, agriculture and live stock, but these books treat of tropical agriculture, if at all, only so far as developments in Florida and California are concerned. No American writer has heretofore presented a general account of tropical agriculture.

The present volume is written from the standpoint of the general reader, business man and agricultural student. I have attempted to present in a brief form what everybody ought to know about the Tropics. Such details regarding the cultivation of crops as are of interest only to the actual planter in the Tropics have been omitted. Particular attention has been given to the nature, source, and commercial importance of tropical products. Not all economic plants of the Tropics have been included, for thousands of these plants are known and of interest only in a restricted locality. The volume contains an account of about 350 tropical products of peculiar interest and commercial importance. I have also attempted to present an intelligible picture of animal industry in the Tropics as well as of climate, soils, and economic conditions.

This is a book on tropical agriculture in the commercial sense, the production of things to eat, wear, and use in technical industries. Without extending its limits too greatly no room was found for a discussion of the tropical diseases of live stock or of insect pests and fungous diseases. With some regret, too, I have found it necessary to omit the subject of ornamentals—the endless list of vines, shrubs, and trees which paint the tropical landscape with their brilliant flowers.

The literature of tropical agriculture abounds in exaggerations. One reads of yields of two pounds of coir fiber per coconut, of 240,000 pounds of bananas per acre, along with similar astonishing statements. If a New York farmer should read that yields of 1,800 bushels of potatoes per acre had been obtained in Oklahoma he would question the statement at once even if he had never been in Oklahoma. But if the same farmer should read that 6,000 avocados were borne on a single tree, or that a vanilla plantation yielded 15 tons of vanilla beans per acre, he might be bowled over by the news, but he would probably have no basis in experience or knowledge for denying the statement. I have tried to present the important facts of tropical agriculture without the glamor of romance, but I hope the account will be none the less interesting to the general reader.

No one who has long lived in the Tropics can ever forget, and few can resist, the call to return where snows and the other discomforts of northern winters are mere memories of less favored climates. The multitude of curious fruits, the brilliant butterflies, the gorgeous birds, the flowering trees, the endless summer, the coral islands, the jungles, the strange peoples and their still stranger customs—all these are woven into the life and literature of the Tropics. In fact, we can almost forgive the early writers on the Tropics for their exaggerations. But sufficient romance still lingers about the picture of the Tropics even when viewed in the full light of day.

The personal contact of the writer with the subject matter of this volume was gained during a residence of more than six years in Hawaii in charge of the Hawaii Agricultural Experiment Station and by visits to California, Florida, and Cuba. Hawaii is sometimes called the crossroads of the Pacific. Every ship that calls at Honolulu carries one or more agricultural experts. They come from Formosa, the Philippines, Java, Malaya, Ceylon, India, Fiji, Australia, Mauritius, Egypt, the Congo, the West Indias, Mexico, and elsewhere. Opportunity was thus had to discuss the progress of agriculture with men from all parts of the tropical world.

The purpose of this book is to stimulate an interest in

tropical agriculture. We, as a nation, need to know more of the Tropics, of the opportunities they offer and of their great commercial importance. We need to know more of the stupendous racial and economic problems involved in the further development of tropical agriculture. We need especially to know more of our Latin American neighbors. If this book serves to some degree in focusing the earnest attention of the American reader upon the wonderful possibilities of the Tropics, it will have fulfilled its purpose.

During the preparation of the volume I received many helpful suggestions from Dr. E. W. Allen, Dr. W. H. Evans, and Mr. E. J. Glasson, all of the Office of Experiment Stations. The proofs were read by Mrs. Mabel R. Wilcox. In the selection of illustrations most courteous assistance was received from Mr. David Fairchild, in charge of Foreign Seed and Plant Introduction, U. S. Department of Agriculture, who has perhaps done more than any other man in the United States in stimulating a general interest in tropical agricultural products.

E. V. WILCOX.

WASHINGTON, D. C.

CONTENTS

LIST OF ILLUSTRATIONS

xvii

LIST OF ILLUSTRATIONS

TROPICAL AGRICULTURE

CHAPTER I

TROPICAL CLIMATE AND ITS EFFECTS ON MAN, FARM ANIMALS AND CROPS

INFORMAL observations concerning the weather often serve as a prelude or introduction to discussions of serious moment concerning affairs of religion, science, or business. It is perhaps well to begin the present volume with a brief account of tropical climate. Questions concerning the nature and effects of the tropical climate are among the first which are asked by those who are planning to visit the Tropics for the first time. Among persons who have never lived in tropical countries, a vast deal of incorrect notions exists as to the nature of the climate in these countries. A part of the misconception regarding weather conditions in the Tropics is perhaps due to the unfortunate use of the term "temperate climates" for the intermediate zones north and south of the Equator. If one has regard to the real meaning of the word temperate, this word should be applied to tropical climates rather than to the climates commonly called temperate, for it is in the temperate zones that the greatest extremes of weather conditions, particularly temperature, occur. In the temperate zones, for example, are recorded temperatures ranging from 40° or 50° below zero to 110° or 120° F. This would give a total annual range of temperature of 150° to 170°. In the Tropics, on the other hand, the temperature seldom rises above 90° and rarely sinks below 75° at sea level. This is truly a temperate climate since it is devoid of both extremes and shows a range of only 15° of temperature.

As is well known, the Tropics are included within a zone about the center of the earth extending 23½° north and south of the Equator. The northern and southern boundaries of the Tropics coincide nearly with the isotherm 68° F. for the coldest month of the year. If, therefore, the Tropics are defined not as a geographical zone 47° wide, but as the area bounded by the isotherm just mentioned, it will be found that this area is only about 30° wide at the west coast of Africa and of America instead of the normal 47°. As is already indicated, it is in the subtropics or so-called temperate climates that the highest temperatures and greatest range of temperature are recorded. For example, temperatures of 110° to 120° F. during the summer months are not of rare occurrence in certain parts of the mainland of the United States. In Jacobabad, India, a temperature of 127° F. has been recorded. This locality is outside of the tropical zone. Moreover, the high temperatures which occur in summer in mainland cities like Washington, Cincinnati, St. Louis, and Chicago, are frequently accompanied with a high relative humidity making the weather combination as a whole much more trying and difficult to endure than the times of highest temperature in strictly tropical climates. Temperatures in the Tropics are affected by elevation in the same manner as in temperate climates. Everywhere the mean temperature falls about 4° for every 1,000 feet of elevation. At the Equator the elevation at which frost occurs is about 18,000 feet. On the Island of Hawaii at an altitude of 20° north the frost elevation is about 4,500 feet. An idea of the range of temperature in certain well known tropical cities may be gathered from the following data: In Cairo, Egypt, the mean winter temperature is 56° and the mean summer temperature 83° F. Bogota, Colombia, lies at considerable elevation and possesses the advantage of perhaps the most remarkably uniform temperature of any city in the world. Its average daily temperature is 60° F. the year round. In Colombo a rather uniform temperature alternation occurs, giving a daily range of only about 11°. At this city the night temperature is about 75° and the day temperature about 86°. In Honolulu, the lowest temperature recorded in 30 years is 52° and the highest 89° F., giving a total range of 37° F.

With the very slight range of temperature in tropical countries, it is obvious that no sudden changes of temperature can possibly occur. There is, therefore, ordinarily no occasion for any changes in the nature or weight of clothing from one season to another. So far as the extremes of temperature and the range of temperature and consequent necessary adjustments of the body are concerned, the Tropics possess a decided advantage over all temperate and less favored climates.

The crops which are characteristic of the Tropics extend for considerable distances outside of the strict boundaries of the tropical zone. It is necessary, therefore, in a discussion of tropical agriculture to include subtropical countries in order not to be forced to draw too arbitrary boundaries. In the matter of tropical climate an important factor in further softening and ameliorating the tropical heat is found in the trade winds. These winds rise about 30° north and south of the Equator and blow toward the Equator with a slight westerly deflection as far as the doldrum belt. North of the Equator, therefore, the trade wind is a northeast wind, while south of the Equator it is a southeast wind. The "trades" are universally gentle winds and in most of the countries within the trade-wind belt, especially in islands, the trade winds blow practically continuously night and day for from 250 to 280 days of the year. These gentle winds are dry and cooling. When the velocity of the trade wind is relatively high the evaporation caused by the "trades" is very great. They therefore not only serve to cool the body, but also to lower the temperature of plants by transpiration.

At irregular intervals the trade winds are interrupted by winds variously known as reverse trades, monsoons, kona winds, etc. The southeast trades become southwest monsoons in southern India about the middle of June when the rainy season begins. This change from southeast to southwest wind occurs every year on almost the same day of the year so that it is possible to know in advance almost the precise day on which the rainy season will begin. In Hawaii the regular trade-wind season extends ordinarily from April to October. During this time there is, for the most part, little interruption of the trade wind. During the winter season and less frequently during the summer the trade wind may be interrupted by periods of from one to seven or more days, during which there is either no definite wind or more frequently a southerly or southwesterly wind. This is known in Hawaii as the kona wind and invariably is accompanied by a period of high relative humidity and consequent discomfort. The natives in Hawaii call the kona wind the sick wind on account of the lassitude and depression which are felt while it prevails. It seems curious that on a group of islands like Hawaii from which the nearest land is distant more than 2,000 miles, a wind from one direction should be dry, while from another direction it is decidedly moist.

The occurrence of thunderstorms is a matter which varies greatly in different parts of the Tropics and this variation is thus far without any very satisfactory explanation. For example, in Cuba rather furious thunderstorms occur during the summer season, whereas in Hawaii a thunderstorm is a rare event and occurs only during a period of kona wind and never during the prevalence of trade winds.

While the Tropics are temperate in the matter of temperature, they show enormous variation in rainfall in different countries and in different localities in these countries. The range of variation in the matter of rainfall runs from a condition of almost absolute desert to an average rainfall of 450 inches per year. Some notion of the range of rainfall in well known localities of the Tropics and subtropics may be gained from the following data: The average annual rainfall for

Singapore is 94 inches, for Bangkok 67 inches, for Formosa 43 inches, for Manila 75 inches, for Vera Cruz 68 inches, for Habana 52 inches, for Honolulu 28 inches, for Burma 99 inches, and for Bengal 188 inches. The Kamerun district has a rainfall of about 350 inches a year. Cherrapongee in Assam has an average annual rainfall of 458 inches and in one year the annual precipitation reached the enormous total of 905 inches.

Within the trade-wind belt on small islands like those which constitute the Hawaiian group, the climate of the lee and windward side of the islands is decidedly different. The windward side receives a much heavier precipitation and is, on the whole, cooler than the lee side. The variation in rainfall on these small islands is a strictly local matter and the most astonishing differences in vegetation in localities separated only a few miles occur as the result of this extreme variation in rainfall. For example, at one of the substations of the U. S. Experiment Station on the Island of Hawaii, a rainfall of 360 inches was recorded for one year, while at a point 28 miles away the annual rainfall for the same year was 6 inches. It is possible, therefore, in the space of an hour's ride to pass from a desert covered with cacti and other drought-resistant plants into a dense tropical jungle reeking with moisture.

In all tropical countries the clearing of forests makes the climate decidedly drier and warmer. The effects of the removal of forests in tropical countries are in various ways far more conspicuous than in northern climates. Stock grazing in forests on account of the destruction of undergrowth and young trees may change a given tract of country from a wet jungle to an almost desert condition. This change may be followed by more disastrous wind erosion than is perhaps ever witnessed in northern climates. The islands of Kahoolawe and Lanai, particularly the former, perhaps illustrate the fearful effects of wind erosion to the best advantage. These islands were formerly well covered with native forest growth,

With the extension of stock grazing, the forest trees were destroyed, especially on the upper elevations, and the forest destruction was soon followed by the loss of moisture from the soil due to the increased evaporation under the exposure to the constant trade winds. The soils of these islands are fine clay in mechanical texture and are readily carried away as dust in the wind. During a period of moderately strong trade winds a continuous dust cloud from the Island of Kahoolawe is visible for 50 to 75 miles. Parts of the island have been eroded by the wind to a depth of over 200 feet since the destruction of the forest growth on the higher elevations. Similar results from wind erosion are to be seen on Lanai, but the damage has not progressed so far as on Kahoolawe. On Lanai there are regions where the soil has been carried away to a depth of 50 feet, in some cases leaving columns with a small shrub or a bit of grass or native plants which escaped destruction and have remained in their original position, thus holding the soil in place and checking the action of the wind while all of the adjacent soil is blown away. A few of these isolated columns of soil standing at a height of 30 to 50 feet give an extremely bizarre aspect to the landscape.

While the old contention as to the effect of forests upon the rainfall of a given locality has been unfortunately obscured and unnecessarily complicated by exaggerations on both sides of the argument, it is certain that the presence of a forest covering on the tops of the mountains of islands lying within the trade-wind belt actually increases the rainfall and is of great benefit in regulating the distribution and conservation of the water of these islands. It should be remembered that rain storms on islands in the trade-wind belt are of a decidedly different nature from those which occur on continental areas, particularly in northern climates. As a rule, precipitation during the prevalence of the trade wind occurs not as a result of the formation of a definite storm area, but as a result of a cooling and compression of air due to its impinging upon the mountains of small islands and being forced to rise in order to pass over the mountains. The water is thus in a sense squeezed out of the atmosphere in passing over the high points of islands lying in the trade winds. It may thus often occur that during the prevalence of clear weather on the windward side of an island, an almost constant precipitation of rain occurs high up on the mountain side and this rain is frequently blown over upon the lee shoulder of the mountains, sometimes reaching almost to the sea on the lee side of the island. Such rains are brought about merely by the presence of the mountains and occur in an area in which no storm conditions in the ordinary sense exist. The higher the mountain the heavier the rainfall caused by its presence. In the case of mountains of no more than 4,000 or 5,000 feet elevation, the presence of a forest growth upon the upper ridges exercises a great influence in increasing precipitation. A part of the explanation of this fact is to be found in the radiation of heat from forests and the consequent cooling of the trees and increase of precipitation as a result.

At any time of the day or night, therefore, at least during the prevalence of the trade-wind season, the atmosphere may be robbed of a portion of its moisture by coming in contact with the mountains and being forced to rise to a height of 5,000 feet or more before passing on in the general course of the trade wind. This peculiar cause of rain storms brings about the frequent occurrence of light showers in a perfectly clear sky, the rain being precipitated from the atmosphere at the tops of the mountains and being blown down over the lee side of the island by the trade winds. This condition is often referred to by the natives as liquid sunshine and gives rise to the almost daily occurrence of brilliant rainbows and the frequent occurrence of lunar rainbows.

The effect of tropical climate upon plants is manifested in various ways. Some plants which are annuals in cold climates become perennials in the Tropics. Similarly, some plants which remain strictly herbs in cold climates become shrubs or small trees in the Tropics. The Lantana, which is cultivated as a more or less delicate greenhouse plant in cold climates, becomes a shrub varying in height from 4 to 15 feet and shows an aggressiveness which makes it one of the very worst of the weed pests. Cotton, which is cultivated strictly as an annual in the cotton belt of the mainland, grows as a perennial in the Tropics and will live and bear for 25 to 40 years, although the best yields are obtained by cutting it back after each crop and treating it practically as an annual. The pigeon pea, which is a useful leguminous cover crop will, if left to itself, become practically a small tree attaining a diameter of eight inches or more. The formation of annual rings in trees is, as is well known, due to the difference in rapidity of growth during the height of the growing season and the fall season just before growth ceases. Since no such seasons prevail in the Tropics there are no definite annual rings in forest trees.

Most trees in the Tropics are evergreen, shedding their leaves the year round a few at a time. A few trees, however, shed their leaves all at one time. The Ceara rubber tree and kapok are conspicuous examples of this sort. Notwithstanding the absence of temperature seasons in the Tropics, plants nevertheless have seasons of growth and periods of rest. There are, therefore, best times to plant in the Tropics as in cold climates. The reason for recommending particular seasons for planting is usually based on the prospects of rainfall and relatively cool weather. A number of plants thrive best in their early stages if planted at the beginning of the winter season. This is perhaps nearly always true for Irish potatoes and corn, which in Hawaii, at any rate, make a much better growth if planted in November or December than if planted in April. Even this recommendation, however, must be limited strictly to sea level, for at high elevations, particularly above 4,000 feet, the best season for planting these crops is in March or April. Many tropical plants, as is well known, bear the year round without any evidence of a particular season of activity. Bananas and papayas are conspicuous examples of this kind. From a plantation of either bananas or papayas fruit can be picked during any month of the year. In fact, with papayas there are ripe fruit on the tree every day the year round. Mangoes and avocados show a tendency to flower and produce their fruit within a relatively restricted season. By the use of early varieties, however, it is possible to extend the season of these fruits over a period of six months or more.

Most tropical plants can be acclimated in subtropical countries. In southern Florida, for example, nearly all of the well known tropical plants, with the exception of breadfruit, cacao, and rubber can be grown with more or less success. Some, however, cannot be acclimated even in the subtropics. This is conspicuously true of such plants as cacao, which will thrive only in the true Tropics near sea level, protected from the wind, and favored with an abundance of rainfall. Conversely, many plants from northern climates cannot be successfully acclimated in the Tropics. This is true to some extent of a large percentage of the well known trees of temperate climates. The oak, for example, does not appear to be able to adjust itself to tropical conditions. It remains ever green, shedding a few leaves occasionally, but showing an extremely poor growth. There are specimens in Hawaii 20 to 25 years old not higher than four or five feet. Apples and peaches behave in a peculiar manner in the Tropics. These fruits are not well adapted to tropical conditions and do not yield satisfactory results except at higher altitudes. Near sea level the peach tree may be seen at almost any time of the year with buds, flowers, young peaches of all sizes, and ripe peaches at the same time. There seems to be no tendency to establish a definite period of fruiting under tropical conditions. Similarly with apples, one branch or one side of the tree may bear at one season and another branch at another season, and a given branch may show flowers and green and ripe apples at the same time.

The effect of temperature, so far at least as it is felt by plants and animals, seems to be a relative matter. Plants suffer in the Tropics at times from the low temperatures which prevail, although these temperatures may not be below 65° F. The effect of temperature upon plants appears to be almost entirely a matter of adaptation on the part of the plants. On the high plateaus in the Rocky Mountains of the mainland one may see certain spring flowers which have actually forced their way through an inch or more of ice to bloom above the surface of the ice and snow. These plants are frozen as stiff as icicles every night and yet are not affected by such temperature conditions. In tropical conditions, on the other hand, a temperature of 65° F. at night, especially if accompanied with a rather high wind, may injuriously check the growth of many plants and may even turn the leaves of cotton brown as if from the effects of frost. Similarly with man and animals, the lowest temperatures which occur in the Tropics seem to be felt as cold, and a certain amount of discomfort is experienced by both man and animals when the temperature descends as low as 65° F.

In tropical countries nearly all animals can find food for themselves the year round, and if they escape from domestication on farms they may run wild. We have therefore in nearly all tropical countries wild cattle, horses, asses, sheep, goats, chickens, turkeys, pea fowl, dogs, cats, etc. In some of the rough mountain districts of Hawaii wild goats which are descended from goats escaped from domestication on the farms have become a veritable scourge requiring organized expeditions of hunters for their destruction. Similarly, pigs, cattle, and sheep after escaping from restraint have multiplied rapidly and occupied the rougher mountain regions, destroying much of the grazing which is required for the more improved strains of domestic animals. The common breeds of poultry, after escaping from domestication and breeding for two or three generations in the mountains, develop powers of flight equal to those of the pheasant, and while retaining the color of the domestic strain, gain somewhat in elegance and trimness of form. On the Island of Lanai, turkeys may be found in all stages of domestication and wildness, ranging from those which may be approached and petted near a ranch house to those which fly on the approach of man as vigorously as do the wild turkeys of the Appalachian Mountains.

In general, domestic animals in the Tropics reach a smaller size and produce less milk than in northern climates. This statement, of course, refers only to the improved breeds of domestic animals developed in northern climates and shipped into tropical countries. It is impossible, for example, to bring Hereford or Shorthorn steers in tropical countries up to the standard weight for northern climates. Similarly, with the best strains of Holstein, Jersey, Guernsey, or other dairy cows, it is impossible to secure a heavy milk yield even with the best and most expensive rations. It is a rather rare accomplishment for Jersey or even Holstein cows in the Tropics to produce 5,000 pounds of milk in a year, and the average yield is far below that, probably not more than 2,500 pounds. The tendency to produce less milk and to reach maturity at a smaller size than in the northern climate may be considered as the result of an unexplained influence of the tropical climate.

The weather problem, however, which is uppermost in the mind of the tourist and intending settler in the Tropics, is concerned with the effect of tropical climate upon man and with especial precautions which he may need to take in order to live comfortably and in health. In former days travelers were wont to regale us with tales of the frightful ravages of the tropical diseases. Many of these diseases were, and still are, in some localities of serious consequence. So much attention was, and still is, paid to them that the reading public became quite thoroughly familiar with the general aspects of the problem of tropical hygiene. As a result of the great amount of medical and popular attention which has been given to these diseases, the average reader who has not been in the Tropics probably has the fixed notion that the chief dangers likely to be met in the Tropics are the specific tropical and Oriental diseases, such as typhus fever, yellow fever, amebic dysentery, Asiatic cholera, plague, leprosy, etc. This, however, would be a highly erroneous conception regarding many districts and cities of tropical countries. On account of the universal fear of tropical diseases felt by the white settlers of tropical countries, an unusual effort has been put forth in nearly all parts of the Tropics to bring about sanitary conditions with reference primarily to the specific diseases which inspire an almost universal terror of the Tropics.

The results of this unusual medical and sanitary campaign have been surprisingly effective, producing, in the case of several tropical cities, sanitary conditions superior to those of northern cities. All the world knows how Habana and Panama were freed from yellow fever. The city of Habana now has a lower death rate than has any city on the mainland of the United States. Likewise in Honolulu, there is no reason for fearing tropical diseases. The most serious diseases in Honolulu are precisely the same as those which prevail throughout the United States, namely, pneumonia, tuberculosis, and typhoid fever. Cases of leprosy, plague, and Asiatic cholera are of such rare occurrence as to be negligible in reaching a conclusion as to whether or not to visit Honolulu. The clean-up campaigns which have been carried on in many tropical cities have reduced the fly and mosquito nuisances to a minimum. In so far as mosquitoes, flies, cockroaches, rats, and the other annoying and disgusting pests of cities are concerned, Habana, for example, is superior to any city of the United States. An incidental result of the application of sanitary methods for the control of tropical diseases is also seen in lowering the number of cases of other diseases.

In tropical countries, the nights are almost universally cool and comfortable. The range of temperature, as already stated, is never great, the total annual range rarely being greater than 30°. Moreover, there are no extremes of temperature to be endured. It is possible in all tropical countries to live practically out-of-doors, at least with doors and windows constantly open. The question of fresh air and ventilation is, therefore, solved automatically. The same weight of clothes can be worn the year round, thus avoiding the necessity for the bodily adjustments rendered inevitable by the rigors of the northern climates.

Notwithstanding the fact that many of the tropical cities have been rendered even more sanitary from the viewpoint of specific diseases than are northern cities, and notwithstanding the fact that tropical cities possess almost none of the ordinary discomforts of climatic conditions and changes, it still remains doubtful whether the Tropics are well adapted for the permanent residence of the white man. It has not been adequately explained, and perhaps may never be fully explained, why the delightfully uniform and comfortable climate of the Tropics lowers the vitality and vigor of a considerable percentage of the white men who go to live in the Tropics. While it may not be possible to explain this, it is nevertheless a fact. Some persons are affected by a general lassitude and depression within a few days after landing in a tropical city, others are not affected at all, or only after a long residence without any trips in the meantime to colder climates. There is no way of predicting who will be injuriously affected and who not by going to the Tropics. The depressing influence of climate may be shown most strongly in a vigorous, healthy individual and may not be manifested at all in invalids or weakly persons who go to the Tropics for a visit or for permanent residence.

It is a common and apparently well founded belief that most white races of the Tropics should pay a visit to some cold climate at intervals not greater than once in three years. In most instances, women probably feel the depressing influ-ence of tropical climates more keenly than men. This fact also is still without any satisfactory explanation.

One may venture the suggestion that a part explanation of the lowering of vitality experienced by white persons after a long residence in the Tropics is found in lack of exercise. One feels so completely comfortable at all times in tropical cli-mates that there appears to be no immediate necessity for exercise or exertion. It may not occur to the ordinary indi-vidual for some time that he is taking less exercise than was his custom in colder climates. It is, however, a matter of common observation that no one can remain well in tropical countries without regular exercise or physical work. The assertion may therefore reasonably be ventured that the one universal enemy of the white man in the Tropics is not tropi-cal disease, but plain laziness.

This laziness is of such an insidious nature that one readily yields to the tradition quite apparent in tropical countries that it is actually dangerous for the white man to work. This con-clusion is the more readily accepted when one realizes that practically all of his fellows have accepted the same conclu-sion and have become surrounded with the swarm of Oriental servants so ready to perform every service involving manual labor. In Cuba, Porto Rico, and Hawaii, on the other hand, there are colonies of white farmers working in the fields at heavy physical labor in the manner to which they were accus-tomed in northern regions and remaining in the most vigorous health during their whole life time. In view of the accumu-lated experience of white farmers and business men through-out the tropical countries of the world, one would seem to be justified in coming to the conclusion that the necessity for physical exercise is not removed by settling in the Tropics.

In connection with the general sanitary conditions of the Tropics, many questions arise in the minds of visitors as to the healthfulness and nutritive value of tropical foods. On this point it is not necessary to dwell at any length. In all tropical countries, all tropical foods are safe, except vegetables to be eaten raw, and surface water. Lettuce, celery, radishes, strawberries, etc., irrigated by Chinese methods, are not safe foods, particularly in case of an outbreak of Asiatic cholera, and, moreover, are not appetizing under any circumstances, if one knows by first hand observation something of the methods of Oriental irrigation. Surface water can nowhere be recommended for use without boiling. This is equally true for northern climates. In the Tropics, however, there are added dangers from the prevalence of minute worms as well as the possibility of typhoid and cholera infection.

The main point in keeping well in the Tropics is to remember that a reasonable amount of physical exercise is absolutely necessary, notwithstanding the fact that the general comfortable feeling may easily persuade one to think that exercise may be omitted from the daily routine. It is perhaps well for everyone to continue the same form of exercise to which he was accustomed in the colder climates. Some exercise hobby, however, seems to be strictly required, and the Tropics offer the same list of recreations as colder climates, namely, tennis, golf, baseball, football, horseback riding, rowing, mountain climbing, and hunting.

CHAPTER II

TROPICAL SOILS

MANY chemical changes are hastened by the application of heat. This is illustrated by the rapidity with which chemical changes take place in soils under the influence of constant warm weather. Rocks and soils decompose with remarkable rapidity in the Tropics. Even fresh lava flows in a district of abundant rainfall may become sufficiently disintegrated in five to ten years to furnish suitable conditions of growth for a considerable variety of plants. In fact, volcanic cinder, if blown out in a state of sufficiently fine fragmentation, is immediately available as a soil. The only element of plant food in which such material is deficient is nitrogen. In regions of modern volcanic flows and eruptions, there are, therefore, many soils of very recent origin. These soils differ greatly in physical and chemical composition from the familiar soils of temperate climates. The basaltic lava from volcanoes may be disintegrated in place to form soils containing a mixture of mineral elements in essentially the same proportion in which they occurred in the original basalt. These soils have not been altered like the old alluvial soils by ages of secondary chemical changes and by the slow process of segregation of certain mineral forms so characteristic of secondary rocks and their resulting soils.

Notwithstanding the recent origin of many tropical soils, particularly in volcanic regions, it is obviously impossible for these soils long to retain the composition of the original basaltic lava. Extensive leaching takes place under the influence of heavy tropical rainfall.' This leaching affects not only the original constituents of the disintegrated lava, but also the fertilizer materials which are applied to such soils. Lime and nitrate of soda are readily leached out of volcanic soils, while ammonium sulphate and phosphates are fixed in the soils to a rather surprising extent. The humus content of tropical soils is ordinarily high. This is due to the great mass of vegetation produced under tropical conditions. If, however, there are long intervals between the rainy seasons, the humus in soils is rapidly decomposed under the influence of heat and aëration.

Practically all tropical soils contain a relatively high percentage of iron. In Hawaii, the iron content of soils is 10 to 45 per cent. (usually about 20 per cent.); in Samoa, 15 to 20 per cent.; in Kamerun, 7 to 14 per cent.; in Madagascar, about 10 per cent.; and in India, 2 to 48 per cent. This iron commonly exists in the condition of three oxids, the ferrous, ferric, and magnetic. Fortunately for the farmer the ferrous iron is usually very insoluble except when the soil becomes puddled so that suitable aëration can not take place. Granules of magnetic iron oxid are of much more frequent occurrence in volcanic soils than in the old soils of temperate climates. In Hawaii, for example, magnetic iron is present to an appreciable extent in all soils, as may be seen by passing a magnet over a sample of pulverized dry soil. These magnetic iron granules are black, but soon assume the red color of ferric oxid as the result of further oxidation. In certain localities there are immense quantities of volcanic cinder or black sand which have resulted from volcanic explosions. Several crops make a satisfactory growth upon pure deposits of this volcanic cinder. In some localities in Hawaii the cinder contains a much higher content of potash than the ordinary lava resulting from a flow. While the lava obtained from ordinary flows contains slightly less than one per cent. of potash the cinder may show from two to five per cent. of potash. This potash is, however, not immediately available, but becomes soluble slowly through the gradual disintegration of the cinder. The volcanic cinder is quite commonly used in lawns and gardens for mixing with the heavy soils to improve the aëration and the drainage.

The so-called clay soils of certain tropical countries are often clay only in mechanical analysis, not in composition. These clays are not aluminium silicate but are high in their content of iron and aluminium hydrates and low in silicates. These soils are commonly referred to as laterite soils. The term is not easily defined, but is usually taken to mean heavy tropical soils formed from decomposing lava under the influence of heat, tropical downpours, and periods of drought.

Laterite soils are not only extremely heavy, but pack and puddle badly. The texture is injured by any manipulation while the soil is too moist. Even when allowed to stand after a year or two without cultivation the soils become so badly packed as to become almost impervious to air and water. During periods of drought wide, deep cracks form in such soils and the cracks are quickly filled again by the swelling process which occurs with the return of the rainy season. As already stated, however, these soils are not true clay and cannot be used for the formation of brick. If bricks are made from laterite soils they will readily disintegrate under the influence of weather conditions. The huge lumps which are turned up in plowing laterite soils gradually slack like lumps of lime under the influence of moisture and sunshine.

Mention may well be made of a few peculiar soils which occur in Hawaii and elsewhere in the Tropics. The most highly manganiferous soils thus far studied occur in Hawaii. In the mainland soils of the United States manganese may be found as a mere trace and usually not to an appreciable extent. In Hawaii, however, nearly all soils contain from one-quarter to one-half per cent. of manganese and in certain restricted areas the content of manganese rises to 10 per cent. Soils which contain three per cent. of manganese or more are floury, of a chocolate color, and will not pack like the ordinary laterite soils, but remain always in a fine state of tilth. Not all crops, however, will grow satisfactorily on highly manganiferous soils. Pineapples, for example, cannot be made to yield satisfactory returns on soils containing more than 2½ or 3 per cent. of manganese. The presence of large quantities of manganese in the soil has the peculiar effect of disturbing the mineral balance, forcing the pineapple to absorb lime out of all proportion with magnesium. The result of this unbalanced soil solution is that the pineapple leaves lose their green color, becoming yellowish and finally dying, while the fruit turns pink at an immature stage and always remains much more acid than normal fruits.

In a few localities, soils of a very high titanium content occur, the titanium sometimes amounting to 35 per cent. This element, however, has no apparent effect upon the growth of plants. In one restricted locality in Hawaii pineapples thrive well on a soil of which iron and titanium alone constitute 85 per cent. Soils with a high titanium content have a bluish or black color, especially when slightly moist, and will stain the hands almost as effectively as a paint pigment.

Near the seashore of all tropical islands surrounded with coral reefs occur areas of soil constituted largely of coral sand. The chief constituent of this sand is carbonate of lime. Coral sand mixed with a small percentage of soil washed down from upper levels and containing minute quantities of humus is quite satisfactory for the growth of watermelons, sweet potatoes, coconuts, and a number of other crops. The coral sand is also extensively used for the purpose of liming soils.

One of the peculiarities of the laterite soils of the Tropics is their high hygroscopic moisture content. Many of the deep, rich soils of the Western States have a hygroscopic moisture content of about 12 or 13 per cent. The laterite soils of the Tropics, however, may contain 24 per cent. of moisture in an air-dry condition. It is quite plain, therefore, that these tropical soils require a much higher total moisture content for the satisfactory growth of crops than is the case with the common soils of temperate climates.

It is a peculiar fact that on tropical islands in the trade-wind belt drainage is a difficult matter on the lee side, while little or no attention need be given to drainage on the windward side of the island. The heavy laterite soils on the lee side of the Hawaiian Islands require extremely deep plowing, the addition of green manures, and sometimes the use of dynamite and other treatment in order to provide suitable drainage for moisture movement and for the process of aëration. On the windward side of the same island, however, under a much greater rainfall there are commonly few running streams and apparently almost no superficial runoff of water. In some farming sections of the windward side of the island of Hawaii, water for household use must be obtained from rain water caught from the roofs of buildings, although the rainfall for months at a time may average an inch a day. This water passes through the soil and on into the porous lava rocks underneath, furnishing no running streams or standing water.

The use of dynamite in improving the drainage conditions and tilth of soil has been adopted in a number of tropical countries. The object in using dynamite in the Tropics is not always precisely the same as that which prevails in cold climates where a distinct subsoil or hardpan may underlie the arable soil. In the laterite soils of the Tropics there is little or no distinction between soil and subsoil, the only apparent change being one of color in passing from the top layer to a depth of four or five feet. Since, however, these soils pack very firmly during the long intervals between plowing, it is obvious that some method of providing better subdrainage is necessary. This perhaps has been accomplished in many instances by the use of dynamite. The best results have been obtained by exploding sticks of low-grade dynamite at a depth of 3½ to 4 feet and at distances of 10 to 20 feet apart both ways. The effect of the dynamite is to form cracks and crevices extending downward and in all directions so as practically to meet the crevices formed by neighboring explosions.

On account of the fact that most tropical crops are allowed to remain in the soil for five years or more the soil is evidently subjected to a slow packing process which interferes with aëration and consequently with nitrification. In almost any sample of laterite soil which has not been disturbed for a year, nitric nitrogen occurs only as a mere trace, while the total nitrogen may indicate a fertile soil. By thorough tillage and furnishing proper drainage conditions, aëration may be set into active operation, thus providing the proper conditions for the rapid growth of all plants which require nitrogen in the nitrate form.

In the growth of sugar cane, the usual system of taking one plant crop and two rattoon crops requires from 4½ to 5 years. In order to prepare the soil as thoroughly as possible for this long period of plant growth, deep plowing has been adopted. This is accomplished either by traction engine, by ox and mule teams, or still better by stationary engines and cable. By the latter means, it is possible to plow from 16 inches to 3 feet in depth. Obviously, the greater the depth of soil thus stirred up and pulverized, the longer the time required for it to become packed and impervious again. When plowed by steam plows to a depth of two feet or more, laterite soils are thrown up largely in huge lumps which require exposure to the sun and water for slacking into a granular form.

In some of the sugar-growing countries, notably in Hawaii, it was long maintained by the sugar planters that no attention need be paid to cover crops or humus. It was assumed that the soils were inexhaustible and that efforts put forth to restoring humus were merely lost and useless. During a considerable series of years, the sugar cane was harvested by setting fires in the fields at the time of maturity. These fires went raging through the field like a forest fire, destroying everything except the green stalks of cane. These were immediately harvested and ground. This system of burning the cane resulted, of course, in the total destruction of the leaves and other trash which would otherwise have been returned to the soil. The folly of this tremendous waste of vegetable substance has at last been realized, and the cane tops and leaves are returned to the soil, supplemented with green manuring crops which are planted immediately after the second rattoon crop is removed. The same change of habit has occurred among the pineapple growers, who found that a good tilth of laterite soils cannot be maintained without giving strict attention to the humus content of the soils.

In Hawaii, an excellent opportunity was offered for the study of the leaching and weathering processes which naturally occur in the lava rock. A chemical study was, therefore, made of the life history of Hawaiian soils. For this purpose, samples of lava were taken from the historic flows known to have occurred in 1910, 1907, 1883, 1868, and 1823. These flows were all from the same volcano. It appeared from a chemical study of these samples of lava that lime is the element which is leached out to the greatest extent. This also gives an indication of the necessity of supplying lime to these soils in order to balance the loss from excessive rainfall and leaching. The supply of suitable lime for agricultural purposes is at hand in the immense deposits of coral sand on the seashore.

From the standpoint of cultivation, many tropical soils are exceedingly heavy. The power required, for example, in plowing soils in Hawaii and in Poona, India, is much greater than would be needed in plowing to the same depth in the familiar soils of the United States. Three or four mules are required for an ordinary mold-board plow turning the soil to a depth of six inches. The difficulty of plowing these heavy soils has induced most planters to resort to power plows. In very heavy soils, as already indicated, the most satisfactory device is the system with two stationary engines, one at either end of a long cable which hauls a heavy, single mold-board or gang plow back and forth across the field. Outfits of this sort cost about $25,000 and are sufficiently strong to endure the great strain required to turn up the clod-packed, laterite soils. Traction engines have been found rather unsatisfactory for these heavy soils, although in some instances it is possible to plow 12 inches deep with a traction engine.

Another difficulty encountered in plowing laterite soils of the Tropics lies in the fact that these soils do not scour the plow. Experiments have been carried on in modifying the surface of plows with the idea that they might be made to scour, even in the gritless laterite soils. No success, however, has ever been achieved along this line, either by modifications of the surface of the plow or of the kind of metal in the mold board or by the use of a slat mold board in place of a solid one. The only condition under which laterite soils will scour is the muddy stage in which some of the rice soils are plowed. The draft upon the plow in soils which do not scour is of course much heavier than in scouring soils.

The investigations which have thus far been made on heavy tropical soils, particularly laterite soils, have shown clearly that the mechanical condition of soils is of prime importance in their use for agricultural purposes. Most of these soils contain plant food in abundance, but when the soils become thoroughly packed and impervious to air and water the chemical compounds in soil become less soluble or fixed in combinations from which plants cannot take sustenance. The thorough aëration of these heavy soils not only brings about the rapid nitrification of the organic nitrogen and ammonia, but renders all chemical compounds more soluble and increases the rate of movement of soil moisture. Under proper tillage it has been found that fertilizers applied to the soils are much more beneficial than when applied to improperly tilled soils. If the laterite soils are allowed to become thoroughly packed, it has been found that fertilizers are fixed by these soils beyond the power of plants to take them up.

CHAPTER III

AGRICULTURAL METHODS PECULIAR TO THE TROPICS

THE climatic and cropping conditions which prevail in tropical countries make necessary certain characteristic practices which are more or less different from the farm practices of temperate climates. A large variety of crops need shade while young and provision is made for satisfactory shade in various ways, sometimes by the use of muslin, palm leaves, or slats, and frequently by the use of trees or shrubs planted with the crop. In the case of nursery beds for young seedlings of coffee, tea, cacao, etc., shade is almost always provided úntil the seedlings are nearly ready to transplant. They may then be held for a short time in a slightly shaded locality in order to season them to some extent for standing in the full glare of the tropical sun. With slow growing tree crops like those just mentioned the practice prevails in some localities of interplanting with some rapid growing plant which will over-top the young trees and furnish a certain amount of shade for the first year or two of growth. Among the plants which have been used for shading crops in the Tropics we may mention bananas, castor bean, Ceara rubber, silky oak (*Grevillea robusta*), and a great variety of leguminous trees, including dadap, madre de cacao, and several species of Albizzia and of Inga. Quite spirited controversies have been carried on regarding the need of permanent shade for coffee, cacao, and certain other tropical crops, but the practice in this regard is by no means uniform in tropical countries. Some growers use no shade for coffee or cacao except in the nursery beds during the early growth of the young trees. Other growers claim

24.

to have best results from permanent partial shade furnished by ceara rubber or other shade trees in the plantations.

In exposed localities windbreaks seem to be perhaps more urgently needed in the Tropics than in temperate climates. Tropical plants are extremely sensitive to change of temperature, especially to relatively low temperature. The constant blowing of the dry trade wind causes rapid transpiration of plants and a consequent lowering of the temperature of the plants. Rows of trees planted for the purpose of furnishing windbreaks are therefore of great benefit when running at intervals of 100 to 200 yards across the fields at right angles to the prevailing wind. In fields thus furnished with windbreaks many tropical crops show a regular gradation in size from the lee side of each row of windbreak trees to the windward side of the next row of trees. Some crops in the most exposed situation do not attain a size greater than half that of the plants in the lee of an effective windbreak.

The choice of a plant for windbreak purposes depends somewhat on the nature of the crop to be protected and the strength of the winds. For low growing plants, pigeon pea furnishes an excellent protection against the wind. This may be grown in dense rows and pruned back annually so as to form a close hedge somewhat resembling the privet hedge in appearance. The pigeon pea is a perennial and may best be used as a windbreak in gardens and for the protection of truck crops under field conditions. The castor bean grows rapidly and is an excellent plant for withstanding fierce and continuous winds in exposed localities. It will continue to grow rather rapidly even when the winds are so strong as to prevent the development of a symmetrical bush.

In exposed localities in the immediate neighborhood of the seashore, the Majagua or hau (*Hibiscus tiliaceus*) is an excellent shrub for use as a windbreak. It will thrive with its feet in salt water and is not destroyed by salt spray, the foliage being promptly restored after burning by the salt water. The ironwood or Australian pine (*Casuarina equisetifolia*) does excellent service as a windbreak in almost any situation. It will thrive in brackish or actual salt water at sea level, grows well where the rainfall is relatively heavy, and is also extremely drought resistant. After becoming well established, it will readily withstand droughts in which all species of eucalyptus die out. Where there is a reasonable amount of rainfall, eucalyptus is an excellent tree for use as a windbreak. Perhaps *Eucalyptus robusta* is the most satisfactory for this purpose. It may be planted in three rows of trees alternating in position so as to make a dense windbreak zone. Under favorable conditions they may be expected to reach a height of 15 to 20 feet in two years.

The number of trees used for windbreaks is legion and in different tropical countries the choice of planters for windbreak trees naturally varies according to their experience in their own locality. In all tropical countries lying within the trade-wind belt it is well to plant rows of trees adapted for windbreaks at suitable intervals across the fields of arable land. Windbreaks are useful and almost necessary in the case of the more tender and sensitive tropical plants, but of course are not required on plantations of sugar cane and pineapples.

On account of the fact that weeds grow the year round in tropical countries, certain special methods of weeding have been adopted in order to reduce the expense of the constant cultivation for the destruction of weeds. In the case of many tropical crops, such as sugar cane, coffee, bananas, etc., the crop itself even before it reaches full size so completely shades the ground as to destroy most of the weeds between the rows. During the early growth of these crops, however, attention must be given to the destruction of the weeds. In some cases the use of leguminous cover crops has given excellent and economic results in weed destruction. In Hawaii, Crotalaria has been used for this purpose with good results. The cover crop must be a quick and vigorous grower in order to rise above the weeds and kill them out by shading, after which the cover crop itself may be plowed under or cultivated into the soil in order to improve the physical condition of the soil.

In localities of excessively high rainfall it often happens that the rain occurs daily and almost continuously for periods of several months. Under such conditions it is impossible to destroy weeds by cultivation, and cultivation, moreover, injures the texture of the soil when it is in a muddy condition. In Hawaii the use of a spray of arsenite of soda has found great favor as a weed destroyer under such circumstances. It has been used for this purpose for six years or more on thousands of acres of land devoted to rubber ranching, sugar cane, and pineapples, and in all cases with satisfactory results. The spray is prepared by boiling two pounds of sal soda and one pound of arsenic in a gallon of water until the mixture is clear. The mixture is then diluted to make from 20 to 24 gallons of spraying material. If desired, seven ounces of caustic soda may be used in the place of two pounds of sal soda. For the successful application of this spray it is merely necessary to have a few hours of weather without rain. The spray is applied to the green growing parts of the weeds and produces the effect of prompt burning of the foliage and tender stems. Special machinery has been devised which prevents the spray from coming in contact with sugar cane, pineapples, or other crops. The cost of application even on rough land has been found to be about $1.25 an acre. Arsenite of soda destroys all ordinary herbaceous weeds and has also been found to kill wild raspberries, Lantana, and various other weedy shrubs.

Insects, like weeds, are busy the year round in tropical countries. The cost of making frequent applications of insecticides month after month and the impossibility of applying insecticides under any circumstances to sugar cane and certain other tropical crops have necessitated the adoption of other methods than artificial insecticides for the control of injurious insects. One method which has perhaps come most prominently to public attention consists in the artificial propagation and distribution of insect parasites. Perhaps the best results with insect parasites have been obtained in Hawaii, where by this means complete control was secured over the sugar-cane leaf-hopper and the sugar-cane borer. Recently, moreover, the insect parasites imported for the control of the Mediterranean fruit fly appear to be giving promise of efficient help.

Similarly with plant diseases, the favorable conditions for fungous and bacterial growth furnished by continuous warm weather and moist atmosphere make these enemies of crop production more serious at times perhaps than is ever the case in temperate climates. Certain notorious diseases of plants have made the cultivation of certain crops impossible in some localities. Thus, we have the well known case of the coffee leaf blight *Hemileia vastatrix* which totally destroyed the coffee industry of Ceylon and parts of India, forcing the coffee growers into the production of tea. In parts of Central America and the north coast of South America, the Panama disease of bananas has caused such ravages among susceptible varieties of bananas in certain localities that the industry had to be abandoned. In a few instances, resort was had to the Chinese banana, which is not susceptible to the disease. Notwithstanding the great economic disturbances caused by the prevalence of such diseases, the abandonment of one crop and adaptation of another crop were accomplished without staggering financial loss and in the end to the benefit of the planters concerned. On the whole, insect pests and plant diseases are no more serious obstacles to agricultural production and development in the Tropics than in the temperate climate.

CHAPTER IV

IMPORTANCE OF TROPICAL PRODUCTS IN COMMERCE

THE importance of tropical agricultural products is often little realized even by persons who use or consume these products daily. This is perhaps partly due to the fact that aside from fruits the products come to the consumer as finished manufactured articles and bring with them no hint of their tropical origin. There is nothing, for example, suggestive of the Tropics in rubber bands, chewing gum, gunny bags, binding twine for harvesters, and chocolate candy. Nevertheless, the essential constituents of all of these products come exclusively from tropical countries. There are a few tropical products which have recently assumed much commercial importance, particularly in the United States. It is reported, for example, that the inhabitants of this country spend more than $10,000,000 annually on chewing gum, the basis for which is chicle, a strictly tropical product.

With tropical fruits the case is somewhat different. The most casual observer recognizes at once the foreign and tropical character of the avocado, papaya, mango, mangosteen, custard apple, and various other tropical fruits which occasionally find their way to the markets of colder climates. All the world has become familiar with citrus fruit, bananas, and pineapples. The other tropical fruits are less familiar to the inhabitants of cold climates and their ultimate commercial importance in cold climates is still somewhat uncertain. Avocados are generally relished even upon first acquaintance. This is not always true, however, and many persons fail to acquire a liking for them even after long acquaintance. Similarly with papayas, they are considered by different individuals as fit for the gods, or fit for pigs, according to individual taste. Mangos offer another illustration of this point. Some of them taste so strongly of turpentine and contain so much fiber that they can hardly be considered more than a mere unpleasant curiosity. Other varieties, however, have extreme delicacy of flavor and the prospect of a commercial market for them is probably greater than for avocado or perhaps for any tropical fruit aside from citrus, bananas, and pineapples.

One of the possible reasons, however, for the slow progress which many tropical fruits have made in cold climate markets is that there are no commercial orchards of these fruits in existence. Notwithstanding the fact that mangos, avocados, papayas, carambolas, custard apples, mangosteen, guava, and many other strictly tropical fruits have been cultivated throughout the Tropics for hundreds, and some of them for thousands, of years, there are still no commercial orchards of these fruits. In every dooryard in tropical countries one finds one or two trees of nearly all of these fruits and the householder is therefore supplied with the quantity which he may need. On this account no occasion has arisen until recently for engaging in the production of these fruits on a commercial scale. It is a curious fact that perhaps the largest avocado orchards in the world are at present located in Florida, although the industry has only recently been taken up in that locality. When a greater variety of tropical fruits is raised in commercial orchards in tropical countries, it may be possible that more of them will become familiar to the inhabitants of cold climates and that a demand of commercial importance will arise for these fruits. Experiments recently conducted at the Hawaii Experiment Station showed that most tropical fruits could readily be held in cold storage for one to three months. It will therefore be possible, if the demand arises, to supply the tropical fruits to the markets of colder climates by means of refrigeration on steamship and freight car.

It is unlikely, however, that any large proportion of these fruits will ever assume the importance now held by apples, pears, and peaches as well as by citrus, bananas, and pineapples for the reason that few persons care for tropical fruits as a regular daily diet. Many of them have a peculiar delicacy which seems very agreeable, but one is often astonished to find that he does not care for another fruit of the same sort for several days. Although the praises of the mangosteen, for example, have been sung by many travelers, the majority of dwellers in the temperate climate would prefer the apple to the mangosteen as a regular part of the daily fare. Many of the less common tropical fruits are insipid or generally lacking in flavor, so that a mere taste is all that one cares for. As oddities, such fruits may always find a small sale, but as commercial fresh fruits, the Tropics appear to offer at present only citrus, bananas, pineapples, mangos, avocados, and possibly papaya, passion fruit, and custard apple.

The commercial future of tropical agricultural products other than fruits rests, however, on a somewhat different basis. The world's demand for oils, fibers, rubber, gums, tanning materials, beverages, coconuts, and sugar is thoroughly established and is increasing every day. In 1914, the United States imported tropical agricultural products to the value of $600,-000,000, the total imports of all sorts for the same year being $1,789,000,000. Some idea of the importance of tropical agricultural production may be gained from the following figures, showing exports from certain tropical countries in 1914: India, $500,000,000; Ceylon, $49,000,000; Indo-China, $52,-000,000; Brazil, $343,000,000; Gold Coast, $9,900,000; Dutch East Indies, $436,000,000; Jamaica, $13,500,000; Ivory Coast, $3,500,000; Cuba, $164,800,000; Philippine Islands, $51,000,-000; Hawaii, $41,500,000; Porto Rico, $43,000,000; and Egypt, $158,300,000.

The amount of tropical products imported by the United

States is shown in somewhat more detail in the following table:

TROPICAL AGRICULTURAL IMPORTS OF THE UNITED STATES DURING
THE FOUR YEARS ENDING JUNE 30, 1914.

	1911	1912	1913	1914
Silk (lbs.)	26,666,091	26,584,962	32,101,555	25,650,383
Ostrich feathers (value)		$3,806,696	$6,252,298	$3,944,928
Buffalo hides (lbs.)	3,425,307	4,906,362	16,234,751	13,042,828
Kangaroo hides (lbs.)			1,097,038	1,007,562
Cocoa and chocolate (lbs.)	140,970,877	148,785,846	143,509,852	180,548,794
Coffee (lbs)	875,366,797	885,201,247	863,130,757	1,114,195,777
Curry (value)	$11,333	$10,441	$11,191	
Ixtle or Tampico fiber (tons)	6,874	9,835	9,573	12,727
Jute (tons)	65,238	101,001	125,389	84,144
Kapok (tons)	2,070	2,099	2,842	2,349
Manila (tons)	74,308	68,536	73,823	51,417
New Zealand flax (tons)	2,679	5,364	7,827	4,828
Sisal (tons)	117,727	114,467	153,869	213,048
Cinchona bark (lbs.)	3,826,048	2,891,823	3,553,239	3,944,509
Logwood (tons)		39,571	37,027	40,862
Camphor (lbs.)	4,204,741	2,398,941	4,200,520	3,488,271
Chicle (lbs.)	6,508,208	7,782,005	13,758,592	5,896,556
Copal, kauri, and dammar (lbs.)	23,021,822	25,115,739	28,573,201	28,647,148
Gambier or terra Japonica (lbs.)	18,764,507	21,002,795	17,064,998	13,706,205
Balata (lbs)	878,305	1,517,066	1,318,598	2,015,158
Guayule gum (lbs.)	19,749,522	14,238,625	10,218,191	2,275,540
Gutta Joolatong or East Indian gum (lbs.)	51,420,872	48,795,268	45,345,338	18,663,898
Gutta percha (lbs.)	1,648,921	1,204,406	480,853	1,923,138
Rubber (lbs.)	72,046,260	110,210,173	90,170,316	143,065,161
Mangrove bark (tons)		21,779	15,187	5,568
Rattan (value)	$925,269	$898,552	$1,040,121	$958,418
Bananas (bunches)	44,699,222	44,520,539	42,357,109	48,683,592
Dates (lbs.)	29,504,592	25,208,248	18,145,341	25,786,468
Figs (lbs)	23,459,728	18,765,408	16,837,819	20,506,563
Lemons (lbs.)	134,968,924	145,639,396	151,416,412	
Olives (gals)	3,044,947	5,076,857	3,946,076	5,743,130
Ginger, preserved (lbs.)	350,177	468,329	551,320	
Coconuts, unshelled (value)	$1,704,105	$1,949,406	$1,781,377	$1,805,909
Coconut meat or copra (lbs.)	37,817,051	69,912,496	40,870,367	60,076,664
Coconut oil (lbs.)	51,118,317	46,370,732	50,504,192	58,012,425
Chinese nut oil (gals.)		4,767,596	5,996,666	4,018,254
Palm oil (lbs.)	57,100,406	47,159,238	50,228,706	49,092,150
Olive oil (gals.)	4,405,827	4,836,515	5,221,001	6,780,936
Lemon oil (lbs.)	430,458	357,174	381,093	486,371
Rice (lbs.)	208,774,795	190,063,331	222,103,547	255,064,251
Castor beans (bushels)	745,035	957,086	887,747	928,322
Cassia vera (lbs.)		6,795,943	6,853,915	6,261,851
Ginger root, not preserved (lbs.)		5,979,314	7,756,090	3,528,142
Pepper (lbs.)	22,065,074	25,802,252	27,562,361	25,297,726
Sugar (lbs.)	3,937,978,265	4,104,618,393	4,740,041,488	5,417,995,129
Tea (lbs.)	102,653,942	101,406,816	94,812,800	97,809,571
Tobacco (lbs.)	48,203,288	54,740,380	67,133,963	57,406,522
Vanilla beans (lbs.)	1,140,650	841,628	1,049,497	835,271

Among the largest items of imports in the United States in 1914 were cane sugar, coffee, and silk, the aggregate value of these three imported products being $354,000,000. Other items, as will be noticed in the above table, vary in amount imported from year to year according to the changes which occur in the extension of manufacturing of various products. Some articles imported from the Tropics appear to have reached their maximum, at least with the present population, and to be increasing slowly with the increase of population.

The control and proper development of the Tropics is a problem of tremendous consequences. Year by year more tropical products become necessities in cold climates. This is apparent from the mere casual consideration of a list of the commonly imported tropical products, such as cane sugar, coconuts, tea, coffee, cocoa, bananas, pineapples, citrus fruits, olives, dates, figs, sisal, Manila hemp, jute, kapok, raffia, rubber, balata, gutta-percha, chicle and other gums, cinchona, tans and dyes, rice, sago, cassava, cinnamon, pepper, cloves, nutmeg, vanilla, and other spices, oils, such as palm, China wood, candlenut, castor, olive, cotton, lemon oil, etc. How many public men in the United States are really giving attention to the tropical question? Some energy has been expended in the introduction and popularization of tropical fruits in order to make our citizens familiar with these products and in order to learn whether the fruits may be cultivated in southern Florida and California. This, however, cannot solve the whole problem. It concerns merely one phase of the question, the other and more important phase being the production of the articles in question in tropical countries which are best suited to the cultivation of such crops.

The total land surface of the earth is estimated at 52,500,000 square miles. Of this area about 29,000,000 square miles is considered as fertile land. The total land area of the Tropics and subtropics is about 15,000,000 square miles. In the Tropics it has been estimated by Willis that 50,000,000 acres are devoted to the production of export crops and 275,000,000 acres to the maintenance of the inhabitants of tropical countries. This total of 325,000,000 acres cultivated in the Tropics is about 30 per cent. of the tropical land area, and is probably too high an estimate. In the United States mainland the total improved land equals 25 per cent. of the total area, being 49 per cent. in the North, 27 per cent. in the South, and 5 per cent. in the West. In tropical countries, there are about 86,-300,000 acres in rice, 4,000,000 acres in sugar cane, 3,500,000 acres in coconuts, 2,000,000 acres in tea, 2,000,000 acres in tobacco, 3,000,000 acres in jute, 1,500,000 acres in rubber, 3,300,000 acres in coffee in Brazil alone, and 40,000,000 acres in millet. In addition to these areas devoted to tropical crops large areas are utilized for the production of agricultural crops which are grown also in temperate climates. For example, India exports 260,000,000 bushels of wheat annually, and corn is a crop of great importance in many strictly tropical countries.

The English and Dutch and, more recently, the French and Belgians have made great progress with their tropical colonies. This progress is solidly based on a careful consideration of the natural resources of their colonies, the needs, rights, and welfare of the native races in these colonies, and the possibilities of commercial development in response to the demand of modern markets. The combined trade of England and the United States with tropical countries is estimated at $3,000,-000,000 yearly. The Tropics have one-half the arable land surface of the earth and this land is capable of continuous uninterrupted production the year round. The native tropical races are capable under proper treatment and guidance of making very effective farmers. Moreover, we should not forget the opportunities for white farmers in tropical countries. Colonies of American farmers are giving a good account of themselves in Cuba and Porto Rico. The possession of the Philippines, Porto Rico, Hawaii, American Samoa, Guam, and the Panama Canal Zone makes it necessary for the United States to show an active interest in the tropical problem in all its phases.

CHAPTER V

ECONOMIC AND SOCIAL CONDITIONS AND OPPORTUNITIES IN THE TROPICS

WHEN the white man first began to visit tropical countries for adventure or discovery or curiosity or business, he found these countries in the possession of native races, mostly brown and black. Tropical agriculture was originally, of course, altogether in the hands of these native races. Until the organizing and commercial mind of the white man interfered in the development of possibilities in the Tropics, practical agriculture was to a large extent confined to the collection of wild products growing naturally in abundance in the primitive jungles or as the result of simple methods of cultivation in small areas about native huts.

The European explorers at once recognized the commercial possibilities in tropical countries. The white man's attitude toward the Tropics from the very first has been one of exploitation. This has involved the use of the native as a peon belonging to an inferior race. In the early literature regarding agricultural and commercial possibilities in the Tropics, it is usually stated with refreshing frankness that the native races are obviously inferior to the white race and that their supposed rights to property in tropical countries must yield to the superior demands of the white race.

As rapidly as men of finance could be interested in tropical development, huge corporations began to be formed involving absentee landlordism in its purest and most exaggerated form with practically all the stock owned in European countries. It is a notorious fact that the native tropical races have usually had no such idea of the value of land as is possessed by the white race. Most of these lands were held by them in common and if an individual wished to move to another locality he readily found in his new place of abode suitable land for his simple wants. It was in no instance, therefore, a difficult matter to persuade the natives to sell their land for a very small mess of pottage, or to force them to sell by economic pressure. The white race assuredly cannot point with pride to the methods which it has used in gaining land in the Tropics.

At the present time there are extremely few, if any, localities in the Tropics in which the individual settler from temperate climates can establish himself without the possession of considerable capital. Such a settler must at least have enough to tide him over the first two or three years. It should be remembered that most tropical crops require three years or more of growth before they begin to bring in returns. The cost of clearing land and preparing it for cultivation is greater in tropical countries than in cold climates and the expense of living may be correspondingly high. The labor which one will be forced to employ in carrying on large agricultural operations is cheap in price but not very effective. In large plantations the usual system of managing labor is the gang method in which a group of laborers are worked together under a field boss. Various devices have been used in different tropical countries to improve the effectiveness of labor and especially to attach the laborer more permanently to the land. For this purpose cheap shacks are built for the laborers, these shacks being arranged in groups so as to constitute labor camps located conveniently to the fields in which the laborer will be required to work. The laborer is usually furnished free fuel and medical attendance. In many cases a so-called homesteading system has been adopted by which the laborer is given from one to six acres of land as a small farm upon which he may raise fruit products. For the most part, however, these small homesteads have not been designed as real homesteads but merely as a bait to hold the laborer permanently attached to the plantation.

On most of these small so-called homesteads little work is done except occasionally by the women and children. The time of the men is all required on the plantation and they have no leisure nor energy for work on their own little plat of land. As a rule, plantation laborers are expected to trade at the plantation stores. At such stores their credit is good up to the extent of their wages and the proverbial improvidence of the coolie laborer usually keeps him either in debt to the plantation store or with his head barely above the financial pool in which he is forced to swim. Most of the labor employed on the large sugar and other plantations succeeds in making a bare living. Theoretically these laborers are free, but economically they are slaves.

The white man can work in the Tropics and it is better for him to do so. On account of the fact that in most tropical countries the best opportunities have already been seized by large corporations it is sometimes difficult for the individual farmer to find a location where he can make a reasonable living without much annoyance and trouble. By means of coöperative associations, however, many of the difficulties of destitution and financial embarrassment are overcome. In Porto Rico, white men working coöperatively have developed a $3,000,000 fresh fruit industry ·from nothing in a period of ten years. Moreover, white colonies of fruit and truck gardeners are prospering in Cuba, particularly in La Gloria, Herradurra, and Isle of Pines. The fruit raiser or truck gardener who requires some additional labor to run his place will have choice among various races. Of all the kinds of labor available in the Tropics, the Chinese is probably the best, being willing, tractable, and of unusual skill and endurance.

Social groups in the Tropics are prone to split up along racial lines with the assumption of inferior and superior races. An endless amount of intermarriage between various races has occurred largely as a result of the white man's interference in the development of the Tropics. Not only have the various races of European origin freely intermarried with other races of darker color, but they have been instrumental in bringing together a hodge-podge of races in nearly every tropical country as a result of the constant endeavor to secure cheap and abundant labor. Of all the races which are found in tropical countries, the Japanese perhaps intermarry least frequently.

The social and business standing of half-breeds varies greatly, according to country and locality and according to the apparent merits of the mixed races. In Hawaii, for example, the half-whites, born of white fathers and Hawaiian mothers, mingle with the best of society just as do the pure native Hawaiians. The point of race inferiority has never been raised by the white man in Hawaii, at least as applied to the Hawaiian. The intensity of race prejudice, however, varies greatly with locality and individual. Even in a city like Honolulu, where nearly all the human races and practically all possible mixtures of these races occur, there is growing intensity of race feeling which in all probability will ultimately lead to a decided diminution in race mixtures and to a reëstablishment of purer races. While it was once thought to be of no consequence whatever that an Anglo-Saxon in Hawaii should marry a pure Hawaiian, there is a growing feeling that an individual with pure ancestry running back for a thousand years or more should have too much race pride to allow his family tree to terminate in a nondescript twig of the half-breed type.

The opportunities offered in the Tropics to the intending settler from colder climates depend on many factors, such as physical acclimatability of the settler, the amount of his capital, his special training, and, above all, his grit and common sense. The white laborer will find little opportunity in tropical countries for, in the field of labor, either skilled or unskilled, he will have to compete with the ubiquitous Oriental or some other race of a low standard of living. The best opportunity which the Tropics offer is farming in coöperative communities favorably located as regards markets. Residents of the Tropics are often consulted for advice regarding the stock-selling companies dealing with agricultural products. There seems to be only one answer that can be made to such inquiries and that is, in general, do not buy stock blindly in tropical agricultural companies. The frauds and failures of rubber companies in Mexico and elsewhere have not only brought financial ruin to hundreds of individuals but have greatly injured the development of legitimate enterprises of this sort. Companies which pretend to be developing rubber and fiber industries in newly opened tracts of tropical land may well be carefully investigated before any stock is purchased. Hell is paved with prospectuses of fiber and rubber companies, some of which have never actually developed an acre of land upon which they have pretended to hold option.

The Tropics offer rather abundant and brilliant opportunities for trained men from various lines. The Tropics need trained chemists, agronomists, horticulturists, entomologists, pathologists, and veterinarians. For the substantial development of tropical agriculture there is great need of white settlers like the type of men who settled our West, but with more money. There is need of colleges of tropical agriculture in the Tropics. At present there can hardly be said to exist a college of tropical agriculture, and yet there is constant call for men especially trained in the production or manufacturing processes connected with various agricultural crops. The Tropics need broad-minded sociologists, or rather social workers, prepared to study and to help solve the endless interracial problems. The Tropics need also the enlightened interest of the genuine statesmen of the dominant races of the world. If these needs are all adequately met the Tropics may contribute greatly to the necessities and luxuries of the world and may not become the battlefield of armed greed.

The accounts of profits from tropical agriculture are often greatly exaggerated and are usually stated on a misleading basis. As a matter of fact, most of the profits of tropical agricultural corporations are profits on cheap labor, not profits from agriculture. A corporation with 2,000 laborers receiving 50 cents a day but really earning $1 a day makes a clear profit of $250,000 a year over and above its legitimate agricultural profit as a result of underpaying the labor. As already indicated, the laborer employed on tropical plantations is nearly on the same basis as the mule, that is, working for his board.

As an example of the agricultural profits from the tropical industries we may take the economics of sugar production. The contract by which the small sugar planter disposes of his cane to the sugar mill in Hawaii varies somewhat according to the company. According to one scheme the small planter receives 48 cents of every dollar obtained for the raw sugar in San Francisco or New York. In other words, when sugar brings $75 a ton the homesteader or small planter gets $36 a ton and the sugar mill company gets $39 a ton. The sugar mill is at an expense of $5 per ton for milling and $9 for freight and the mill profit is, therefore, $25 a ton. On the other hand, it costs the small planter $4 a ton to produce his sugar cane and it requires at least 8 tons of cane to make one ton of sugar. The total cost to the small planter, therefore, of producing a ton of sugar is $32. The small planter, therefore, makes a profit of $4 a ton on his sugar when the sugar sells for $75 a ton. Now an average yield of sugar in Hawaii is about 4½ tons per acre and the small planter's profit-per acre is therefore $18 on an 18 months' crop, or $12 per acre per year. The average size of the sugar cane homestead in Hawaii is about 10 acres. The homesteader's profit from his whole homestead is therefore $120 per year. If, however, sugar falls to $60 per ton the small planter actually loses. Moreover, many of the plantations pay for cane according to another plan by which the small planter or homesteader receives $4 a ton for his cane. This is just the cost of production. In other words, the small planter works 18 months to get back after a few months' additional delay what he expended in the production of his crop. The Porto Rico sugar mills, on the other hand, pay the planter 60 to 75 cents out of every dollar received for the sugar. The Porto Rico method allows a square deal to the small planter.

Similarly with pineapples, the actual agricultural profits are not large as compared with mainland crops. In Hawaii, it costs from $11 to $14 to produce a ton of pineapples, the average cost being perhaps $12. In 1914, the pineapple canneries of Hawaii reduced the prices which they offered to the pineapple growers to $5 to $9 per ton. Previously the prices had been about $18 per ton. At the latter figure there was a profit of about $6 per ton to the grower. The average yield per acre is about 6 tons of pineapples, giving a total acre profit of $36 for an 18 months' crop, or $24 per acre per year. The cost of producing bananas may be set at about 30 cents a bunch. The grower receives on an average about 40 cents a bunch, which gives him an apparent profit of 10 cents per bunch. The average yield of bananas is about 230 bunches per acre per year, thus yielding a total acre profit of $23, but it is unnecessary to elaborate statements of profits in connection with other tropical crops. The figures in any case are valid only for one locality and must be constantly revised on account of the changes in market facilities, prices of labor, and other factors. There are no huge profits from tropical agriculture for the small grower. In fact, his profits can in no event be larger than he can obtain from a smaller amount of effort in cold climates. The one hope for the homesteader or farmer or small grower in the Tropics is in the formation of coöperative communities, such as are already giving great promise in Porto Rico, in Cuba, and in Hawaii. While it is evident from the figures just given of profits from sugar cane and pineapples that the small grower does not receive any large acre profit, it should be remembered that the profits of large corporations growing cane and pineapples in Hawaii average over $75 to $100 per acre per year as compared with the $12 to $20 profit to the small grower. This difference, however, is due not to better management but, as already indicated, to the underpayment of labor.

In connection with our tropical possessions we need a consistent and definite policy, a policy scientifically and economically sound, a policy in which all interests will receive due consideration, namely, homesteaders, laborers, capital, and the welfare of the United States as a whole. It is perfectly futile to set ephemeral politicians at the business of running and developing the Tropics. Thus far such a system of managing the Tropics has merely developed a feudal system for the exploitation of land and of cheap labor. The whole problem presented by the tropical possessions of the United States should be in the hands of trained men and should involve the coöperation of the Departments of Agriculture, Interior, Commerce, Labor, War, and Navy. A definite policy could then be framed, announced, and consistently pushed forward with the assurance that greater and greater beneficial results would flow from it every year.

CHAPTER VI

SUGAR CANE

SUGAR CANE is a tall, rank-growing grass, presumably a native of India, Malaya, and Cochin China, and now cultivated throughout the Tropics and subtropics. It is doubtful whether the strictly wild species from which the cultivated varieties of sugar cane have been developed has been preserved in any of its original habitats. Sugar cane is not only an extremely vigorous grass of rapid growth, but is of considerable ornamental beauty, especially when in tassel.

The sugar cane is generally recognized as one of the most important commercial crops of the world. The world's trade in sugar is about 10,000,000 tons annually, of which 6,000,000 tons are beet sugar and 4,000,000 tons cane sugar. India also produces about 2,500,000 tons of cane sugar annually which does not come into commerce but is consumed locally. Large quantities of sugar are also consumed in other sugar-producing countries. The total world production of sugar is about 20,885,000 tons.

Sugar cane is referred by botanists to the species *Saccharum officinarum*. There are several species of this genus, but *S. officinarum* is the only one with which we are concerned as a commercial sugar-producing plant. This species has been divided for purposes of classification into the groups *genuinum* (pale green or yellow canes), *litteratum* (greenish or yellowish canes with red stripes), and *violaceum* (violet-colored canes). These groups in turn are divided into the numerous varieties of cane which are cultivated throughout the tropical countries. The stalk of sugar cane varies from 3 to 25 feet in length and from ½ to 3 inches in diameter. The length of the stem varies greatly according to variety, locality, and length of time during which it is allowed to grow. The length of the internodes between the joints commonly varies from 4 to 10 inches, depending in turn primarily on the rate and vigor of growth. The roots of sugar cane, like those of most other grasses, are delicate and fibrous, varying in length from 18 inches to 10 feet and distributed therefore widely throughout the soil, and under favorable conditions to a great depth. Sugar cane has no tap root. The leaf sheath of cane is about one foot long on an average and the leaves vary from two to four feet in length and two to three inches in width. At maturity, sugar cane forms long, beautiful silky tassels of panicled flowers. Seed is formed rather sparingly but persistent search has been kept up for seed in order to use it in producing seedlings. Millions of seedlings have been raised, especially in Java, Barbados, and Hawaii. As with other cultivated plants, so with sugar cane, a great variation of characters has been thus obtained. Some of the seedling varieties which have been produced are of striking promise, producing not only a heavy growth of cane but an enormous yield of sugar. In a few instances, yields as high as 16 tons of sugar per acre have been obtained from seedling canes.

In the sugar-producing countries, 100 or more varieties of sugar cane have received serious commercial attention. In most varieties the stalk is recumbent at the base, thus requiring more labor in harvesting. The stalks are erect, however, in the Demerara canes, particularly D. 1135, and in Yellow Caledonia, Japanese cane, and a few other varieties. The sucrose content of sugar cane varies from 7 to 20 per cent. and the water content from 70 to 75 per cent. The sugar content is much affected by weather and soil and is probably less a function of variety, although it should be said that in Hawaii the Lahaina cane is always sweeter than Yellow Caledonia. It will at once be seen that the percentage of sugar developed in sugar cane has been exceeded in sugar beets and even in some of the saccharine sorghums. For this reason, it has been felt that possibly long-continued selection might result in an increase in the sucrose content. Some increase in the sugar content has been brought about in Java by a process of chemical selection. In this work seed sticks were selected from canes showing the highest percentage of sugar. So far as may be judged by experiments thus far carried on, however, there is little prospect of greatly increasing the sugar content of cane. The average sugar content of Louisiana cane is about 13.5 per cent. The sugar content diminishes from the base to the tip of the cane. Since it is the common practice to use the upper part of the cane for seed purposes, certain experiments have been carried on to determine whether such practice is calculated gradually to reduce the percentage of sugar in the cane. These experiments have indicated little, if any, advantage from planting the lower segments of cane over the use of the upper segments of the stalk.

The extreme geographical limits of cane at present are 37° N. in Spain and 37° S. in New Zealand. The higher the temperature the faster the growth and the longer and thicker the internodes. This applies almost without exception in all sugar-producing countries. In Demerara, with an almost constant equatorial temperature, only 270 days are required from planting to tasseling. In Hawaii, on the other hand, 500 days are required for the same stages of growth. The length of time required for sugar cane to reach maturity varies greatly in different parts of Hawaii according to altitude and the amount of rainfall and sunshine. In general, the variation is from 18 months to 2½ years.

On account of the cool winter weather in Louisiana, cane must be harvested in an immature condition. The juice is therefore impure, containing a high amount of reducing sugar and being relatively low in sucrose. The same condition, however, is also found in equatorial regions where the temperature is always hot and where the seasons show the least variation. Under the latter conditions the growth is constant and the cane never comes to so complete a maturity as occurs on the borders of the Tropics where also the greatest purity of cane juice is obtained.

Throughout the Tropics there is an almost universal system of nomenclature for the crops of cane as well as for many other tropical crops. The first crop from seed planting is called the plant crop, and subsequent crops obtained without replanting are called rattoon crops. In Java, most of the sugar cane crop is plant cane. In Louisiana, the crop is made up of plant cane and first rattoons. In Hawaii, the common practice is to harvest a plant crop and two rattoon crops. In Mauritius, three rattoon crops are taken, and in Cuba and the West Indies it is customary to continue without replanting up to the fifth rattoon crop or in certain fields as long as 25 years or more. The number of crops taken without replanting is, of course, not determined by theoretical considerations of the possibility of the successful growth of cane after being cut, but strictly for economic reasons. In some localities the third rattoon crop is so light and the yield of sugar so low that it is more profitable to plow and replant than to allow the plant to remain for the production of a third rattoon crop. In a few localities in Hawaii, for reasons which are not at all apparent, sugar cane has continued to yield excellent crops without replanting for a period of 25 years. This would not be considered an unusual performance in Cuba and the West Indies.

The optimum quantity of water for cane, either as rainfall or irrigation water, depends to a large extent on the physics of the soil, the rate of evaporation, and the farming system according to which the soil is handled. The rate of evaporation, as is well known, varies greatly in different localities and this naturally has much to do with the amount of water required for the growth of cane. The optimum quantity of

· water for a crop of sugar cane in Louisiana is about 60 inches, in Demerara about 100 inches, and in Hawaii about 150 inches. There are many known cases of special adaptability of variety to climate; for example, D. 74 Louisiana, Lahaina cane on irrigated lands in Hawaii, and Yellow Caledonia on unirrigated plantations and at higher elevations in Hawaii. It has been fairly well shown that cane soils should have a high water-holding power and that on this account clays, lateritic soils, and alluvial soils are perhaps best for the growth of cane.

The use of fertilizers in the production of sugar cane has received a great amount of attention in all cane-growing countries. In Hawaii, a profit has been shown from the use of fertilizers even on soils which will produce 11 tons of sugar per acre, and naturally fertilizers give still more profitable returns on poorer soils. In Hawaii, the tendency now is to use more nitrogen and less potash than in former years. This change in formula came about as a result of extended experience in which it was found that potash was not required to the extent which had previously been considered necessary. Lime is used extensively in cane production. In Hawaii, coral sand is much used for that purpose. It has generally been found that nitrogen should be applied early in the growth of the cane. Nitrate of soda may easily be applied in solution in the irrigation water. This practice is followed on a number of Hawaiian plantations. No specific effect has ever been shown of fertilizers on the composition of cane juice. The mud press cake is usually returned to the soil and on some of the Hawaiian plantations all the molasses from the mills is returned to the soil as fertilizer. Sugar cane causes little soil exhaustion if all trash is returned to the soil. In Hawaii and in many of the cane-growing countries, the practice was adopted years ago of burning all cane leaves and tops left in the field after harvesting. In recent years, this tendency was· further extended in Hawaii where the cane fields were burned off before harvesting, thus destroying all material which would otherwise have been returned to the soil and leaving nothing but the bare stems standing. This practice was adopted on account of the supposed reduction which is brought about in the cost of harvesting. With the exception of two or three plantations no effort was made at all within recent years on any of the Hawaiian plantations to conserve the humus of the soil, to practice green manuring in any way or to adopt any system of rotation. This deceptive and suicidal system of robbing the soil finally led to so-called physiological diseases and diminished yields which require serious attention. It was soon found that the so-called senility of the Lahaina cane was due entirely to the destruction of the humus in the soils and the consequent deterioration of the physical condition of the soil. By returning to the soil the natural cane trash, together with legumes and other weeds which were allowed to grow in the interval between harvesting and plowing, it was found possible to bring the yield back to standard and to demonstrate that the so-called senility was not a disease of cane but merely an indication of poor soil management. In Java, Louisiana, Mauritius, British India, Egypt, and certain other cane-producing countries, some form of rotation is practiced. No rotation system, however, has been adopted in Cuba, Hawaii, Trinidad, or Fiji, but in Hawaii the present tendency to plow under the cane trash and to secure as much green material as possible from a quick growing legume, such as Crotalaria or Jack bean, may be said to take the place of the regular system of rotation.

According to results thus far obtained, it appears that in Hawaii about 1,000 pounds of water are required for the production of a pound of cane sugar. The average application of irrigation water in Hawaii is about 75 inches in a district where the normal rainfall is 25 inches. Outside of the districts of heavy rainfall cane is irrigated in nearly all parts of cane-producing countries On the lowlands near the sea-

shore the irrigation waters usually contain a certain amount
of salt. It has been found that water may be safely used for
irrigation if it contains no more than 100 grains of salt per
gallon.

In plowing cane lands quite different practices prevail in
different countries. In Poona, India, the land is plowed with
mold-board plows drawn by ox teams and the depth of plowing is 10 to 12 inches. In Cuba, the cane soils are likewise
plowed with ox-drawn mold-board plows but usually not to
a depth exceeding 8 or 10 inches. In Hawaii, steam power is
chiefly used in plowing cane soils and the depth of plowing
is from 12 to 24 inches, usually about 16 inches. It has been
definitely shown that deep plowing is beneficial. Moreover,
as it has recently been demonstrated to the satisfaction of
plantation managers that cane trash and green manuring crops
are necessary for a continued high yield of sugar cane, the
managers have adopted special plows for turning under the
cane trash and legumes and weeds.

As is generally known, even to those who have never visited
cane plantations, cane seed means segments of the stalk of
the cane cut in lengths of 8 to 10 inches. These sticks of seed
cane are commonly cut from the top of the cane and are
planted in furrows or holes, mostly in furrows. They are
usually dropped in a continuous row at the bottom of the furrow or sometimes a double row, as, for example, in Louisiana.
These rows are from 3 to 7 feet apart. The amount of seed
required per acre varies from 1½ to 4 tons, according to the
distance between the rows and whether or not two rows of
sticks are dropped in each furrow. In Louisiana, seed cane
has to be preserved over winter by burying in the ground.

On irrigated plantations, weeding must be done by hand and
not by machines, for horse or power machines would spoil or
fill up the furrows and thus prevent irrigation. Various kinds
of cultivators, row straddlers, and other implements are used
on nonirrigated cane. Recently in Hawaii, particularly in the

districts of heavy rainfall, the use of arsenite of soda has been adopted in destroying weeds. This chemical method of destroying weeds is much cheaper than mechanical methods and in seasons of almost continuous rain can be applied without injuring the soil, whereas cultivation of the muddy soil would not only not destroy the weeds but would injure the texture of the soil. The practice of stripping the lower leaves from the cane at two or three periods during the growth of the crop has been practiced quite commonly on some of the Hawaiian plantations and elsewhere, but the results show that this practice is of doubtful value. Cane leaves by analysis as well as by field experiments have been shown to have large value in nitrogen and humus for the maintenance of soil fertility.

The harvesting season for cane varies in different countries. It extends over a rather long period in Hawaii, commonly from December to the following September. In Louisiana, the harvesting season extends from October to January. The tasseling of cane marks the end of growth. Cane may, however, be allowed to stand for at least six months after tasseling before any loss of sugar occurs. There is a great variation in the yield of cane per acre in different countries, the limits of variation being perhaps 6 and 120 tons. In Louisiana, the yield is about 20 tons, in Java about 40, and in Cuba about 17. Hawaii has perhaps the highest yield. The average yield of sugar per acre in Hawaii is 4½ tons and the average yield of cane is about 50 tons. In Hawaii, yields of 15 tons of sugar per acre have been obtained in localities where the soil and climatic conditions are especially favorable. The number of tons of cane required to produce a ton of sugar naturally depends on the percentage of sugar in the juice and purity of the juice. In Hawaii, from 8 to 10 tons of cane are required to produce a ton of sugar.

Thus far no successful cane harvester has been devised, although repeated efforts have been made to perfect a machine which would economically harvest cane and save a great part of the hand labor required in this operation. Cane is therefore cut with a cane knife and is carried to the mill in special cane cars on permanent or portable tracks, in water flumes, by ox carts, in canals, especially in Demerara and Straits Settlements, or on aërial cables.

In most modern sugar mills cane is crushed and the juice is expressed in three-roller-units. In each unit the rollers are so placed that their centers are at the angles of an isosceles triangle. The rollers are commonly 30 by 60 inches, or 34 by 78 inches, are made of steel, and are variously grooved and ridged. Sugar mills may be 9, 12, or 15 roller mills, that is, contain a series of 3, 4, or 5 three-roller-units. These rollers are often preceded by a forced feeding device and a shredder or crusher. It has been found in Hawaii that a 12-roller mill with rollers 30 by 60 inches would treat 50 tons of cane per hour. The pressure on the upper roller varies from 200 to 400 tons in different mills and the surface of the rollers revolves at a speed of 16 to 25 feet per minute.

Another method for extracting sugar is the diffusion process. This process depends upon the principle of osmosis. The method has been adopted on many plantations in different countries and is still in operation. In extracting sugar by this method cane is cut into thin slices about 1-20 inch thick. The juice is then allowed to diffuse into pure water or into dilute juice in a series of vessels. While this method, as just stated, is still in use, it is for the most part in operation only on small plantations. At the annual meeting of the Hawaiian Sugar Planters' Association in November, 1915, some interest was manifested in experiments with this method in Hawaii and one manager stated that a large plant would soon be installed to give the method a thorough test.

By the usual process of sugar extraction, the juice from the crushed cane is at once heated to a temperature of 190° to 200° F. to clarify it. Lime is added to the juice at the same time to assist the process of clarification. Sulphur, phosphoric acid, and other chemicals have also been used for the same purpose. The purpose of adding lime is to precipitate various impurities out of the juice. After this process of clarification the juice is at once filtered in large filter presses for the purpose of removing the mud and the precipitated impurities. The juice is then boiled in a multiple series evaporating apparatus to the consistency of sirup. It contains in that stage about 55 per cent. solids in solution. The sirup is then boiled in vacuum pans until it is condensed to the point where it separates into crystalline sugar and uncrystallizable molasses. The whole mass at this stage is called massecuite. The crystallized sugar is then separated from the molasses by centrifugals, the sugar crystals being caught on a fine wire gauze strainer with 400 to 500 meshes to the inch, while the molasses is thrown out by centrifugal force. The crystallized sugar is removed from the centrifugal and at once packed for export as raw sugar.

The machinery concerned in the manufacture of sugar has reached a stage of great elaboration and of striking perfection. The whole process is a continuous one from the time the cane arrives at the mill until the sugar is sewed up in the bags.

Molasses resulting from the manufacture of cane sugar varies greatly in composition but contains on an average about 25 per cent. water; 50 per cent. sugars (40 per cent. sucrose and 10 per cent. glucose and reducing sugars), 15 per cent. organic material (nonsugar), and 10 per cent. ash. The lowest percentage of reducing sugar occurs in Hawaii and the highest in Demerara and Louisiana. The chief constituent of the ash of molasses is potash in the form of a sulphate. In fact, sulphate of potash constitutes about 4 per cent. of the molasses. The amount of molasses obtained in the manufacture of sugar is about 20 per cent. that of the sugar in Hawaii and 40 per cent. that of the sugar in Demerara. Waste molasses is used in making denatured alcohol and rum, as a fuel along with bagasse in boiler furnaces, and as a fertilizer. As a stock feed, waste molasses must be used with certain restrictions for the reason that the high content of sulphate of potash causes digestive troubles and even more serious physiological disturbances. When molasses is used as a fertilizer the ash is, of course, directly beneficial since it contains a high percentage of sulphate of potash and the sugars in molasses perhaps serve as food for nitrogen-gathering bacteria.

Bagasse as it comes from the last battery of rollers contains sometimes as low as 40 per cent. water but usually 45 to 50 per cent. Bagasse makes a satisfactory fuel for boilers with or without further drying. In fact, on most plantations bagasse constitutes the chief fuel used in sugar mills.

Java has made a greater scientific contribution than any other country to the whole subject of sugar cane, including field culture, chemistry, manufacture, diseases and insect pests, and selection of cane. The scientific investigation of sugar cane in Java is under government supervision. In Hawaii, on the other hand, the Sugar Planters' Experiment Station is a private institution supported entirely by assessments on the sugar plantations of Hawaii and controlling absolutely the results of its investigations. Most of the publications of the experiment station of the Hawaii Sugar Planters' Association are not available except to members of the Association and certain libraries and other institutions.

The production of beet sugar passed that of cane sugar in 1883 and maintained its lead until recently. Sugar and molasses are also obtained from various other sources, especially sorghum, a considerable variety of palms, maple, etc., but all sources of sugar except sugar beet and sugar cane are of very minor importance.

The most recent available statistics on cane sugar showed the following annual production: Cuba, 3,000,000 tons; British India, 2,534,000 tons; Java, 1,591,000 tons; Hawaii, 612,-000 tons; Porto Rico, 364,000 tons; Argentina, 304,000 tons;

Louisiana, 293,000 tons; Mauritius, 271,000 tons; Queensland, 263,000 tons; Philippine Islands, 235,000 tons; Brazil, 228,000 tons; Formosa, 213,000 tons; Peru, 212,000 tons; Mexico, 143,000 tons; British Guiana, 114,000 tons; Fiji, 112,000 tons; Dominican Republic, 87,000 tons; and lesser amounts in the various other cane-producing countries.

The methods of cultivation and manufacture of sugar vary greatly in different countries. Sugar manufacture may be carried on in central coöperative mills patronized by small planters or in mills owned by corporations to which cane is furnished by independent growers or in mills owned by companies which raise all their cane on owned or leased land or by several other systems of organization. The mill company contracts for buying cane vary greatly in different countries and with different plantations in the same country. Where the plan of paying for cane on a cash basis is determined by the price of sugar, the amount received by the homesteader or small cane grower varies from 48 per cent. in Hawaii to 70 per cent. in Porto Rico. Another method of paying for cane in Hawaii consists in a flat rate price of about $4 per ton for the sugar cane. This contract removes all possibility of the small grower making a profit from his operations. Contracts for cane buying vary in other particulars from fairness to various degrees of unfairness up to a practical condition of peonage. The complaint which most small growers make about cane-buying contracts, aside from the obvious fact that they cannot make a profit according to the terms of contract, is that the contracts are ordinarily stated in such involved legal phraseology as to be practically unintelligible to the average man and always ambiguous. For the most part, these contracts leave certain points to be determined by the sugar mill company.

Cane sugar is shipped from the producing countries either as raw or refined sugar. Java does its own refining, while Cuba and Hawaii ship nearly all their sugar in the raw condition just as it comes from the centrifugals.

Modern methods described above are not everywhere in use in the manufacture of cane sugar. In India, for example, cane is crushed by wooden rollers with ox power, the juice is boiled in open pans, and the process results in the production of gur or jaggery, which goes into local trade in hard crystalline masses weighing 50 to 75 pounds.

CHAPTER VII

COCONUTS

THE coconut (*Cocos nucifera*) is a native of the Malay Archipelago and Africa. It has been carried accidentally and intentionally to all parts of the Tropics and subtropics where it may now be found growing especially along the seashore, but occurring also up to an elevation of 2,000 feet. The coconut is one of the most graceful and beautiful of the palm tribe of trees. It commonly reaches a height of 50 to 80 feet but often attains a considerably greater height. The trunk is slender and never straight. It is usually swollen and bottle-shaped at the base. The roots are very numerous and long and fibrous. The peculiar leaning or almost reclining habit of the trunk of the coconut palm seems to be one of the natural characteristics of the tree and readily distinguishes it from the habit of growth of most other palms. The leaning habit is not caused by winds for the reason that, in any grove of coconuts, trees may be found leaning with the wind, directly against the wind, and in all other directions without any apparent order or preference. In many cases the trunks lean as much as 15° away from the perpendicular and in the case of very tall trees this must cause a great strain upon the fibrous roots. Notwithstanding the height of coconut trees and the fact that all of the leaves are confined to a large cluster at the tip of the trunk, the trees are seldom injured by winds except in the case of the most violent typhoons or hurricanes.

The graceful, pinnate leaves of the coconut are 6 to 12 feet long and 18 inches or more in width. The flowers appear in a large compound spadix and, as in the case of many other palms, are at first inclosed in a spathe.

The coconut is one of the world's most important economic plants. Its uses are almost innumerable. The nut yields coconut oil, copra, coconut meal, coir, desiccated coconut, coconut milk, and hard shells used in making utensils, and a fine quality of charcoal. By tapping the inflorescence before the spathe opens one obtains a sweet liquid called toddy, which on evaporation yields a crude sugar known as jaggery. Moreover, the leaves yield fiber, paper-stock, material for making hats, baskets, mats, thatching, etc. The cross-laced fiber at the base of the leaves is used as sieves and for other purposes by natives. The trunk of the coconut tree is used for making walking sticks, for construction purposes, as dugout canoes, and in various other ways.

Estimates of the world's total production of coconuts are not very complete and are therefore somewhat unreliable. Probably 50 per cent. of the total amount of coconuts produced is consumed in the producing countries. The world's trade in copra at the present time is about 700,000 tons annually and is increasing in amount quite rapidly. There are about 3,500,000 acres in coconuts with an average of perhaps 100 trees per acre. Of this area about 800,000 acres are in Ceylon, 500,000 in the Philippines, 500,000 in tropical South America, 380,000 in British India, 370,000 in Central America, 270,000 in the small islands of the Pacific, 250,000 in New Guinea and Straits Settlements, and smaller areas in Java, Sumatra, Mauritius, Madagascar, Zanzibar, Seychelles, Reunion, Siam, Cochin China, the West Indies, including Cuba, Jamaica, Porto Rico, etc., and tropical America.

The question of coconut varieties is much muddled. There are, perhaps, 25 or 30 varieties. Simons used such descriptive variety names as green, yellow, black, red, heavy, and globular. Other writers on coconuts have used merely geographical names for varieties, such as Coromandel, Malabar, Maldive,

Siamese, Samoan, Ceylon, Pemba, etc. Until more work has been done in the identification of coconut varieties, it is quite useless to present elaborate descriptions of these varieties.

The coconut is essentially a tropical plant and thrives best inside the boundaries of the true Tropics from sea level up to an elevation of about 2,000 feet. It appears to thrive equally well in almost any kind of soil, even in coral sand and in brackish water. In fact, it grows well along the actual fringe of the sea beach where its roots stand in salt water.

For planting, mature nuts from trees which regularly yield a heavy crop are selected. The nuts are held for thorough curing for a period of 2 to 4 weeks before planting. They are then planted in rows 4 to 5 feet apart in the nursery and barely covered with earth. The nuts are laid on one side and mulch of straw or leaves may be placed over the germinating nuts. The coconut nursery should have some shade for the best results. Germination requires 3 or 4 months and about 90 per cent. of the nuts germinate. The seedlings are transplanted at about one year of age. The nuts are often planted in the field without the use of a nursery but the care required during the germination is much more expensive in the field than in the nursery. The planting distances vary greatly in different localities. As a rule, in commercial coconut plantations, the number of trees per acre ranges from 50 to 150. In some old coconut groves there are 300 or even 400 trees per acre. With such close planting, however, the results are not at all satisfactory.

The growth of coconut trees is much improved and earlier fruiting is promoted by clean cultivation or intercropping with sweet potatoes, soy beans, or some other suitable crop during the first two or three years. The trees in plantations treated in this manner develop a much larger trunk and come into bearing two or three years sooner than would be the case in a neglected or uncultivated plantation. After coconut plan-

CROWN OF COCONUT TREE WITH NUTS IN VARIOUS STAGES OF GROWTH

tations come into bearing the use of cover crops and light applications of potash and phosphoric acid will help to maintain the yield. Some irrigation may be necessary until the young trees have become thoroughly established with roots reaching down to water. The growth periods of the coconut are about as follows: Leaves with the mature pinnate form appear at 15 months, a beginning of a trunk appears at 4 years, the first flowers are commonly observed at the age of 5 years, and the first fruit at 6 years. These figures perhaps represent the average conditions in the Tropics at sea level. In higher altitudes or latitudes the growth is slower. Even in the Tropics most trees do not begin to bear on a commercial scale until they reach the age of 7 to 10 years. In some extra tropical localities, however, as for example, in southern Florida, coconuts may begin to bear at the age of 4 or 5 years. The reasons for this early maturity are not well understood.

Flowering and fruiting of the coconut goes on almost continuously and ripe nuts are to be had every month of the year. The nuts are usually picked every two months, but in Zanzibar only four pickings a year are commonly made. It is not rare to find individual trees which mature 15 nuts per month or at the rate of 180 nuts a year. I have seen a yield of 200 nuts from one tree in 12 months, but one cannot depend upon more than 100 nuts per tree per year even under the best conditions. In fact, the commercial average is probably not above 50 nuts for each mature tree per year. On poor, thin, and sandy soils the average may be reduced to 15 to 20 nuts per year. The coconut comes into full bearing at the age of 18 to 20 years.

The size of the coconut varies according to variety. Depending upon the variety, from 3,500 to 7,000 nuts are required for the production of a ton of copra. A ton of copra in turn will yield 1,200 pounds of coconut oil and 800 pounds of coconut meal or poonac. In the experience of the Ceylon planters, 165 pounds of coir fiber are obtained from every

1,000 nuts. The meat of the fresh coconut contains about 53 per cent. of water and 30 per cent. of oil, and dried copra contains 2 to 7 per cent. of water and 64 to 71 per cent. of oil.

Coconuts are husked by hand by means of a sharp steel pike or similar instrument securely fastened in a block of wood. The coconut is grasped firmly in the hands and driven upon the pike after which a wrenching motion splits off a portion of the husk. Two or three motions of this sort are sufficient to remove the husk from the nut. An experienced laborer will husk 1,200 to 2,500 nuts per day. The husked nut is easily broken into two hemispheres by a sharp blow with a heavy dull knife, either a cane knife or machete. The nuts are then dried in the sun or in kilns. About one-half of the world's supply of copra is dried in the sun. Within a few hours the meat curls away from the hard shell and is easily removed. The sun drying process requires 2 to 4 days, while artificial driers may produce the same result within 3 to 20 hours. Experiments are now being made with several kinds of desiccating apparatus in an attempt to hasten the process of drying and thus to produce a better quality of product. The dried coconut meat is the copra of commerce. In the ordinary sun-drying processes the copra obtained is a dark brown or black product of extremely uninviting appearance. An almost white copra, resembling the desiccated, shredded coconut in color, may be obtained by the use of artificial driers.

. Coconut oil was formerly used chiefly in the manufacture of soap and candles. Methods of purifying the oil have been devised and it is now extensively used for human food, especially in coconut-butter, also called nut-butter, vegetaline, and palmine, a product extensively manufactured in Marseilles and elsewhere since 1897. Both the solid and liquid portions of coconut oil are also used in various cooking oils and margarines. Coconut oil is yellow or pale in color and the best and clearest grade of the oil comes from Malabar. At temperatures below 74° F. the oil becomes solid. The oleic and stearic portions of the oil may easily be separated as is the case with many other oils. Coconut oil is obtained from the dried copra by pressure. For food purposes only cold pressed oil is used, while hot pressed oil is used for soaps, candles, and various other purposes. The present methods actually recover 60 to 65 per cent. of the weight of copra in oil. The new style of hydraulic presses leave only about two per cent. of the oil in the pressed cake or poonac. Coconut meal usually contains 8 to 12 per cent. of fat and 18 or 19 per cent. of protein. It is an excellent stock feed, as shown by the numerous experiments which have been carried on in the United States and elsewhere. In feeding experiments in India, where coconut meal is called poonac, equally satisfactory results have been obtained.

The world's supply of desiccated shredded coconut comes almost entirely from Ceylon. The supply of this product is now about 31,500,000 pounds annually, and a large percentage of it is used in the United States. In making desiccated shredded coconut the best mature nuts are selected. These nuts are cured for about three weeks, then cracked, and the meat removed while fresh. . The brown skin on the surface of the meat is scraped off, the meat is immediately shredded, and then dried in hot-air ovens at a temperature of 160° F. The product is sorted according to the length of the shreds or strips and is packed in tea boxes or other packages containing about 130 pounds each. One laborer will crack about 5,000 nuts a day.

In preparing coir, or coconut fiber, the husks are retted in tanks of water or steamed until they become soft. They are then beaten and dried and the broken powdery waste material is separated from the coir fiber by hand or machinery. The fiber is carded by special machines, washed, dried, again carded, this time by hand, sorted, and baled. Coir fiber from old nuts is dark brown, but from young nuts the fiber is lighter in color. It cannot be artificially bleached without causing great injury to the fiber. Coir is extremely resistant to salt water. For this purpose it has been much used for ship cables. It is also extensively used for ropes, mattresses, cushions, door mats, coarse hall matting, nose bags for horses, bags for oil presses, yarn for weaving into finer matting, brushes, etc. The coconut waste obtained in cleaning the coir fiber is used as bedding for animals, as packing material for nursery stock, as insulating material for cold storage, and for other purposes. Coir fiber brings from 2½ to 6 cents a pound.

By incising or bruising the flower spadix about 3 or 4 months after the spathe appears and before it has opened, a considerable quantity of toddy is secured containing 14 per cent. of sugar. This sweet juice may easily be fermented into arack, or vinegar, or may be condensed by boiling into jaggery or raw sugar.

Of the territory belonging to the United States, the Philippines are most active in the production of coconuts. In the Philippine Islands, there are at present about 30,000,000 mature coconut trees and 20,000,000 young trees. Interest in the coconut industry in the Philippines is active and further planting is going on quite rapidly. About 175,000 tons of copra annually, or one-fourth of the world's output of copra, is produced in the Philippines. In southern Florida coconuts are being planted by the thousand. Little interest, however, has thus far been taken in them as a commercial crop. For the most part they are considered merely as ornamentals. They come into bearing early, however, in Florida, and the time is coming when the product of these trees will be of sufficient importance to attract the attention of coconut buyers.

The coconut is one of the hardiest and longest-lived crops in the whole list of agricultural products. After the trees have become mature they require little or no attention except for the occasional application of fertilizer. On account of the profits which have been obtained from coconut plantations in full bearing, a wide commercial interest has been manifested in further planting. A great increase in the total supply of coconuts has thus been brought about, but limits of the demand for coconuts seem not yet to have been approached. The price of copra has steadily risen even with the increased supply. So far as may be judged by present appearances, especially taking into consideration the additional modern uses of coconut and its products, the coconut industry seems to be about as safe and secure from a financial standpoint as any tropical agricultural industry. There is one serious enemy of the coconut which has wrought havoc in Cuba, Jamaica, and a few other localities in the West Indies. This is the bud rot, which has been shown to be a bacterial disease. Whole groves of coconuts have been annihilated by this disease within 3 or 4 years, and Cuba perhaps has suffered most severely from the disease. It appeared seriously in Cuba about 35 years ago and its progress has caused the almost complete disappearance of coconuts from the island of Cuba except in the Baracoa district of the extreme eastern end of the island. In 1906, Cuba was the main source of supply of coconuts for the United States. At present, the Baracoa district furnishes 10,000,000 to 15,000,000 nuts annually for the American trade.

An indication of the importance of the coconut industry may be obtained from the mere casual consideration of the United States imports of coconut products. In 1914, the United States imported 60,000,000 pounds of copra, 58,000,000 pounds of coconut oil, and unshelled coconuts to the value of $1,800,-000. These unshelled coconuts were largely used in the retail trade and in the manufacture of desiccated shredded coconut.

CHAPTER VIII

BEVERAGES

Of the large list of plant substances used in tropical countries for preparing beverages only a few have attained commercial importance. These are coffee, tea, cacao, maté, and kola nuts. There are many other tropical plants which furnish beverages, used on account of their flavor or as stimulants, but for the most part they are consumed only by natives of tropical countries and are not prepared on a commercial scale. In the United States the only tropical beverages used in considerable quantities are coffee, tea, and cacao. Coffee stands at the head of the list in commercial importance, but in recent years the consumption of tea is increasing in the United States. At first green teas were preferred but recently the demand for black teas is increasing.

COFFEE

There are several species of coffee of which the berries are used in preparing the familiar breakfast beverage. Chief among these species are *Coffea arabica, C. robusta,* and *C. liberica.* The first named species is commonly known as Arabian coffee, a native of Abyssinia. The Liberian coffee is native of west tropical Africa, while *Coffea robusta* comes originally from the Congo. Coffee was apparently first used as a beverage in Aden and later in Constantinople. It appeared in Venice in 1615, in Paris in 1645, and in London in 1650. The habit of drinking coffee spread rapidly in all towns in which the product was introduced. Until 1690 the world's supply of coffee came from Arabia and Abyssinia. Coffee was introduced from Mocha in Arabia to Java in 1690 and to Ceylon at about the same date. It was in Ceylon and Java that the first great development of the commercial coffee industry took place. Coffee production in Ceylon assumed enormous proportions between 1830 and 1875. Soon after the latter date a leaf blight caused by *Hemileia vastatrix* appeared and rapidly destroyed the whole coffee industry in Ceylon and India. The immense areas devoted to coffee were then gradually planted in tea and this was the beginning of the present huge tea industry of India and Ceylon.

Coffee was brought to the West Indies in 1720 and to Rio de Janeiro in 1770. The relative commercial rank of different countries in coffee production has undergone many changes and fluctuations since the time when the whole supply of coffee came from Arabia and Abyssinia. At present the total area devoted to the production of coffee is about 5,000,000 acres, of which Brazil has 3,300,000. The world's production of coffee is about 2,500,000,000 pounds annually, of which Brazil produces 1,750,000,000 pounds. From the standpoint of the amount of coffee exported, coffee-producing countries stand in the following order: Brazil, Venezuela, Colombia, Guatemala, Salvador, Haiti, Mexico, Java, Porto Rico, etc.

Coffee extends about 25° north and south of the Equator and from near sea level to an altitude of 6,000 feet. The plant thrives best, however, at altitudes between 500 and 5,000 feet. Coffee will endure a quite heavy rainfall but does not thrive satisfactorily where the annual rainfall is less than 50 inches. The extremes of rainfall between which coffee may be said to grow most satisfactorily are 50 and 200 inches.

Coffee is planted either directly in place in the field or in nurseries from which seedlings are later removed for planting. Young seedlings in the nursery bed require some shade for their best development and are usually seasoned by removing to half shade for a short time before planting in the field.

More frequently shade is furnished the young plants in the field until they become thoroughly established. The planting distance for coffee trees varies from 6 by 6 to 12 by 12 feet, according to variety, locality, and opinion of various planters. Coffee trees left to themselves will attain a height of 30 or 40 feet. The trees are usually topped off at about 6 to 15 feet. This operation not only keeps the tree from growing out of reach of the coffee pickers but seems to have the effect of increasing the bearing of the vigorous lateral branches.

Coffee is one of the most beautiful of all the agricultural crops. The dark, glossy green leaves, thickly scattered along the horizontal branches, are always an attractive sight and when the great profusion of white flowers appears upon the upper surface of these branches the trees somewhat resemble the holly in a snow storm. Later, when the red cherries appear, the coffee tree is also a very attractive sight. The coffee tree begins bearing at from 2 to 5 years. The bearing age occurs somewhat earlier in Asiatic countries than in Brazil. The full mature crop does not occur until about 7 to 10 years. Under ordinary conditions the limit of profitable bearing age of coffee is about 30 years. The yield varies enormously in different countries and in different localities. Under favorable conditions the yield of dried coffee per acre ranges from 500 to 1,200 pounds. It may ordinarily be considered that 1 to 1½ pounds of dry coffee per tree is a satisfactory yield.

The crimson fruit of the coffee is known as the coffee cherry and the seed as the coffee berry. From a botanical standpoint the fruit itself is a berry, but the trade names cherry and berry have become very firmly established and are so generally well known that there seems little reason for attempting to change the terminology. The cherries are pulped as soon as they are brought in from the field by the pickers. Numerous improvements have been made since the days of hand-pulping, until at present very efficient pulping machines are in use on

COFFEE TREE IN BLOOM IN COSTA RICA

all coffee plantations. The mucilaginous material left around the berries after the removal of the pulp is in turn removed by fermentation or soaking in water for a few hours. The berries are then dried in the parchment. The term parchment is applied to the tough, leathery skin surrounding the coffee berry. Inside of the tough parchment is a very thin, filmy layer of tissue closely adhering to the coffee berry and known as the silver skin. The parchment and silver skin are removed by coffee hulling machines and the berries are then thoroughly cleaned by winnowing. Coffee may be handled and sold either in the parchment or after hulling. For the most part, however, coffee is hulled before being shipped for the reason that hulling removes some of the useless material and makes a saving in freight.

In the process of roasting, coffee loses from 15 to 20 per cent. in weight and gains from 30 to 50 per cent. in bulk according to the degree or extent of roasting. Roasted coffee has the following average composition: Water, 1.1 per cent.; protein, 14 per cent. (including 1.2 per cent. caffein); fat, 14.5 per cent.; nitrogen-free extract, 45.8 per cent.; fiber, 19.9 per cent.; and ash, 4.7 per cent. About 25 per cent. of the total solids in coffee is soluble in water.

The temperature used in roasting coffee and the length of the roasting period vary somewhat in different countries and in different grades of coffee. All coffee users who buy the unground roasted berry are familiar with the different shades of brown which are characteristic of different brands and grades of coffee. These browns range from almost black to an extremely light shade of brown. It has been found by experience that in order to bring out the best flavor and aroma different lengths of time are required for roasting different grades of coffee. Some require to be roasted nearly black, while others, particularly Hawaiian coffee, would be nearly ruined by overroasting.

In the amount of coffee consumed, some of the most important coffee-drinking countries stand in the following order: United States, Germany, France, Austria-Hungary, Italy, Switzerland, Norway, Russia, etc. The wholesale prices in New York for coffee of different grades in the last 15 years has ranged from 6¼ to 30 cents per pound. For many years the coffee market was so manipulated that a surprisingly large margin uniformly existed between the wholesale and retail price. The trade sorts of coffee from Brazil are commonly called Rio Nos. 1-9. From Venezuela we receive grades of coffee called La Guiara and Maracaibo, while coffees from Bolivia are commonly called Yungas, and from Hawaii, Kona and Hamakua. Mocha is a trade name applied to a pea berry coffee grown in various countries. It is obvious from this statement that the term Mocha does not in any sense indicate, that the coffee came from Mocha, Arabia. Pea berry is a term applied to a round-berried coffee obtained from cherries which produced only one berry. The ordinary coffee berry, as all coffee users know, has one flat side due to the fact that the ordinary coffee cherry contains two berries closely pressed together. Whenever the cherry contains only one berry that berry shows no flat side and is rounded somewhat in the form of a pea, thus giving occasion to the name, pea berry coffee. Java coffee is a trade name for coffee like the typical brand which is found in Java. From Ceylon we obtain Native Plantation, Liberian, and Mountain coffees and the coffees which enter into trade from Abyssinia are called Harrar and Abyssinian. In addition to these few trade names there are also dozens of geographical names of various brands of coffee, while the trade names for coffee as a whole are almost innumerable. Most coffees, like teas, are not composed of one strain but are blended by the use of coffees from several localities.

The Liberian coffee is a considerably larger tree with larger leaves, much larger cherries, and a firmer pulp. This coffee has a poor aroma but is more resistant to the devastating leaf blight and is therefore cultivated to some extent in Java, Ceylon, and elsewhere. The Liberian coffee thrives at lower elevations than the common varieties of Arabian coffee. *Coffea robusta* is another species of coffee which has recently come into some prominence as a rival of the Arabian and Liberian coffees for certain purposes. This species grows faster than the Liberian coffee and the leaves are thinner. Moreover, the branches have a more decided habit of drooping and the cherries occur in larger clusters. The cherries are smaller than is the case with the Liberian coffee but the berries are about the same size. This species flowers the year round, is decidedly resistant to leaf blight, and the aroma is much better than that of the Liberian coffee. In Java, there are at present about 15,000 acres devoted to the cultivation of Liberian coffee. Sierra Leone coffee (*Coffea stenophylla*) was introduced into Ceylon in 1894. This species develops black cherries instead of the usual crimson cherries and possesses an excellent aroma. *Coffea excelsa* is also under experiment in various coffee-producing countries, but its value has thus far not been established.

The coffee industry of the United States is largely confined to Porto Rico and Hawaii. Porto Rico exports coffee to the value of about $8,500,000 annually and the industry is showing quite rapid progress. The improvement of the coffee industry of Porto Rico is due to better cultivation, higher prices, and the use of superior varieties. Little demand has been created in the United States for Porto Rican coffee, and practically all of it is sold in foreign countries. The export of Hawaiian coffee amounts to about 25,000 bags annually, with a value of $175,000. The prevailing prices for Hawaiian coffee have been relatively high in recent years, reaching 18 to 20 cents per pound wholesale. The prospects for the coffee industry in Hawaii are brighter than has been the case in former years. The Army has adopted Hawaiian coffee for use in Hawaii and the Philippines.

TEA

Tea is a beverage which ranks second only to coffee in commercial importance and, in fact, is used in many countries far more extensively than coffee. The tea plant is called *Camellia thea* and the variety name viridis is used for Assam tea and the name bohea for China tea. The tea plant is a native of China, Japan, and India. The China tea is a low bush, while the Assam tea is taller, reaching even a height of 40 feet and becoming a tree of large proportions if unpruned and left to itself. Tea has been cultivated in China and Japan since the dawn of history and in India since 1875. At that date the seriousness of the leaf blight of coffee had become apparent and the coffee growers began to experiment with tea. These experiments rapidly led to the general adoption of tea as a crop for replacing coffee in India and Ceylon.

Tea requires a heavy rainfall for its most vigorous growth. It thrives best in a rainfall of 90 to 200 inches. The Assam tea does best at low altitudes, while China tea gives satisfactory results at elevations up to 5,000 feet.

Tea is propagated from seed planted either directly in the field or in seed beds from which the seedlings are later transplanted in the field at distances of 4 by 4 or 5 by 5 feet. In commercial plantations tea is usually prevented from growing more than 5 feet high by repeated pruning. The first picking takes place about 3 years from the time of planting the seed and full bearing begins when the plants are about 6 years old. The crop of leaves continues unabated for 50 years or more. In fact, by means of severe pruning after a plantation has apparently almost run out, a renewed vigor may be reëstablished for a considerably longer period.

The yield of tea ranges from 200 to 1,000 pounds of' cured leaves per acre, according to the number of flushes, the nature of the soil, the variety of tea, and the locality in which it is grown. In Ceylon, there are about 400,000 acres devoted to

TEA HEDGES IN YENDO, JAPAN

FIELD OF SMOOTH CAYENNE PINEAPPLES IN HAWAII

the production of tea and the exports from that country amount to 190,000,000 pounds of black tea annually. The total exports of tea from tea-producing countries are about 810,000,000 pounds per year. Tea-producing countries stand in the following order from the standpoint of the amount of tea produced: British India, Ceylon, China, Dutch East Indies, Formosa, Japan, and Singapore.

Tea leaves are picked from 10 to 25 times a year. In Ceylon a picking occurs every 10 to 12 days. Tea, like many other tropical plants, shows at intervals an unusually vigorous growth in which fresh leaves are developed very rapidly. These periods of unusually active growth are known as flushes. For the highest grades of tea only the tip of the actively growing shoot and one or two of the youngest leaves are plucked. A few older and coarser leaves go into the cheaper grades. The tea leaves are brought from the field by pickers and at once undergo a withering process in the sun, in open sheds, or under the influence of low artificial heat for a period of about 18 hours. The leaves are then rolled by hand or by machine, after which they are fermented in piles or in drawers for a period of 2 to 10 hours. The piles of tea are covered with a clean cloth wrung out in cold water. The appearance of a coppery yellow color in the leaves and the characteristic aroma indicate the time to stop the process of fermentation. The tea then goes at once into the drying or firing machines, where the leaves are completely dried by currents of hot air. The process just described produces black tea.

Fermentation of the leaves is carefully avoided in making green tea. The fresh leaves on being brought in from the field are at once heated in a pan or are steamed until they wilt and are then put immediately into the drier. This process effectively prevents fermentation and consequently prevents the development of the dark color characteristic of black tea. Green teas, however, are not all green in color. In fact, they have no uniform color. Green teas usually show a gray or brown as well as a green color. On account of the lack of uniformity in the color of green teas it was formerly a widely prevalent custom to color green teas artificially with soapstone, turmeric, gypsum, indigo, and other materials. This process was sometimes called facing the tea leaves.

China produces both green and black tea, while Ceylon tea is almost all of the black sort. Oolong tea from Formosa is manufactured like green tea, except that it is allowed to ferment only slightly. Oolong tea therefore has the appearance of black tea and flavor of green tea. The Japanese manufacture two chief grades of green tea known as gyokuro and sencha and also a low-grade tea from old leaves known as bancha.

As already indicated, the highest grades of both black and green teas are prepared from the terminal bud and the youngest leaves. In the order of quality, the grades of black tea from Ceylon and British India run as follows: Orange Pekoe, Pekoe, Pekoe-souchong, Souchong, Congou, and Dust. The green teas from China are commonly graded in the order of their quality as follows: Young Hyson, Hyson No. 1, Hyson No. 2, Gunpowder, and Dust. Nearly all of these trade names are common Chinese words derived from the tea industry. The young flushing leaves of tea are covered with a fine gray pubescence which turns to an orange color during the process of curing. This pubescence is partly rubbed off the leaves during the process of handling but is sufficiently evident to give the term Orange Pekoe to a high-grade Pekoe tea. The presence of the pubescence in the tea is taken as an evidence of the fact that the tea is made of the youngest leaves. Brick tea, as made in China, is of two forms: That which is commonly used in Tibet is made of old leaves and twigs with a glutinous substance added, while the Brick tea used in Russia is ordinary Dust tea pressed into bricks.

In the list given above of tea-producing countries mentioned in the order of their importance only a few countries of greatest importance as sources of tea were given. Tea is also a commercial product in Natal, the Caucasus, Jamaica, Fiji, Java, the Andamans, Tonquin, Burma, etc. The importation of tea into the United States has fallen from 102,653,000 pounds in 1911 to 97,800,000 pounds in 1914. In the amount of their tea imports the first three countries are Great Britain, Russia, and the United States, in the order named.

The United States has taken little part in the business of producing tea. It has been grown experimentally at Pinehurst, South Carolina, and also in Hawaii. It is impossible, however, for us to compete with the cheap labor of China and India. While the planting and cultivation of tea requires no more hand labor than is customarily applied to fruit crops, the picking of the leaves is a tedious process of hand labor which would make the cost of production disproportionately high, except where labor is very cheap. From statistics prepared in recent years by tea companies in Ceylon, it appears that the cost of production, plus the freight to London, is 8 to 14 cents per pound of tea. The wholesale prices of tea in New York in the past 10 years have ranged from 12 to 39 cents per pound. This indicates only a narrow margin between the cost of production and wholesale price and shows quite clearly that any considerable increase in the cost of hand labor would necessarily involve an increase in the wholesale price of tea in order to keep the industry in a prosperous condition.

CACAO

The cacao tree, being a native of the American Continent, was not known to the European world until sometime after the discovery of America. As compared with tea and coffee, its history as a commercial beverage is therefore relatively short. The importance of cocoa and chocolate, the two chief trade products derived from cacao is, however, increasing from year to year.

. Cacao, known botanically as *Theobroma cacao,* is a native of the regions along the Orinoco and Amazon and of Central América. The tree normally attains a height of 15 to 40 feet. It bears large, oblong, rather thin, shiny leaves and large pods 6 to 9 inches long of a red-gray or yellow color when ripe. The pods are ridged lengthwise and are variously covered with wartlike protuberances. Each pod contains from 20 to 45 large seeds, or cacao beans, closely packed in a gelatinous mass. The pods are borne, for the most part, along the trunk of the tree or on the sides of the large branches.

The cacao tree is considerably injured by temperatures below 60° F. It therefore does not thrive beyond 20° north or south of the Equator. The cultural 'requirements for cacao are very similar to those for coffee, but it must always be remembered that cacao is more sensitive to cold, drought, and wind. The rainfall requirement for cacao depends much upon the drainage and the physics of the soil. The limits of rainfall for good vigorous growth of cacao lie perhaps between 60 and 190 inches per year. It is often stated that for the vigorous development of cacao the soil must contain an ample supply of potash and nitrogen and a medium amount of phosphoric acid. This, however, is little more than a guess since few experiments have been carried out with fertilizers in the production of cacao. The tree is quite tolerant of salt and will grow even in brackish soil.

The pod husks constitute 79 per cent. of the weight of the whole pod, while the seeds together with the pulp make up the remaining 21 per cent. An analysis of fresh cacao beans will show a water content of 37.6 per cent.; proteids, 7.2 per cent.; theobromin, 1.4 per cent.; caffein, 0.1 per cent.; fat, 29.3 per cent.; glucose, 1 per cent.; starch, 3.8 per cent.; fiber, 8.1 per cent.; cocoa red, pectin, and astringent matters, 8.7 per cent.; tartaric acid, 0.6 per cent., and ash, 2.35 per cent. During the process of fermentation cocoa red, the coloring matter of cocoa and theobromin, the stimulant constituent of cocoa, are

TRUNK OF CACAO TREE BEARING RIPE PODS

probably formed by the oxidation of a glucosid. At the same time, the essential aromatic oil appears and the bitterness disappears. The fermented and dried bean contains 6.3 per cent. water, 52.1 per cent. fat, 6.1 per cent. proteids, 6.8 per cent. carbohydrates, 1.7 per cent. theobromin, 6.3 per cent. cocoa red and astringent matters, 1.8 per cent. ash, and 18.9 per cent. cellulose. It is apparent from these figures that one-half the dry cacao bean is made up of cocoa fat or cocoa butter, which is extensively used in making chocolate, perfumes, and many pharmaceutical preparations. Cocoa fat is a yellowish-white fat with a melting point of 35° C.

About 20 species of Theobroma are known, of which *T. cacao* and *T. pentagona* (usually considered a variety of *T. cacao*) are grown commercially. The cacao tree reaches full growth at 10 to 12 years. The red-fruited varieties have darker leaves, and the flowers and fruit are borne on the trunk or large branches as indicated above. There are three principal groups of the varieties of cacao, Criollo, Forastero, and Calabacillo. The Criollo group is quite superior in quality. The wall of the pod is soft and the round white beans are only slightly bitter. The Forastero group has a much harder pod and flat violet-colored beans. The Criollo varieties came originally from Venezuela, but are now cultivated in many tropical countries. A very smooth fruited subvariety of the Criollo group is known under the name Porcelaine. The Forastero group of cacaos is more variable. The fruit is usually yellow and the trees are more hardy than those of the Criollo group. The Forastero cacao, therefore, seems to be gradually taking the place of the better varieties even in Venezuela.

For cacao plantations openings in forest or areas protected by windbreaks are commonly selected. Perhaps the best shade for the first three years of growth can be obtained by interplanting with bananas, cassava, or pigeon peas. The usual planting distance for cacao is 9 to 20 feet apart both ways with perhaps 15 by 15 feet as the average spacing. In certain localities permanent shade has been used with success. For this purpose kapok, castilloa, hevea, coffee, etc., have served excellently well. The idea underlying this interplanting of cacao with other trees is to arrange the plantation in such a manner that at full growth the cacao will utilize all the space. The cacao beans are planted either in nurseries or directly in place in the field. The advantages are rather in favor of planting in nurseries and in transplanting the seedlings for the reason that the young trees are more easily cared for during their first year of growth when close together in a well protected nursery than when planted at the usual spacing in the open field. Budwood of superior varieties may be used for topworking old trees or inarching may be practiced with good success. These methods, however, have not come into use on commercial plantations. In a few instances grafted trees have borne as high as 30 pods each 2½ years after grafting. The permanent shade trees which are most commonly used for cacao are leguminous. Cacao is grown, however, without shade in Brazil, Grenada, St. Thomas, and several other localities. If, however, leguminous shade trees are not used good tillage is required, otherwise profitable yields may not be obtained. Little systematic work has been done with fertilizers in the growth of cacao trees. In Dominica the best yields have been obtained from the use of mulch of leaves and grass. In pruning cacao, it has been found best to remove all suckers and diseased branches. In a few instances one sucker has been left near the base of the trunk, but this has proved to be a wrong practice. The removal and burning of dead branches, twigs, and diseased pods help greatly to prevent the spread of cacao diseases.

Pods when ripe are removed with a knife or hook, leaving a clean wound. The pods are then gathered and opened the same day or within three days at the outside. The contents of the pods are removed at once to the fermentation house. The cacao tree begins to bear at 3 or 4 years of age, and the full yield is reached at about 7 or 8 years. The maximum yield occurs perhaps at about 12 years of age. The Criollo varieties, however, begin bearing at 5 years. The yield of cacao ranges from 100 to nearly 1,000 pounds per acre and 500 pounds may be considered a good acre return. Individual trees sometimes bear as many as 400 pods, but an average of 50 pods per trees is satisfactory. It requires about 15 pods to make one pound of cocoa.

The fresh cacao beans as they are removed from the pod are large, somewhat flattened seeds about ¾ inch in width. They are of an ivory white or delicate violet color. The beans are at once placed in boxes and covered with banana leaves or other suitable material. The boxes used for this purpose are of such size as to allow the beans to be packed in to a depth of 6 or 7 feet. While held in these boxes the beans undergo a process of heating and of fermentation. They are transferred daily into other boxes for a period of 4 to 6 days in order to equalize the temperature throughout the mass of beans. During this process the slimy pulp around the beans ferments into a vinegar-like liquid and flows away. During the process, also, the red color and the characteristic aroma develop in the beans. The fermentation process with cacao beans is, however, not adopted in all countries. In Ecuador, the beans are not fermented at all and are dried at once and packed for shipment. On some plantations the beans are washed after fermentation, but washing is hardly to be recommended since the beans lose flavor in this process. After fermentation, beans are dried in the sun or in an artificial drying apparatus. On account of the trade demand for a rich red color in cacao beans, this color has been given to the beans on some plantations by the process called dancing and claying. In this process a small quantity of clay of a rich red color is sprinkled over the beans, after which the beans are trampled by the bare feet of natives.

Loss of weight in fermenting and drying cacao beans is

about 60 per cent. This gives a means of estimating the approximate weight of the cured crop from the weight of the fresh beans. The brands of cacao which come into the market from Ecuador are commonly known as Balao, Arriba, Machala, Manabi, and Esmeraldas. From Brazil we receive brands of cacao known as Bahia and Para, and from Venezuela come the Caracas, Maracaibo, and Cabello cocoas. The most important cocoa markets are Hamburg, Havre, London, Amsterdam, Lisbon, and New York. The wholesale Hamburg price for cocoa ranges from 12 to 24 cents per pound for various sorts of this product.

The similarity in names in a number of tropical agricultural products has led to much confusion in the minds of readers not intimately acquainted with the Tropics. It may be well, therefore, to call attention to some of these terms which have caused confusion, particularly in connection with cacao products. It should perhaps first be mentioned that cocoa butter is the fat of cacao bean and, therefore, differs utterly from coconut butter, a product manufactured from coconut oil. It is unfortunate that coconut has been frequently spelled cocoanut, thus causing further confusion with cocoa, one of the products manufactured from the cacao bean. The confusion has been worse confounded by the fact that the specific botanical name of cocain is coca and that kola nuts have been spelled indifferently cola and kola. The tree from which cocoa and chocolate are derived is properly known as cacao and the beans produced by the tree are usually known as cacao beans, although occasionally they are also called cocoa beans. There has also been considerable looseness in the use of the terms cocoa and chocolate. In preparing cocoa powder for use in manufacturing cocoa for drinking, a considerable part of the cocoa fat is removed by hydraulic pressure and the residue is treated with carbonates to produce a better suspension in water. Cocoa, as properly used, therefore means the ground mass obtained from the fermented and roasted cacao bean after the removal of a considerable portion of the fat naturally contained in the bean.

In manufacturing cocoa and chocolate, the dried beans are roasted at a temperature of 250° to 275° F. for a short time in rotary drums. The beans are then cracked and the skins removed by an air blast, after which the beans are ground into cocoa powder. Sweet chocolate consists of cocoa powder to which are added sugar, spices, starch, flavors, and other adulterants. Chocolate, whether of the sweet or bitter sort, therefore, contains all of the cocoa fat originally present in the bean. Plain or bitter chocolate is the firm mass obtained by grinding the fermented and roasted bean without removing any of the fat. Bitter chocolate is, therefore, merely the ground cacao bean without any further alteration, either by removal of the fat or by the addition of other substances, while cocoa is the original cocoa powder from which a part of the fat has been removed by pressure.

The total exports of cacao beans from producing countries are about 260,000 tons annually. Of this amount the Gold Coast exports 65,500 tons, while other producing countries range in the following order: Ecuador, St. Thomas, Nigeria, Brazil, Trinidad, Dominican Republic, Venezuela, Grenada, Lagos, Ceylon, etc.

In territory belonging to the United States, cacao is grown to some extent in Porto Rico and the Philippines and experiments have also been made with cacao in Hawaii. Conditions for the growth of cacao seem to be quite favorable in Porto Rico and the Philippines. In Hawaii, on the other hand, there is little basis for a cacao industry for the reason that the continued prevalence of the trade winds appears to increase transpiration from the leaves to such an extent that they are unduly chilled and turn brown along the edges. The growth of cacao in Hawaii has not been satisfactory from a commercial standpoint, although an excellent quality of cacao has been produced in the neighborhood of Hilo.

MATÉ

Maté, or Paraguay tea, is a common South American drink prepared from the leaves of *Ilex paraguayensis*. This is a common bush in South America occurring in particular abundance in Brazil and Paraguay. The leaves of the bush are 3 to 4 inches long, serrate, and somewhat resemble tea leaves. The crop is taken largely from wild plants, but is cultivated to some extent. Like coffee and tea, the beverage contains some caffein. The consumption of Paraguay tea in South America is enormous and there is a small export trade with Europe. Elsewhere the habit of drinking Paraguay tea has not taken root.

Brazil is the chief producing country and exports about 140,-000,000 pounds of maté annually to Argentina. Paraguay exports about 5,000,000 pounds of this product every year. In preparing the material, young twigs are cut from the bushes and thoroughly dried over a fire of aromatic wood, after which the dry leaves are beaten off, ground to a coarse powder, and packed for the market. There are three recognized grades of maté, the caa-cuys made from the partly expanded leaf buds, the caa-miri prepared from the unroasted leaf, and the caa-guaza prepared from roasted leaves and leaf stalks.

KOLA NUTS

The seeds of *Cola acuminata* are used to some extent in the preparation of a drink which carries a high content of caffein. The tree is a native of West Africa from Loango to Senegambia. It attains a height of 20 to 40 feet and bears warty pods 4 to 6 inches long with 4 to 10 white or pink seeds, which turn brown on drying. The seeds contain about $2\frac{1}{2}$ per cent. of caffein and some theobromin and are chewed or used as a beverage for the stimulating effect. The tree begins bearing at the age of about 6 or 7 years and yields two crops annually, amounting in all from 500 to 700 pods, or about 75 pounds of kola nuts per tree. The planting distance for the kola nut is about 20 by 20 feet. In preparing the product for the trade, the pods are merely removed and the nuts dried in the sun. Considerable effort has been put forth to extend the use of the kola nuts as a beverage. Some hesitation must be felt, however, in recommending the use of such material on account of its high caffein content. In Europe the kola nut has been used to some extent with cacao in making a beverage.

GUARANA

The woody climber, known as *Paullinia sorbilis,* native of South America, particularly in Brazil, bears seeds which are used in the preparation of the beverage known as guarana. This woody climber bears flowers in axillary panicles and an ovoid fruit about the size of the grape, ripening its seed in October. The seeds are removed from the hard shell, washed, roasted about 6 hours, and then removed from the inside paperlike shells by beating. In preparing the beverage, the seeds are ground, moistened, made into a paste, rolled into cylinders, and dried. This material is then used in producing an infusion which is consumed as a beverage. The flavor somewhat resembles cocoa, but is bitter. The beverage is occasionally called Brazilian cocoa. It is used only in South America and chiefly by the Indians. The seeds contain about 4 per cent. of caffein and the beverage is highly stimulating.

CHAPTER IX

FRUITS AND NUTS

TROPICAL fruits are gradually becoming more familiar objects in the markets of the United States. Citrus fruits, bananas, and pineapples have for years been of nearly as general distribution as apples and peaches. Pomegranates and fresh figs are to be seen here and there in fruit markets and on the carts of the street venders. Preserved figs and dates may be obtained in any grocery store, and these products have become a part of the ration of a large percentage of our population. Occasionally, mangos and avocados make their way to the markets of larger cities, where they are sold mostly as luxuries. These fruits are not yet produced in sufficient quantity to bring the market price down below the level of luxuries. Avocados sell at retail for prices ranging from 15 to 75 cents which, like the price of the occasional mango which appears on the market, is too high to allow this fruit to be considered a regular part of the diet. Now and then one sees the sapodilla, or papaya, on the market, particularly in the Southern States. While the most of the tropical fruits, except bananas, citrus fruit, and pineapples, are still for the most part curiosities in the general market of the Northern States, a widespread interest is being awakened in tropical fruits and a taste for these fruits is being gradually developed.

It is possible that larger quantities of these less familiar tropical fruits may reach the northern markets with the use of cold storage. The only systematic experiments thus far carried on in the cold storage of tropical fruits have been conducted at the Hawaii Experiment Station. In these experiments it was found that most tropical fruits could be safely held for a period of 1 or 2 months at a temperature of 32° F. Some fruits can be held longer. For example, the waterlemon retains its flavor and texture for a much longer period and seems, in fact, not to be badly affected by cold storage for a period of 3 or 4 months. The use of cold storage makes it possible to pick pineapples, avocados, and mangos at a riper stage than would otherwise be possible. These fruits are easily injured in shipment, and, therefore, it has been customary to pick them while very firm and green in order to avoid losses as far as possible. By means of cold storage it will be an easy matter to handle these fruits without loss, even if they are picked only 2 or 3 days before the stage of complete ripeness.

The discussion of tropical fruits in this chapter does not by any means include all edible tropical fruits. There are a great number of fruits in tropical countries which have never become known outside the Tropics and which never enter into commerce. In fact, many of them never appear even on the local markets in the countries where they grow. They are known and eaten only by natives and by others who may occasionally visit tropical countries. The number of such fruits is so great and their economic importance so slight that their discussion in any adequate manner would unduly lengthen the present chapter.

Questions may have arisen in the mind of the reader as to the behavior of our familiar temperate climate fruits in the Tropics. Little need be said on this subject. Apples, peaches, and pears, at least, at sea level, behave in a very erratic manner in tropical countries. Flowers, green fruit in all stages, and ripe fruit may be seen on a tree almost at any season of the year. A few apples and pears which have occasionally been produced at sea level in tropical countries are of poor flavor and texture. Some varieties of peaches do fairly well in so far as the flavor is concerned, but the yield is almost invariably low. At elevations of 3,000 to 5,000 feet, however, considerable success has been had in several tropical countries in growing apples, peaches, pears, plums, and cherries. Strawberries and grapes thrive fairly well in nearly all tropical countries but, for the most part, neither one of these fruits has acquired much commercial importance in any strictly tropical country. Considerable interest has been added to the study of tropical fruits within the past 15 or 20 years by the quite important developments which have taken place in Florida and southern California, particularly in Florida. Practically all of the well known tropical fruits, except perhaps breadfruit, have been successfully grown to a bearing age in Florida and some of these fruits will doubtless acquire enough commercial importance to attract serious attention. This is, of course, particularly the case with avocados and mangos.

BANANAS

The banana is a native of India and southern China. It is a rapid-growing, herbaceous, treelike plant attaining a height of 4 to 25 feet, according to variety and location. The large, glossy, and graceful leaves have an even entire margin and attain a length of 2 to 6 feet and a width of 1 to 2 feet. The stem or false trunk is succulent and is composed of concentric layers, being really made up of the bases of leaf sheaths. When the plant reaches the flowering age a flowering stem rapidly grows upward from the bulb through the center of the trunk, appearing at the center of the crown of leaves and bearing several clusters of irregular flowers protected by large purple bracts which later fall off. The clusters of flowers produce the "hands" of the future bunch of bananas. The male flowers appear near the tip of the flowering stem and later fall off, leaving the tip of the flowering stem quite bare. With the growing weight of the bananas, the fruiting stem turns down, becoming pendulous, while the individual bananas stand up-

Popoulu Banana, a Hawaiian Variety To Be Eaten Baked

right. The base of the flowering stem is thus curved into a loop which forms a convenient hook by means of which the bunch of bananas may be held after removal from the stem. There are a few varieties of bananas in which the fruiting stem does not turn downward, but remains erect during the whole fruiting period. This is particularly true in the Fehi and Kusaie bananas.

The flowering or "shooting" of the banana occurs about 7 to 9 months from the time of planting. About 2½ to 4 months are required from the shooting stage to the development of the full-sized bananas ready for shipment. In the case of the Chinese banana the end of the flowering stem carrying the male flowers is cut off after the fruit has set. This operation, however, is not necessary with the Jamaica banana.

The banana is propagated by suckers which are usually from 2 to 8 months of age. The suckers grow from the base of the parent stem and are readily detached by means of a mattock or cane knife. Cultivated bananas never bear seeds, with the exception of the Fehi banana and various supposedly wild species of banana. In these so-called wild forms and in the Fehi banana, as well as in the Manila hemp, which is a closely related species, the fruit contains a number of well developed black seed.

In the West Indies, March is the favorite month for planting bananas. In the case of the Chinese banana, the leaves are left on the sucker, but the leaves are cut off from the sucker of the Jamaica banana before planting. With reference to general cultural methods for bananas, it may be said that various systems have been adopted. In some localities a dust mulch is maintained. Other growers prefer a leaf mulch or use a system of green manuring. For the most part not more than 2 or 3 suckers are left to grow about the mother plant. These suckers are always of different age and represent the coming generations of banana plants on a given plantation. The banana plant bears but once and is not renewed by growth from the stump of the old plant, but by suckers attached to the base of the stump.

The total time required from planting to the fruiting period ranges from 12 to 14 months. The first rattoon crop will appear within 12 to 16 months later. The time required for the production of the first crop, or the rattoon crops, is much longer in the subtropical regions and at higher elevations. At Glenwood, Hawaii, it requires nearly 3 years from planting to produce a marketable bunch of bananas. The old leaves are usually not stripped off during the growth of the banana crop, but are allowed to droop and fall upon the ground as they gradually die.

Each banana trunk bears one bunch of bananas. Rarely 2 or 3 smaller bunches are borne, especially in the case of the Chinese banana, but this is an unusual performance and may be almost considered in the nature of a curiosity. In harvesting the Jamaica banana, the trunk is cut off 5 or 6 feet from the ground and the bunch is caught as the trunk falls in order to prevent the bananas from being broken from the stem. The ground is plowed and replanted every 3 to 7 years. In some localities it is considered necessary to replant at intervals not longer than 3 years. The length of time during which satisfactory yields of bananas may be obtained without replanting will in all cases, however, depend upon the physical properties of the soil and the amount of fertilizer and cultivation which the crop receives. In some cases good yields have been obtained for 10 or even 12 years continuously without systematic cultivation.

The yield of bananas ranges from 225 to 300 bunches per acre per year. Each bunch carries from 6 to 12 "hands" or clusters of bananas. A payable bunch of bananas is considered by banana dealers as meaning a bunch containing 9 hands or more. The banana grower receives from 30 to 60 cents per bunch, according to the size of the bunch and the locality. The American market for bananas is best during the months from

March to June, and an effort is made in planting bananas to time the crop so that a considerable proportion of the bananas may be marketed during these favorable months.

According to the experience of most banana growers, not much fertilizer is required for bananas. If lime, humus, drainage, and good cultivation are supplied, and if a rotation system is adopted or replanting is done every 5 years, good results may be expected without the use of other fertilizers. Some growers, however, apply about 150 pounds of potash, 75 pounds of phosphoric acid, and 50 pounds of nitrogen per acre per year. An abundant rainfall is necessary for the satisfactory growth of bananas, otherwise irrigation is required. The rainfall should be from 60 to 100 inches. The banana will not tolerate brackish water. If the irrigation water or ground water contains even small percentages of salt the banana will never produce a marketable bunch of fruit.

There is a large but indefinite number of varieties of bananas. Plantain and banana are not definite terms used with the same significance in all countries. All varieties of bananas are called plantains in Ceylon and India. In the West Indies, bananas is the term used for varieties which are eaten raw and plantains for those varieties which are eaten cooked. In Hawaii, the corresponding terms are bananas and cooking bananas. All the varieties of bananas belong to the genus Musa and several species of Musa produce edible fruit. *Musa sapientum*, in full development, produces a trunk 20 to 25 feet high with leaves 4 to 8 feet long. The flower bracts are of violet color and 6 to 12 inches long. The male flowers are deciduous and the fruit is slightly 3-angled and about 3 to 8 inches in length. This group of bananas includes the Jamaica, Red Spanish, Apple, Lady Finger, Ice Cream, Brazilian, Hamakua, Largo, and the Hawaiian varieties (Iholena, Maimaoli, Popoulu, Huamoa, etc.). The subspecies *paradisiaca* has a long cylindrical fruit and, for the most part, is eaten only after cooking. This subspecies includes the Kusaie banana and certain semi-wild forms of bananas which bear seed. The species of banana known as *Musa acuminata* bears fruit in bunches of 4 to 6 large hands of 10 to 12 fingers each. The fruit is short, being not more than 2 to 4 inches in length, is beaked, and contains seed. This species is common in the Malay Archipelago.

The Chinese, Dwarf, or Canary banana, known to botanists as *cavendishii*, and also sometimes called Cavendish banana, grows only 4 to 6 feet high and bears 6 to 8 leaves in a close crown. The male flowers are persistent on the tip of the flowering stem. The fruit is slightly hexagonal, about 4 to 6 inches long, and with a rather thick skin and excellent flavor.

The phenomenal rise of the banana industry is one of the most interesting phases of modern commerce. The industry began sometime more than a generation ago with the shipment of a few bunches of bananas to the United States from Jamaica and Panama. In 1878 bananas were imported into the United States to the value of $500,000. By 1900 the value of the banana imports had increased to $6,000,000, and in 1914 to $16,500,000. This industry is concerned almost entirely with one variety of banana, commonly known as the Jamaica banana, but also sometimes called Gros Michel, Martinique, or Bluefields. The Spanish Red or Cuban Red banana is imported into the United States in small quantities, and may occasionally be seen on the markets of our large cities. The Chinese banana is found only on the California markets and in Florida. This banana is grown in Hawaii and has thus far been marketed exclusively in San Francisco. The flavor of the Chinese banana is so well liked that the Hawaiian bananas are all consumed in San Francisco and Oakland. Recently an arrangement has been made for shipping about 15,000 bunches of Chinese bananas per month to Portland, Oregon. The banana industry of Hawaii is a small but slowly increasing one. It began about 1865 and has now reached about 20,000 bunches per month. The United States imported in 1914, 48,-

000,000 bunches of bananas from Jamaica, Costa Rica, Colombia, Panama, Guatemala, Nicaragua, Honduras, Cuba, Dominican Republic, and Hawaii. Large exports are made from these same countries also to Europe. For example, the Canary Islands export about 3,000,000 bunches of the Chinese banana annually to Europe, mostly to England.

The development of the banana industry has been largely due to the efforts of several large fruit-distributing companies which have built and operated for many years steamers specially adapted for this trade. There are now about 300 steamers chiefly occupied in the banana trade. These steamships carry 10,000 to 12,000 bunches of bananas each, but some of the larger ones carry 50,000 to 75,000 bunches. Special arrangements are made on these boats for carrying bananas with a minimum of loss. Forced ventilation is in use on the steamships and in some cases refrigeration has been adopted. Bananas do not endure a low temperature in cold storage and the temperature commonly adopted is not lower than 55° F. In addition to these special banana steamships which are also fitted up for passenger trade in tropical cruises, special trains have been provided for the fast transportation of bananas on arrival at ports of the United States. New Orleans is one of the large distributing points for bananas. On arrival at these distributing centers the bananas are ripened in rooms specially prepared for this purpose at a temperature of 60° to 80° F. for a period of about 48 hours. The Jamaica banana is so compactly arranged in the bunches that the individual bananas are not readily broken off. Special arrangements have been made for carrying these bunches on shipboard with a view to obviating the necessity for wrapping the bunches. The bunches of Jamaica bananas are laid on shelves or are suspended close together so as to prevent rubbing and bruising. The Chinese banana, on the other hand, seldom develops so compact a bunch as the Jamaica banana. For this reason, unless special arrangements are made on shipboard for banana transportation, it is necessary to wrap the bunches in banana leaves or other suitable material in order to prevent the individual bananas from becoming broken off.

The banana is, without comparison, the most important tropical fruit. It may be had every day of the year. The great importance of the banana is not fully indicated by the commercial trade in this fruit. It should be remembered that nearly every inhabitant of the Tropics outside of the large cities has a few banana plants in his garden from which fruit is obtained for table use. / Millions of tropical inhabitants depend upon the banana as one of the staple food products. The chemical composition of the banana shows that this fruit contains 1 to 1½ per cent. of protein and 14 to 26 per cent. of starch. Many persons have found that they can not eat bananas without some distress. This digestive disturbance is apparently due to the large amount of starch in the banana in all stages until it is fully ripe or overripe. In the ripening of the banana practically all of the starch, which constitutes on an average about 15 per cent. by weight of the fresh banana, is changed into sugar. The banana is therefore most digestible when fully ripe. The transformation of the starch into sugar is not completed until the final stages of ripening. It should always be remembered that the skin of the banana is sufficiently thick and tough to protect the edible pulp against dirt or contamination so long as no injury has occurred to the skin. Bananas are therefore a safe and palatable food product, even after the skin has turned black, provided the skin has not been broken. In the final stages of ripening the pulp becomes a soft straw-colored jelly. The softening indicates the complete transformation of the starch into sugar. In this fully ripe or overripe condition many persons who otherwise would have to abstain from the use of bananas have found that they may eat them without the occurrence of digestive disturbances.

One often hears the expression of a desire to pick bananas fully ripened on the plant and to enjoy the superior flavor which is often supposed to be developed under those conditions. This, however, is entirely a misconception. No one in the Tropics would think of allowing the bananas to ripen on the plant. In the first place they do not ripen uniformly. On this account the few fruits which first turn yellow in different parts of the bunch are quickly attacked by birds and insects and are thus destroyed. In the second place, the flavor and nutritive value are not one whit improved by allowing the fruit to ripen on the plant. Fruit picked two weeks or longer before ripening and hung in a cool place on the bunch will develop their flavor and nutritive value as completely as if allowed to remain on the plant. The inhabitants of the Tropics, therefore, commonly cut off a bunch of bananas from time to time for household use and allow it to hang in some cool part of the house, removing the bananas for use as fast as they ripen.

Bananas are eaten not only in the raw condition as fresh fruit, but are preserved in the form of banana figs or as banana flour and a great variety of bananas are eaten only after baking or frying. The product known as banana figs is made in Jamaica, Hawaii, and elsewhere. The method of preparation consists in slicing the pulp of the banana in halves and allowing the pulp to dry either in the sun or preferably in an artificial drying apparatus. The sugar in the fully ripe banana is sufficient to preserve the fruit in that form and the moisture is not all driven out by the process of drying. The resulting product is a soft, flexible, yellow-colored pulp of rather agreeable flavor. Banana flour is made from fully grown unripe bananas which are pealed, sliced, and dried in the sun or in vacuum driers to a moisture content of about 15 per cent. The amount of desiccation undergone in this process may be understood when it is remembered that fresh bananas contain about 75 per cent. of water. The material is then pulverized and sifted, after which it is used for various culinary purposes. Cooking bananas are baked, fried, or cooked in a stew pan after being allowed to ripen fully. In the process of baking, an agreeable flavor somewhat different from that of the fresh fruit is developed, some of the varieties developing a decided sweet, acid flavor. While the ordinary Jamaica banana may be cooked or used in fritters, it is by no means as well adapted for this purpose as the varieties of cooking bananas.

There are a great number of varieties of bananas differing in flavor and appearance as decidedly as the varieties of apples. Some of these varieties may be eaten when they are only half ripe, while others contain in the unripe condition so much tannin as to be quite unfit for food. This is particularly true of the Apple banana, which is no more palatable than a green persimmon until it is completely ripe. Little effort has been made thus far to ship cooking varieties of bananas to the United States.

Waste bananas may be fed to stock, but they should not be used for this purpose until they are entirely ripe. They may also be used in making denatured alcohol. The trunk and leaves of bananas are used as cattle feed. For this purpose they are palatable, but not particularly nutritious. Banana fiber from many localities has been tested, but the commercial use of this fiber offers little prospect at the present time.

The banana differs widely in its chemical composition from the ordinary fruit of the market, such as apples, pears, and peaches. The high percentage of starch in the banana makes this fruit somewhat comparable with potatoes in nutritive value. It is unquestionable that from the standpoint of human food the banana is the most important fruit known in the world's commerce. Unfortunately, however, the obvious merits of the banana have seemed insufficient to some of its most ardent champions and resort has been had to numerous exaggerations which have been repeated parrot-like in the literature relating to bananas. For example, on a basis of the chemical composition of banana flour, comparisons have been drawn showing that banana flour is far more nutritious than

Young Avocado Tree in Fruit, Trapp Variety

Sandersha Mango Tree in Bearing

beefsteak or wheat bread. The absurdity of such claims is sufficiently apparent when one remembers that the fresh banana contains 75 per cent. of water and that a comparison of the composition of the dry substance of one product with another product in a fresh condition is obviously unfair. Many exaggerated statements as to the yield of bananas as compared with the yields of potatoes and wheat have also crept into the literature of this subject. For example, in a recent book on bananas, which is perhaps the fullest and most satisfactory discussion thus far presented of the whole subject from an agricultural and botanical standpoint, the statement was made that the total yield of food material produced by bananas is 240,000 pounds per acre. The utter impossibility of such a yield is apparent from the fact that the average number of bunches of bananas per acre per year is from 230 to 240. In order to secure a total yield of 240,000 pounds per acre it would obviously be necessary that each bunch of bananas weigh 1,000 pounds, whereas the average weight is from 40 to 75 pounds. The banana possesses sufficient well known merits to make its way in the world without the aid of such exaggerations.

The banana is subject to the attacks of various fungi and insect pests, but only one, the so-called Panama disease, is of real serious consequence. This disease causes the wilting down and rotting of the stem and spreads quite rapidly throughout the plantation and from one plantation to another. In parts of Costa Rica, Panama, Mexico, and British Guiana, the disease has caused devastation and abandonment of large areas of bananas. The Panama disease attacks particularly the Jamaica and Brazilian banana. The Chinese banana, on the other hand, is quite resistant. No satisfactory method of controlling the Panama disease has been devised and the substitution of the Chinese banana for the Jamaica banana appears to be the only practical method of continuing in the banana business in the infected areas.

The United States occupies a very unimportant place in the

production of bananas. In the Philippines, bananas are everywhere grown for household purposes, but have never become of commercial importance. Experiments have been carried on at the Bureau of Agriculture in Manila with more than 300 varieties of bananas, but the Philippines cannot be said to have a commercial banana industry. Similarly with Porto Rico, while bananas are grown in all parts of the island, they are raised for domestic use and do not come into international trade. Hawaii is the only part of the United States which produces more bananas than are consumed locally. As indicated above, the shipment of bananas from Hawaii to the United States amounts to about 20,000 bunches per month, and this amount may be nearly doubled within the near future by an effort which is being made to secure the Chinese banana, grown in Hawaii, for distribution in the Northwest. In Florida, the Chinese banana thrives fairly well and produces good bunches of well formed bananas. These bananas are all taken by local markets.

PINEAPPLES

A genuine pleasure is still in store for the individual who has not tasted a pineapple allowed to reach the full stage of ripeness on the plant. The pineapple is perhaps the most conspicuous of the few fruits which do not develop their full flavor if picked when green. The pineapple is a native of tropical America and is now cultivated to some extent everywhere in the Tropics and the subtropics and even in Europe (under glass). It is grown on a large scale in South America, the West Indies, Porto Rico, Cuba, Florida, Hawaii, Federated Malay States, Ceylon, Java, Queensland, Madagascar, and in other countries.

The pineapple is referred by botanists to the name *Ananassa sativa*. The plant is a herbaceous perennial belonging to the family Bromeliaceæ. It reaches a height of 2 to 4 feet, developing only a very short stem, which is commonly called the stump. From the base of the stump fibrous roots develop, and arranged along the upper portion of the stump in a spiral equitant fashion are the numerous long, narrow, serrate, and usually spiny leaves which are channeled above and are about 2 to 4 feet long. In a few varieties the leaves are not spiny along the edges. At blossoming time the plant bears a spike of small lavender-colored flowers and later produces a conical compound fruit which at maturity varies in size from 1 to 15 pounds or more, according to location and variety.

The pineapple is propagated by suckers, slips, crowns, or stumps. The suckers are the small plants which develop in the axils of the upper leaves below the fruit stem. The crown is the cluster of short leaves which are formed upon the tip of the fruit. The slips are small plants which develop from the side of the fruit stem just at the base of the fruit, while the stump, as already indicated, is the short stem of the pineapple plant. Ordinarily, propagation is by means of suckers since plants grown from suckers produce fruit more quickly than from any other method of propagation. If suckers are taken for planting at the right stage of maturity, the resulting plants will produce pineapples within 15 to 18 months. The crowns are allowed to remain on fruit for fresh shipment and can therefore only be secured for planting purposes from the fruit which are canned. It requires nearly two years for plants grown from crowns to ripen fruit. From slips the mature fruit are obtained somewhat more quickly than from crowns, but not so soon as from suckers. Stumps are occasionally used for planting purposes and have the advantage of producing a very vigorous growth. They may be only half buried in furrows or may be entirely covered over. In fact, the methods used in planting pineapple stumps are similar to those employed in planting sticks of seed cane. The pineapple stump is composed largely of starch comparing favorably in this respect with sweet potatoes and cassava. The stump has, therefore, been found more serviceable than the sucker in planting on manganiferous soil since the stump itself furnishes a large store of material for the production of the young plant.

In preparing suckers and slips for planting it is customary to remove some of the leaves at the base of the sucker or slip and to allow the cut end to dry thoroughly before placing in the soil. The suckers or slips are then planted in rows, being inserted only a few inches into the soil. These young plants are extremely drought resistant and will withstand a long dry season, finally striking root and beginning to grow when the rain appears.

The rainfall required for the successful growth of pineapples should be at least 50 inches, but pineapples will endure a much heavier rainfall if the soil is well drained. Good tilth and satisfactory drainage are very necessary for the proper growth of pineapples. The pineapple is a rather anomalous plant in some of its relations with the soil, belonging as it does to a family of plants many of which are epiphytes or air plants. It appears itself to be able to live for considerable periods practically as an air plant. Occasionally, one will find in the case of large vigorous plants that practically all of the roots have died and decayed. The living roots, however, possess an unusually heavy coating of root hairs near their growing tips, and the physical condition of the soil with respect to drainage and aëration appears to be one of the prime factors in the proper growth of the plant. It is necessary to keep pineapple fields as free as may be from weeds. This may be accomplished either by hand weeding, by horse cultivation, or by spraying with arsenite of soda. The chemical method for destroying weeds is used to some extent in the pineapple fields of Hawaii in the same manner as in the cane fields. In seasons when rains occur so frequently as to keep the soil constantly moist for a long period, it may be necessary to resort to dynamiting pineapple fields in order to bring about drainage without puddling the surface layer of the soil by cultivation. Dynamiting has been tested on a considerable scale in Hawaii and with satisfactory results. In fields of growing pineapples the sticks of dynamite are exploded about 20 feet apart both ways at a depth of about 4 feet. This operation, if properly carried out, does not disturb the surface layer of soil and therefore does not interfere with the growth of the plants.

It has been found by practical experience and by scientific investigation that pineapples will not endure an excess of either lime or manganese in the soil. The effect of an excess of lime is to produce a yellowing of the leaves and the development of small fruits in which the normal color does not appear. Manganese, if present in the soil to an extent of more than 3 per cent., has similar effects, but the effects are usually manifested to a much greater degree. On highly manganiferous soil the pineapple leaves turn yellow and the young fruit develops a decided pink color long before it has reached its full size and, of course, far in advance of the process of ripening. These fruits even when ripe are extremely acid and unpalaable. Manganese when present in the soil in excess has the effect of forcing the pineapple plant to absorb undue quantities of lime. Some of this lime is thrown out of solution in the form of needle-like crystals of oxalate of lime. The pineapple leaf apparently has no breathing pores or stomata, at least thorough search has failed to detect any stomata. The chlorophyll of the pineapple leaf is largely located on the under side of the leaf and is protected from the direct rays of the sun by a reddish-colored sap in the epidermis of the upper side of the leaf and by a thick layer of water-distributing tissue above the chlorophyll.

The fruit of the pineapple differs in its composition and ripening process from the banana or apple or pear. At no stage of growth, however small or green, does the pineapple contain any considerable quantity of starch. In fact, there is no measurable quantity of starch in the pineapple at any time except a few small granules in the green tissue of the rind immediately under the eyes of the fruit. As already indicated, however, the stump and the fruit stem are completely filled with starch. The supply of sugar for the ripening pineapple is, therefore, secured from the starch in the stump by transformation and translocation. It is obvious, therefore, that when the fully grown pineapple, still green and firm, is cut from the plant there is no material in the fruit which can be transformed into sugar during the process of ripening. Fruit picked in this condition, however, does undergo a process of ripening. The normal color of the ripened fruit develops and the tissue of the fruit becomes soft and juicy. Fruit picked in a green condition, however, contains no more sugar when it is fully ripe than at the time when it was taken from the plant. In the condition in which pineapples are commonly picked for shipment as fresh fruit, the pineapple fruit contains about 4 per cent. of sugar. In the fully ripe condition, on the other hand, the pineapple contains from 9 to 14 per cent. sugar with an average sugar content of about 11 per cent. It is sufficiently obvious, without argument, that the flavor of a fruit containing 11 per cent. of sugar is far superior to that of one containing only 4 per cent. Pineapples are not harvested for canning until they are completely ripe and are then canned within 24 to 48 hours after being harvested. For this reason the flavor of ordinary canned pineapples is superior to that of the average run of fresh pineapples to be found on the market. Without refrigeration it is impossible to ship perfectly ripe pineapples for the reason that they are too easily bruised and immediately begin to ferment.

The difficulty of placing fresh pineapples in their best condition on the northern markets was not to be overcome without the use of refrigeration. A study was, therefore, made by the Hawaii Experiment Station to determine whether refrigeration was adapted for use for pineapples. These experiments were begun after the Hawaii Station had worked out the essential chemical processes in the ripening of the pineapple fruit. Pineapples were placed in cold storage rooms at temperatures of 32° and 36° F. The fruit used in these experiments was in various stages of growth from green to fully ripe. In the room held at a temperature of 32° F. after one month, ripe pineapples showed a slight deadening of the normal yellow color. The rind was otherwise in perfect condition and the flavor was excellent, being equal in most cases to that of the pineapple freshly cut from the plant. In a few cases the acidity seemed to be less than before refrigeration. After about 45 days a slight withering began to occur. Essentially the same results were obtained in the room held at a temperature of 36° F., except that the flavor of the pineapple began to deteriorate after 35 days in the case of fruits placed in refrigeration in a perfectly ripe condition. These findings of the Hawaii Experiment Station have been put into practice by the pineapple growers of Florida with great advantage to their industry. The pineapple industry had been somewhat on the decline in Florida, no large canning establishments were located there, and fruit consumers did not take very kindly to the sour pineapples which appeared on the northern markets. By means of cold storage, however, it has been found possible to ship ripe fruits to the northern markets, and fruit buyers have been glad to pay $1 a crate more for this fruit than had been the ruling price for pineapples before the use of refrigeration.

The shipments of fresh pineapples from Porto Rico are already large and are increasing from year to year. The fresh Porto Rican pineapples are all shipped into New York. A large percentage of the Florida crop of pineapples is also sent to New York. Recently an impetus has been given to the shipment of fresh pineapples from Hawaii by the activities of the territorial marketing division, which is carried on under the supervision of the United States Department of Agriculture. It has been found that the pineapple rot which caused serious losses in some previous shipments of fresh pineapples from Hawaii is very prevalent in certain localities, while other plantations are relatively free from the disease. Shipments have therefore been obtained largely from plantations where the disease does not greatly prevail. Hawaiian fresh pineapples have recently been shipped in carload lots from the branch office of the territorial marketing division in San Francisco as far east as Chicago and other cities. A large industry has also been worked up for the fancy trade in which 9 and 10-pound pineapples are sent in heavy paper cartons by express to various parts of the United States. The preferred package for this kind of shipment holds four fruit and weighs a little under 50 pounds.

For canning purposes, pineapples weighing from 3½ to 5 pounds are preferred on account of the fact that there is less loss. Some attempt has been made to select plants which produce cylindrical fruit rather than conical fruit, since in cylindrical fruit a large number of slices of the same diameter could be obtained. This also prevented undue loss of fruit. Perhaps the largest and most efficient pineapple canneries in the world are located in Honolulu. The process of canning has been systematized until the whole operation is practically a continuous one from the lug boxes in which the pineapples are brought from the field to the sealed can. The business of pineapple canning has undergone a quite phenomenal development in Hawaii. In 1908 the output was about 350,000 cases, while at present it is nearly 2,000,000 cases. Even the core of the fruit is used. The paring and slicing machinery removes these cores in the form of cylindrical "candles." A great demand has been developed for these candles, all of which are shipped to New York. The candles are cooked in the same manner as the pineapple slices, canned, and shipped to New York, where they are used in the glacé fruit industry.

The pineapple juice was formerly allowed to go to waste in large quantities. At present more attention is paid to the preservation of this material. Some of the canneries offer a bottled pineapple juice, which has been merely sterilized by heat and filtered and is otherwise unmodified. This product for the most part, however, does not have a very agreeable flavor and

PAPAYA TREE IN MIAMI, FLORIDA

does not make a very strong place for itself on the market. Recently a pineapple juice prepared in Cuba appears to be of more promise. One firm in Honolulu prepares a condensed pineapple sirup to which some cane sugar has been added, and this sirup is used for carbonating at soda fountains. A very palatable drink can be obtained in this way. On account of the large amount of sugar contained in pineapple juice, a plant has recently been erected in Honolulu for condensing this juice into a sirup to be used in increasing the sugar content of canned pineapples for the trade which requires additional sugar. The fiber of the pineapple leaf has been used for various purposes and a discussion of its economic value will be found under fibers. Moreover, the stumps are filled with starch and could possibly be used as a commercial source of starch.

The varieties of pineapples grown commercially in Hawaii are Smooth Cayenne and Queensland, particularly the former. In Porto Rico the leading varieties are Cabezona, Red Spanish, Ruby, Sugar Loaf, Trinidad, and Black Jamaica. In Florida the pineapple growers have preferred the Red Spanish, Black Ripley, Egyptian, Golden Pernambuco, Abachi, and other varieties. As already indicated, the shipments of fresh pineapples from Porto Rico, Florida, and Hawaii are quite rapidly increasing, and this may be taken as an indication of the favor with which the pineapple is received in the northern markets so long as the fruit is shipped in a satisfactory condition. With the adoption of cold storage methods, riper pineapples with a larger sugar content and better flavor will reach the northern markets and the demand for fresh pineapples will undoubtedly increase as these improved methods are put into operation.

CITRUS FRUITS

The literature relating to citrus fruit is so extensive and has been so widely distributed in the form of bulletins, magazine articles, books, and newspaper accounts that it seems unnecessary for the purposes of the present volume to deal in much detail with the cultural and industrial methods used in the production of these familiar fruits. Citrus fruits are native of tropical Asia and Malaya. These fruits show such a wide variety of form, structure, flavor, and other characters that a brief reference to some of the distinguishing features of the different groups of citrus fruits may be desirable.

The lemon (*Citrus limonia*) is a small tree with short stout thorns and with leaf stems sometimes narrowly margined. The flowers are rather large, being pure white above and crimson beneath. The fruit is oval, 3 to 5 inches long, and 2 to 3 inches in diameter. The favorite varieties of lemon in California are Lisbon, Villa Franca, and Genoa. The rough-skinned lemon and numerous other varieties are grown in tropical countries.

The lime (*C. aurantifolia*) is a rather small tree with sharp thorns and small leaves with winged petioles. The flowers are small and white and the fruit is nearly round, 1 to 2½ inches in diameter. The lime is grown extensively in the West Indies and Central America and also to a less extent in Florida, California, and in the eastern Tropics and Mediterranean regions. The favorite varieties of lime are Mexican, Tahiti (seedless), Sweet, Kusaie, etc.

The grapefruit (*C. grandis*), also known as pomelo and shaddock, is a larger tree which is spineless, or furnished with flexible spines, and has glossy oval leaves and large white flowers. The fruit is an oblate spheroid, 4 to 6 inches in diameter or in some forms of shaddock which occur in Hawaii and the Pacific Islands the fruit may reach a diameter of 8 to 12 inches with a very thick rind. The supply of grapefruit on the United States markets comes largely from Florida and Porto Rico.

The common or sweet orange (*C. sinensis*) is a small tree without spines or with slender flexible spines with narrow wings upon the leaf petioles and with pure white flowers. The fruit is nearly round and the number of segments in each fruit ranges from 10 to 13. The sweet orange is grown everywhere in the Tropics as well as in California and Florida. The favorite varieties are Navel, Valencia, Pineapple, Thompson, Ruby, Majorca, etc. The sour orange (*C. aurantium*) is a tree of medium size with long flexible spines, white fragrant flowers, and globose fruit 2½ to 3½ inches in diameter. The sour orange is shipped from Spain to England in large quantities for use in making marmalade. Seedling sour oranges are widely used as citrus stock in the United States on account of their hardiness.

The citron (*C. medica*) is a small tree with short, stout thorns, large leaves, and large flowers, white above and crimson beneath. The fruit is oval, 6 to 10 inches long and 4 to 6 inches in diameter, usually with a rough skin. This tree is cultivated to a small extent in Florida and California and generally throughout the Tropics. The chief commercial cultivation of citron is in the Mediterranean region, particularly in Corsica. The dried peel is shipped to the United States to be candied.

The kumquat (*C. japonica*) is a bush 6 to 8 feet high and bears oblong or round fruit about one inch in diameter. The usual form of kumquat fruit is oblong. The Chinese orange is considered as being the variety *hazara* of the kumquat. This tree reaches a height of 10 to 20 feet and bears a great profusion of spherical fruit much used in making marmalade and as a flavor for papaya and other fruits. The bergamot (*C. bergamia*) is grown chiefly for the essential oil contained in the peel. A brief discussion of the preparation of this oil will be found under essential oils. *C. trifoliata* is used largely as a citrus stock on account of its extreme hardiness. The fruit is about 2 inches in diameter, is very acid, full of seed, and not very juicy. The mandarin group of citrus fruit includes the Dancy, the King mandarin, Satsuma, Mikado, and a number of other citrus varieties. The mandarin group is commonly referred to as *C. nobilis* and these varieties are known either as mandarins or tangerines.

In the early years of its development in Florida the citrus industry made a slow and gradual growth until the season of 1884-85, at which time 600,000 boxes of citrus fruits were shipped out of Florida groves. During the next decade the industry increased very rapidly and 6,000,000 boxes of citrus fruits were shipped from Florida in the season of 1894-95. The industry was then greatly crippled by the great freeze, after which it built up rapidly again. For the year ended August 31, 1915, California shipped 40,986 cars of oranges and 6,658 cars of lemons. The popularity of the Valencia orange has so greatly increased that it can no longer be said that the California orange industry consists in growing the navel orange. The lemon crop of California in 1915 was more than twice that of the previous year. There are now in California 20,000 acres of lemons, 21,000 acres of Valencia orange, and 43,500 acres of Washington Navel orange, all 4 years or under in age. When these areas of citrus fruit come into bearing it will greatly increase the output from California. Florida shipped 20,706 carloads of oranges and grapefruit from December, 1914, to August, 1915.

The recent development of the citrus industry in the United States is due chiefly to coöperative organization, regulated distribution, and the scientific study of methods of packing, precooling, and shipment in refrigeration. The organization of the California Citrus Growers' Association was one of the pioneer associations along the line of agricultural coöperation in the United States, and has been frequently used as a model of efficiency and methods in the organization of other similar associations. The Florida Citrus Exchange is of more recent development, but is of almost, if not quite, equal efficiency as an agency for the scientific distribution of the Florida citrus crop. In addition to the citrus fruit produced in this country, the United States imported in 1914 about 160,000,000 pounds of lemons and about 4,000,000 pounds of oranges. At present the consensus of opinion gives the first rank to the grapefruit from Florida and Porto Rico. California grapefruit are more bitter and not so juicy. The lemon industry in the United States, however, is almost entirely confined to California. Little success has been had in growing lemons in Florida except in a few restricted localities.

Citrus fruits run wild in various parts of the Tropics, thus resulting in the development of numerous seedlings. Some Hawaiian and Porto Rican seedling oranges are of excellent flavor and are gradually finding an appreciative market. The Porto Rican seedling oranges are shipped in large quantities to New York City, where they are sold to the poorer inhabitants of the East Side. In the matter of citrus fruit, at least, the East Side residents get a far better bargain than their more prosperous fellow citizens, since the seedling fruit cost much less than the standard varieties of oranges and are for the most part actually of superior flavor to the Navel and Valencia oranges. The same statement applies with equal force to some of the Hawaiian seedling oranges, which are far superior to the California oranges shipped to the Honolulu markets. The citrus industry is rapidly developing in one line or another in various tropical countries. As an example of one special line of development, it may be mentioned that perhaps the chief export from the Dominican Republic is concentrated lime juice.

The orange-producing countries stand in the following order: United States, Spain, Italy, Palestine, Japan, Porto Rico, Cuba, etc. The total production of oranges amounts to 40,-000,000 boxes per year. The lemon-producing countries stand in the following order: Sicily, Italy, California, etc. The total production of lemons is 7,000,000 boxes per year. The citrus industry, as a whole, results not only in the production of enormous quantities of fruit to be consumed in a fresh condition, but also in various by-products, such as lime juice, lemon juice, citric acid, orange juice, orange wine, orange vinegar, lemon oil, bergamot perfume, and various other products.

In recent years a keen rivalry for the early citrus fruit market has developed between California, Florida, and Porto Rico. The highest prices are obtained usually for the earliest shipments of fruit which the market receives. From a financial standpoint, therefore, it has been a point of great advantage to reach the market first with grapefruit or oranges or other fruit in which the shipper is interested. No one of these competitors has any pronounced natural advantage of earliness from climatic conditions over his competitors. The race for the early market has therefore involved certain tricks of the trade, and among these perhaps the most familiar one is the process of artificial ripening. It has been found that by a sweating process under the influence of artificial heat the chlorophyll or green color in the unripe fruit may be made to disappear quickly, thus producing the appearance of ripeness in so far as the bright yellow color of the rind of the fruit is concerned. Of course, the development of sugar in the fruit can not keep pace with this change of color, and artificially ripened fruit may therefore be readily detected by the narrow ratio between acid and total solids in the juice, these total solids being chiefly sugar. After numerous tests on ripe oranges it has been determined that the ratio of acid to total solids in the juice should not be closer than 1 : 8 as a standard requirement. In fruit artificially ripened by sweating the ratio between acids and total solids may be as close as 1 : 5. The United States Department of Agriculture is attempting to prevent the use of this process of artificial ripening for the reason that it is essentially a fraud toward the consumer.

OLIVE

The olive is one of the oldest of cultivated crops. It is native of Asia Minor and is referred by botanists to the name

Olea europæa. The olive is cultivated chiefly around the Mediterranan, particularly in Asia Minor, North Africa, Turkey, Greece, Austria, Italy, France, Spain, and Portugal. It has been introduced and cultivated on a small scale in nearly all subtropical and tropical countries, but aside from the Mediterranean region California is the only district in which olive production has been developed on a commercial scale. The United States imported 5,000,000 pounds of olives in 1914 and 8,000,000 gallons of olive oil. This indicates the increasing favor with which olives are treated in the United States.

The olive is an evergreen tree with narrow, lanceolate, leathery leaves, small white fragrant flowers and a spherical or ovate fruit which is bluish-black when ripe. The olive is ¾ to 1 inch in diameter and has a hard pit. The olive is easily propagated by cuttings or layers as well as by seed. Old trees may be easily improved by budding or grafting. The olive seldom fruits in Ceylon or Hawaii, although the trees reach a large size and show the usual vigor of growth in these countries. The reason for their sterility is not understood. Like citrus fruit the olive is not strictly a tropical plant, but will endure a temperature of 20° F. or in the case of some varieties even a temperature of 14° F. Such temperatures, however, cause injury unless the trees are in the most dormant condition. The olive tree lives to a great age. There are trees in Palestine which are said to be 500 to 1,000 years old. Wild trees, if not cultivated, bear only every 2 or 3 years.

Olive trees reach a height of about 40 feet and have a rounded, dense, and graceful head. The strongest, heaviest bearing and longest lived olive trees are those which are grown from seed. It should be remembered, too, that olive fruit is always borne on 2-year-old wood and that the same wood never bears twice. It is necessary, therefore, to maintain a good growth of new wood every year.

In California the olive region corresponds quite closely with that of the raisin grape. The tree appears to thrive on any well drained soil which is supplied with sufficient lime. If young trees for planting are to be obtained from seedlings, it is well to soak the seed for several hours in a 10 per cent. solution of caustic potash before planting, otherwise they require a long time to sprout. Cuttings of almost any size or age may be rooted in the nursery, but these cuttings should preferably not be less than 3/4 inch in diameter. The young seedlings are grafted near the surface of the ground. The olive requires essentially the same cultural methods as citrus fruits. In California this means clean cultivation, the occasional use of cover crops, and rather heavy applications of irrigation water at long intervals.

The yield of olives in the profitable orchards of California varies from 1,000 to 8,000 pounds per acre. For pickling large olives are selected, while for use in obtaining oils the smaller fruit and culls may be successfully employed. The preferred varieties of olives in California are Mission, Sevallana, Manzanillo, and Ascolano. The process of pickling olives includes three essential steps. The olives are first soaked for about 12 hours in a solution of caustic potash at the rate of 1½ pounds to 12 gallons of water. As soon as the lye has penetrated nearly to the pit the olives are removed to pure water in which they remain for 2 or 3 days, the water being changed at least once a day. After the lye and bitterness have been removed the olives are placed in salt brine of gradually increasing strength. For olives which are intended to be bottled or canned a brine containing 5 pounds of salt to 12 gallons of water is strong enough.

For use as green pickles, olives are picked when fully grown, but before coloring. For use as ripe pickles or for oil olives are picked after coloring, but before turning black. The olive industry in California is a thriving and profitable one. At present the olive industry ranks along with the walnut industry among the most profitable agricultural operations in California. During the development of the olive industry in

FEIJOA TWIGS AND FRUIT

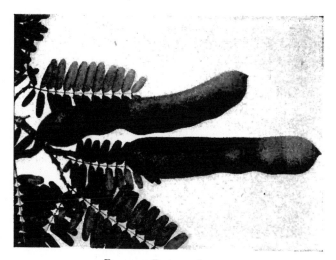

TAMARIND PODS AND LEAVES

California more than 70 varieties of olives have been tested, but the varieties mentioned above have come to be considered as superior.

DATE

The date palm was also one of the earliest plants to be cultivated by man. It is a native of northern Africa and Arabia, but is also cultivated extensively in southern Asia and sparingly throughout the Tropics. Beginnings in date cultivation have been made in Arizona, New Mexico, California, and Florida. The date palm referred by botanists to the name *Phoenix dactylifera* is a tree with a shaggy trunk which often reaches a height of 100 feet or more and continues to bear fruit for 100 to 200 years. The trunk is topped with a large crown of long pinnate leaves and bears 6 to 20 large clusters of fruit, each cluster weighing 20 to 40 pounds. The date palm is diecious, the male and female flowers growing on different trees. The common practice of Arabs is to hang small portions of the clusters of male flowers with the clusters of female flowers. As a rule, it is considered sufficient to have one male tree for each 25 female trees. The ordinary planting distance is 25 by 25 feet. The date palm usually begins bearing at 4 years of age and attains full bearing at about 10 years. The fruit yield ranges from 100 to 600 pounds per tree, being usually 100 pounds or slightly more.

The date palm differs from most other palms in producing suckers at the base of the stem at least during the first 8 or 10 years of its life. Old date palms which have obtained nearly full height do not develop suckers. The date palm does not come true to seed and for the continuation of desirable varieties it is therefore necessary to plant suckers or offsets. Recently an attempt has been made to develop a pedigreed strain of seed from which it is hoped that 30 to 50 per cent. of the resulting trees will bear fruit of the same type as that of the parent tree. It is too early, however, to say whether this expectation will be completely realized. Seedling dates are seldom edible. For the most part they are bitter and do not develop a sufficient quantity of sugar. Even the seedling dates which are sweet enough usually have only the thinnest film of pulp about the seed, so that they are practically useless for table purposes. Occasionally, however, a fairly satisfactory seedling date is obtained.

The climatic and soil conditions necessary for the best growth of date palms include a dry air and high temperature at least during the later stages in the development of the fruit and an abundance of water at the roots of the trees. Provided the water is moving and not stagnant, the date will endure an unlimited amount of moisture. Moreover, it cannot be too hot for the date palm and the air cannot be too dry. The date palm is quite tolerant to alkali water. Among the numerous varieties of dates which have been introduced and grown in Arizona and California the Deglet-noor, Rhars, Wolfskill, Amaree, Tedmama, Hallawee, Zahdee, and Bhar have given excellent results.

For curing dates the whole bunch is removed and confined in a warm, moist chamber at a temperature of 80° to 90° F. It has been found that there are two chemical varieties of dates, one containing cane sugar and the other containing chiefly invert sugar. At some stage of development, however, all dates contain a high percentage of cane sugar. The greatest increase in sugar takes place shortly before ripening. It is impossible to ship fresh dates to any great distance on account of their susceptibility to injury and fermentation. The necessity arises, therefore, of providing facilities for curing near the date plantation. It has been found that artificially ripened dates are superior to the naturally ripened fruit in keeping quality. This is probably due to the fact that the artificially ripened date is more nearly sterilized by the treatment which it undergoes. The dried, cured date as ordinarily obtained on the market contains 1.9 per cent protein, 2.5 per cent. fat, and

70.6 per cent. sugar. The seed constitutes about 10 per cent. of the date by weight.

The commercial date industry of the United States is still in the experimental stage. Dates of excellent quality have been produced in Arizona, New Mexico, and California. There is a market in the United States for far more dates than can be produced in the country for many years to come. The United States imports about 25,000,000 pounds of dates annually.

FIG

The fig (*Ficus carica*) belongs, as the botanical name indicates, to a genus of tropical plants including more than 600 species of which many are familiar as species of rubber, banyan, and related plants. The fig is a native of Turkey and the Mediterranean. It is a shrub or tree of moderate size with palmately lobed leaves and peculiar hollow compound fruits. It is cultivated everywhere in the Tropics and subtropics as well as in the Southern States and California. In California the tree attains a large size. The fig tree is commonly propagated by cuttings. These cuttings are very easily rooted and after they have rooted and developed a few shoots carrying leaves, they are planted in the field at distances 25 by 25 feet. In the Orient, figs are planted much more closely together. For fresh consumption the favorite varieties are Celestial, White Adriatic, Golden, Black Ischia, Black California, etc.

The Smyrna fig is the fig of commerce and appears on the market in the familiar dried condition. The Smyrna fig is produced chiefly in the Mediterranean region and in California. Numerous attempts were made to grow the Smyrna fig in California before the introduction of the Capri fig and the fig wasp known as *Blastophaga grossorum*. The Smyrna fig in order to attain its normal flavor must be fertilized by the fig wasp. This insect was introduced into California in 1889, since which time a highly developed industry in Smyrna figs has come into existence. By means of a number of varieties of Capri figs the fig wasp is carried throughout the year in its different generations and stages. The wasp emerges from the Capri fig and enters the opening in the end of the Smyrna fig, carrying upon itself a portion of the Capri fig pollen and thus fertilizing the Smyrna fig, causing the normal development of seed, flavor, and aroma. It has been found that two Capri figs for each 100 Smyrna fig trees is sufficient for purposes of pollination. California produces about 15,000 tons of Smyrna figs annually, and in addition to this quantity the United States imports about 10,000 tons each year. The fig has a fairly high nutritive value for fruits, especially in the dried condition. The fresh fig contains 1.5 per cent. protein and 18.8 per cent. sugars, while the dried fig carries 4.3 per cent. protein and about 75 per cent. total sugars.

AVOCADO

The avocado (*Persea gratissima*) is a tree native to tropical America. It has become universally distributed through the Tropics and subtropics. The avocado is a tree which attains a height of 20 to 60 feet, has leaves 4 to 15 inches long and 2 to 10 inches wide, varying considerably in thickness and glossiness, and fruits which vary greatly in size and shape. The avocado fruit may be oblong, nearly spherical, pear shaped, or bottle shaped, and may vary in length from 5 to 12 inches, in weight from 1 to 4 pounds, and in color from green through the browns to purple. Moreover, the rind varies from almost the thinness of paper to a thick woody shell. The avocado has also been called aguacate and alligator pear. The last name has become generally distributed and is much used although it is really a barbarous and inappropriate term.

The avocado fruit has one large seed occupying the center of the fruit. In some seedlings and inferior varieties the seed in fact occupies the larger part of the fruit, leaving only a thin layer of pulp between the seed and skin. There are 200 or more known varieties of avocado which are cultivated in various parts of the Tropics and subtropics. The avocado is propagated by seed and by budding, grafting, or inarching. The seed are used merely to obtain the seedlings which can be budded, grafted, or inarched. The avocado does not come true to seed and it is therefore an unnecessary gamble to plant any considerable orchard to seedling avocados. Notwithstanding the great variation which occurs in the seedling avocados some of them possess flavor and other properties fully equal to the most improved varieties.

The avocado tree begins bearing at 5 or 6 years of age. There is occasionally a tree which bears fruit at 3 years and sometimes not until 7 years. The full bearing age may be expected at about 8 to 10 years. A yield of 500 fruits per tree must be considered quite satisfactory although occasionally trees have been reported as yielding from 800 to 2,000 fruits.

In general, the long green-colored varieties of avocado are preferred as being superior in texture and flavor. In Florida the Trapp avocado is generally cultivated. In California the varieties thus far planted have been obtained largely from Mexico and Hawaii. In Hawaii a large number of chance seedlings of superior merit have been propagated and varieties have been introduced from all parts of the world until about 65 varieties have been established at the Hawaii Experiment Station. One of these varieties, known as the Nutmeg, has an extremely hard woody shell covered with roughened protuberances. This is essentially a winter or very late variety and helps to extend very greatly the season during which avocados may be obtained on the market. The greater part of the crop of avocados in Hawaii comes to the market from June to August, but a good supply is maintained from May to September. Avocados arrive on the Honolulu market first from Kona in early April. Attention has been called to the fact that if one has regard to the whole avocado crop from Peru to Florida and including the Pacific Islands there are avocados on the market for all seasons of the year. The season during which fruit of good quality can be obtained in any reasonable quantity, however, is limited to a few months.

As a matter of fact, there cannot be said to be as yet any commercial avocado industry. While this tree has been grown in all localities throughout tropical countries, it has never been planted in commercial orchards except perhaps in Florida. We have, therefore, the curious condition of affairs that probably the largest avocado orchards in the world are now located in Florida in a locality where until recently it was not known whether avocados would thrive at all or not.

The avocado in chemical composition is more like a nut than like a fruit. The fresh fruit contains 1.5 to 2.5 per cent. protein and 13 to 22 per cent. oil depending upon variety and climate. There is practically no starch or sugar in the avocado fruit at any stage of growth. The oil may be easily extracted by pressure and is of a greenish color and excellent flavor. It would be a superior salad oil but would necessarily be extremely expensive since the demand for the fresh fruits is so active as to drive the price of the raw material far beyond the point which would allow an economic production of oil.

The avocado endures cold storage excellently well. At the Hawaii Experiment Station avocados were held for a period of 60 days at a temperature of 32° F. and when removed from the storage room were found to have retained their flavor almost perfectly. This refrigerated fruit held its flavor for a period of 6 days after removal from cold storage.

MANGO

The mango (*Mangifera indica*) is one of a group of about 30 species of trees native to tropical Asia. The mango is the only one in this group which produces fruit of value. It has been cultivated for centuries in India and was introduced into the Philippines in the sixteenth century. More recently much interest has been shown in the mango in Florida, Porto Rico, Cuba, and Hawaii. The mango is a beautiful evergreen tree, with dense foliage, entire leathery lanceolate leaves, and graceful panicles of small reddish-yellow or green flowers. The fruit is borne in pendant clusters on long pedicles and varies in size from 2 or 3 ounces to 3 pounds in weight, according to variety. The tree bears a crop of fruit each year or occasionally two crops will be borne on a few trees in the mango orchard. The mango is now widely distributed throughout the Tropics, where it occurs in a great range of varieties. About 600 varieties have been mentioned as occurring in India alone and new varieties are constantly appearing by the natural variation of seedlings and as a result of cross-pollination in orchards of mixed varieties. Some of these variety names are doubtless synonymous but the number of horticulturally distinct varieties is unquestionably large.

The mango is nowhere grown in large continuous orchards but almost everyone in the Tropics has a mango tree. Some of the most delicious varieties of mangos come from the Philippines, where the chief varieties are Carabao, Pico, and Pahutan. Some of the noted and most highly esteemed Indian varieties of mango are Alphonse, Totapari, Cambodiana, Mulgoa, Mulgoba, Sandersha, Brindabani, etc. In addition to these well known improved varieties of superior flavor and other merits, there are hundreds of varieties of seedling trees, some of which are of rather high merit but which are likely to be full of fiber and permeated with the flavor of turpentine.

The esteem in which the mango is held as a fruit for eating in a fresh condition depends almost entirely on the varieties with which acquaintance has been had. If one's notion of the mango came from attempts to eat the ordinary stringy turpentiny seedling, the mango would be considered as a practically worthless fruit. On the other hand, some of the best varieties have a delicate aroma and a flavor of the highest delicacy. It is unquestionable that if the standard varieties of mangos could be placed on the northern markets in prime condition the demand for them would soon far exceed that for any other fresh tropical fruit except bananas and pineapples. The color and shape of the mango fruit vary greatly as well as the size of the fruit. The color ranges from green to yellow, and various peach tints to a decided magenta, and the rind may be variously speckled with yellow or pink spots or with a blush of high color on one side of the fruit. The amount of fiber in the fruit also varies greatly. In some varieties the slicing of the fruit with a knife makes a noise like the operation of shaving a stiff beard. In other varieties the pulp is so free from fiber and of such consistency that it may be readily eaten with a spoon.

The mango, with the exception of some of the Philippine varieties, does not come true to seed. It should be propagated therefore by the methods of inarching, budding, grafting, or bark grafting. In some of the seedling types, particularly those from the Philippines, the seed is polyembryonic, each seed producing 6 to 8 or more plants. Such types of mangos usually come fairly true to seed. In planting the seed the husk should be removed. This hastens germination and also enables one to see whether he is planting a good kernel or a mere empty husk. It should be remembered that the seeds do not retain their germinating power more than one to two months after removal from the fruit. In many localities in the Tropics seed is likely to be destroyed by the mango weevil, which enters the fruit when it is young and goes through its transformations in the kernel of the seed.

The flower panicles, the young fruit, and the growing twigs are often attacked by the fungous disease known as the mango anthracnose. This causes a blighting of the twigs and flowers and prevents the setting of fruit. It is particularly prevalent

Fruiting Branch of Litchi

in moist weather but it can be controlled by spraying with Bordeaux mixture unless repeated and frequent rain storms occur during the flowering season. The fruit also fails to set if high winds and heavy rains occur during the flowering season even without the attacks of anthracnose. If the setting of fruit should thus be prevented by these causes a new crop of flowers may be produced a month or two later, thus bringing a crop of fruit to maturity out of the regular season. In these respects the mango is like the avocado, which is also affected by anthracnose in the same manner and which may be prevented from setting fruit by persistent rain during the flowering season.

The mango has often been called the apple of the Tropics and sometimes the king of fruits. The term apple of the Tropics is more or less appropriate since it occurs in such great abundance throughout the Tropics, is in everybody's dooryard, and is eaten in the fresh condition, stewed, or made into jellies and marmalade. The comparison appears even more close when one remembers that the green mango, like the green apple, is an important part of the ration of young boys. Wherever the Mediterranean fruit fly prevails most varieties of mangos are seriously attacked by this pest.

The mango is not only a delicious fruit for consumption in the fresh condition but makes an excellent green sauce resembling green apple sauce in appearance and flavor. The fruit when cooked in a green condition jellies readily and may therefore be used for jam, jelly, or marmalade. Moreover, the mango is widely used in the preparation of Chutney sauce which contains mango, raisins, tamarind, chili, mace, cloves, pimento, salt, and mustard seed. The mango endures shipment well and may be held in cold storage without injury for a period of 6 to 8 weeks at a temperature of 32° to 40° F.

The seedling mango tree comes into bearing at about 6 or 7 years of age. Inarched and budded mangos, however, may be brought to bearing within 2 or 3 years. In some cases inarched trees have borne within 18 months after the process of inarching.

The mango was first planted in Florida on the Keys in the forties and on Biscayne Bay, Florida, at about the same time. The first trees to develop in Florida were therefore seedlings. Grafted specimens of the Mulgoba mango were brought to Florida in 1889. The varieties at present grown in Florida fruit from May to September. For shipment to the northern cities mangos are picked after developing their color and before softening. The amount of sugar in mangos range from 11.5 to 20 per cent., depending upon the variety and stage of ripeness. Mangos also contain from 0.5 to 1 per cent. protein and therefore in their nutritive value compare favorably with other common fruits.

PAPAYA

The papaya is native to Central America and the West Indies. The type which has made the greatest place for itself belongs to the species *Carica papaya*. The other common types of papaya are *C. paltata*, *C. quercifolia*, *C. erythrocarpa*, etc. The common papaya, often called papaw, especially in the English tropical colonies but having no close relationship with the common papaw of the central states, occurs everywhere throughout the Tropics and subtropics. It grows wild even in Florida. The trunk of the papaya tree reaches a height of 25 feet and bears long stemmed, palmately seven-lobed leaves, which are about 2 feet across. The leaves are borne in a crown at the top of the tree and fall away as soon as mature, leaving a large characteristic scar on the trunk of the tree. The trunk is sometimes branched but usually is unbranched and erect. The fruit of the papaya varies in size from that of a tennis ball to long watermelon-like fruit, weighing sometimes 18 pounds and measuring 16 inches in length. The fruit varies greatly also in shape from perfectly spherical to elongated or cucumber form and several types of papaya are distinctly pentagonal. The fruit of *Carica erythrocarpa* is similar to that of the common papaya but has a red flesh and an extremely thin rind. This species has sometimes been considered as particularly useful in the production of papain. The fruit of *C. candamarcensis* is about the size of a baseball, rich yellow in color, and five-angled. The flavor is not particularly meritorious. The leaves of this species are cordate, palmately five-lobed, and smaller than in the common papaya. *C. quercifolia* is a curious branched, small-fruited papaya with oak-like leaves and clusters of ellipsoid yellow fruit 1 or 2 inches in length.

The papaya is commonly propagated by seed but does not come true. The variation in the size, shape, and flavor of papayas is therefore without end or restraint. It has recently been found that the papaya may be readily grafted. This furnishes a method of propagating varieties of superior merit. After a tree has come to bearing and has shown a desirable flavor and size of fruit the tree may be beheaded, after which a large number of shoots will appear near the tip of the trunk. These shoots may be grafted by the ordinary wedge process into the trunks of small seedlings about 1 inch in diameter. No difficulty is experienced in propagating by this method.

Another method of establishing a desirable type of papaya has been for some time under investigation at the Hawaii Experiment Station. This method is based on an attempt to eliminate the male papaya and to secure a type which will produce only hermaphrodite plants. It should be remembered that the papaya is normally a diecious tree and that about half of the trees are male and half female. The conditions which appear in the reproductive organ of the papaya, however, are extremely variable. For the most part the flowers on the male trees are small and borne in long branching panicles 2 to 5 feet in length. The flowers on the female trees, on the other hand, are large and nearly sessile along the side of the trunk in the axils of the leaves. In some cases fruit of superior quality is borne on the male trees. Some male trees bear regularly and quite heavily, but the fruit hang suspended on long pedicles rather than being sessile on the side of the trunk as in female trees. Occasionally, a female tree is found in which the flowers are perfect. At the Hawaii Experiment Station a flower on a tree of this type was self-fertilized and protected from cross-pollination. The seed obtained from the resulting fruit were all planted and as soon as the trees came into bearing a selection was made of the most desirable type and on this tree the flower was again cross-pollinated and a second generation of trees obtained. This second generation included 454 trees and a careful examination of these trees showed that 95 per cent. were self-fertile. This gives reason to hope that within a few more generations a self-fertile type will be established which will obviate the necessity of cross-pollination and prevent the endless variation which occurs from this method of propagation.

The papaya comes into bearing perhaps earlier than any other fruit tree. Under favorable conditions large ripe fruit may be obtained within 11 or 12 months from the time of planting the seed. The trunk is succulent and starchy and grows very rapidly. For commercial purposes it is perhaps desirable to cut down the orchard and replant at the end of 3 years since the papaya tree has the peculiar habit of tapering to a point, after which the fruit is extremely small. The papaya is one of the few commercial plants in which it has been found possible to change the sex by mutilation. At the Hawaii Experiment Station, 22 perfectly sterile, staminate papaya trees were beheaded. When the new growth appeared on these trees it was found that two of the trees had become strictly female trees bearing large fruit. Change of sex in papaya has also been produced in one or two instances by other investigators.

The juice of the fruit, stem, and leaves of the papaya contains an active ferment known as papain, a vegetable pepsin.

The milky juice pours out of the rind of the green fruit in abundance after shallow tapping. In an investigation at the Hawaii Experiment Station it was found that if in the early morning a dozen shallow lengthwise incisions, ½ to ¾ inch apart, were made in a papaya fruit of good size, enough juice would be obtained to make an ounce of dry papain. Crude dry papain ordinarily brings about $2 a pound on the market. This ferment is even more active than the common ferment of the pineapple, but like that of the pineapple is destroyed by cooking. The action of the papaya ferment is so well known that it is used for various purposes throughout the Tropics. If a piece of tough steak is wrapped in a bruised papaya leaf the papaya ferment will rapidly make the steak tender. Papain has also been used in medicine in dissolving the membranes which occur in diphtheria.

The papaya is eaten for the most part in a fresh condition and may be had the year round. In fact, there are always ripe and green fruit on the papaya tree. It is also sometimes stewed like a squash and eaten as a vegetable. The fruit contains no starch at any stage of growth. In a ripe condition the papaya contains from 7 to 10 per cent. of sugar and about 0.5 per cent. protein.

GUAVA

The common or lemon guava (*Psidium guajava*) is a native bush or small tree of tropical America reaching a height of 3 to 30 feet. The plant has been introduced into all tropical and subtropical countries, including Florida, where it runs wild, bearing large crops of fruit. In Hawaii and a few other regions the guava has become a fearful pest necessitating the expenditure of large sums of money for its eradication. It occurs throughout the Territory of Hawaii in a wild condition and the fruit are collected for making guava jam or jelly. Guava is cultivated in Florida and California. The leaves of this tree are opposite and bright green, the flowers are four-petaled and white, being nearly sessile in the axiles of the leaves. The fruit is 2 to 4 inches in diameter, with a yellow rind when ripe and somewhat resembling a lemon in appearance. The flesh is pink and full of seeds. The peculiar aroma of the fresh fruit is usually not well liked on first acquaintance. The strawberry guava (*P. cattleianum*) is a small tree attaining a height of 20 feet and bearing thicker and smaller leaves than lemon guava. The fruit is much smaller, being ¾ to 1½ inches in diameter and of a dark crimson or maroon color. For use as a fresh fruit the flavor is far superior to that of the lemon guava but the strawberry guava is less desirable for use in jams and jellies. The tree bears within 2 or 3 years from seeding and is cultivated in both Florida and California. The guava fruit contains 4 to 10 per cent. of sugar and 1 per cent. of protein. As already indicated, the lemon guava is extremely well adapted for use in making jams and jellies. A considerable industry in this product has been established in Hawaii, Cuba, Porto Rico, Florida, and elsewhere. Guava jelly or jam is almost universally well liked even on first acquaintance and there seems to be good prospect for a rather large extension of this industry.

FEIJOA

The feijoa is a guava-like shrub 5 to 15 feet high, native of Paraguay, Brazil, Uruguay, and Argentina. Its botanical name is *Feijoa sellowiana*. The leaves resemble those of the olive and are silver-gray beneath. The flowers are white and with four petals and the fruit is about 2 inches long and 1½ inches thick. The feijoa fruit is of a green color or often with a slight crimson blush on one side, and the seed, while distributed in large numbers through the pulp of the fruit, as in the guava, are less objectionable than guava seed on account of their small size. The feijoa has a flavor somewhat resembling a mixture of the pineapple and strawberry and is

ROSELLE; THE THICK CALYX IS THE EDIBLE PART

CHERIMOYER, ONE OF THE CUSTARD APPLES

eaten fresh or in jams or jellies. The bush thrives best in a moderately dry climate. It is propagated either by seed or cuttings and the usual planting distance is 15 by 15 feet. Outside of South America the feijoa is cultivated in France, Italy, and various other subtropical regions. It was introduced into the United States in 1900 and a considerable industry in producing feijoa has been developed in California, where the fruit may be found upon the market in season.

POMEGRANATE

The pomegranate (*Punica granatum*) is a bush or small tree native to the Mediterranean region and south Asia and is now cultivated everywhere in the Tropics and subtropics, including the Southern States and California. The pomegranate is grown both for ornamental purposes and for its fruit. The bush reaches a height of 6 to 20 feet. The calyx of the flowers is red and thick, the petals are of an unusually brilliant scarlet color, and the leaves are glossy. The fruit when ripe is red, orange, or yellow in color, about 2 to 4 inches in diameter, with a tough rind and with crimson acid pulp in which the numerous seed are embedded. In localities north of the Equator the pomegranate usually fruits from September to December. It is propagated by cuttings. The pulp of the fruit is eaten raw or is used in cooling drinks or sometimes condensed into sirups. Superior varieties may be perpetuated by budding or grafting. Certain varieties of the pomegranate have only a few seed and a much larger percentage of pulp than the common varieties. The pulp of the fruit contains about 6 per cent. of sugar. The rind has a high percentage of tannin and has occasionally been used as a source of tannin. The pomegranate is commonly allowed to grow in dooryards without much attention but where it is cultivated commercially the usual planting distance is 8 by 8 feet.

TAMARIND

The tamarind (*Tamarindus indica*) is a large rather graceful tree, native of tropical Asia and Africa. It is found almost everywhere in tropical countries, being considered as a valuable shade tree and source of food. The tamarind is a stately leguminous tree with pinnate leaves, like those of the acacia, and yellowish-red flowers about 1 inch across. The tree bears jointed moniliform brown pods 2 to 5 inches in length which are filled with a sweet sugary pulp much used in cooling drinks and for making jam and also a medicine. The tree is propagated either by seed or cuttings. In trade "Tamarinds" are the whole pods of the tamarind tree. This tree fruits generally in January and February. On the mainland of the United States it is grown in Florida and California. While the tamarind is a leguminous tree with characteristic pods, it is here classed with fruits because as a food product it is used in jams and for other purposes in the manner of fruits. The tamarind pods contain 3.5 per cent. of protein and 21 per cent. of sugar. In India tamarind seeds are universally eaten by the natives.

LITCHI

The litchi (*Nephelium litchi*) is a small tree native of China with dense foliage of rich green, shiny leaves, racemes of greenish flowers, and clusters of spherical fruit about 1 inch in diameter. The skin of the fruit is wine-red or brown in color, and the fruit ripens usually in June. Each fruit contains one seed in a firm jellylike whitish pulp or aril of delicious flavor. The litchi is cultivated throughout the Tropics, especially in China, Cochin China, and India. In China the production of dried litchi fruit is a large industry. Dried litchis are shipped to the United States and Europe in considerable quantities. There are several varieties of quite unlike excellence. The tree is best propagated by grafting.

When grown from seed the litchi does not fruit until 10 years of age or older. The fresh fruit contains 1½ per cent. of protein and 8.5 per cent. of sugar. In a dried condition the rind becomes a thin papery shell, while the sweet pulp shrinks away from the rind in a mass surrounding the seed. The litchi was brought to Florida in 1886 and is grown in various localities in the southern part of the State but apparently has not done well.

The longan (*N. longana*) is a native of Eastern Bengal. The tree and fruit much resemble those of the litchi but the fruit is of inferior flavor and value.

The rambutan (*N. lappaceum*) is a large fine tree with good spread of branches. It is a native of the Federated Malay States. The fruit is produced in clusters and is orange or red in color and about ½ inch in diameter. Like the litchi, the fruit has one seed which is surrounded with a white acid pulp of rather agreeable flavor. The rambutan is propagated by seed or grafting but as a matter of fact is little cultivated anywhere.

ROSELLE

The roselle (*Hibiscus sabdariffa*) is an annual semishrubby mallow about 4 to 10 feet high with palmately five-parted leaves and handsome sessile yellow flowers with a crimson eye. It is a native of the West Indies and is now quite extensively cultivated in India, Queensland, Ceylon, the West Indies, Hawaii, the Philippines, Florida, and California. The edible portion of the fruit consists of the greatly thickened calyx leaves which are of a brilliant crimson or wine color when ripe. The fruit ripens about 3 weeks after flowering.

The roselle is propagated by seed either planted in the field or in the nursery, from which seedlings are later transplanted when they reach a height of 6 to 18 inches. The best variety of roselle is perhaps the Victor. A poor variety with small fruit has been introduced into various countries from Africa but does not seem to be of much promise. North of the Equator the roselle is planted in February or March with a spacing 4 by 4 feet or 6 by 6 feet. The fruit is ready for harvest in November and December. In Hawaii it has been found that March is decidedly the best month for planting roselle. If planted later it ripens its fruit as early as if it had been planted in March but the fruit is inferior in quality and the yield is considerably reduced.

In 1914, about 220 acres of roselle were planted on the Island of Maui between the young trees of a ceara rubber plantation. The planting distance adopted was 5 by 5 feet. The district in which the roselle was planted was one of high rainfall, averaging about 150 inches per year. The plants yielded at the rate of 10 pounds of fruit per plant or approximately 17,000 pounds of fresh fruit per acre. This is far above the average yield, which may be taken as being about 5,000 pounds per acre. The roselle fruit will not stand shipment in a fresh condition. It must, therefore, be dried on the plantation. Moreover, if the atmosphere is humid it is necessary to provide artificial heat for drying. If large drying rooms are constructed in which a temperature of 120° to 140° F. can be maintained, the fruit requires from 24 to 48 hours for desiccation. In drying roselle it has been found that 10 pounds of green fruit make 1 pound of dried material.

The only portion of the fruit used for edible purposes is the calyx. The seed pod is removed either after picking or is separated from the calyx at the time of picking. The harvesting of the crop is the most expensive operation in connection with the growing of roselle.

A firm has been organized in Chicago to handle the roselle crop on a large scale. This firm has encouraged the production of roselle in Queensland, Hawaii, Mexico, and elsewhere, and has purchased all the product in a dried form. In 1914, the product amounted to about 500,000 pounds of the dried fruit. This material makes a most excellent and delicious jam or jelly and has also been used as a basis of a fruit juice which is proposed as a rival for grapejuice. The color of the juice is a beautiful wine-red and the flavor is quite satisfactory.

The leaves of the roselle are used to some extent for boiled greens in Hawaii and are used in curries in India. Roselle seeds are quite commonly used as poultry feed and the bast in the bark has been extensively used for fiber. In fact, for many years roselle wás grown in India chiefly as a fiber plant. This matter is discussed under fibers.

Roselle is a good example of a fruit which, while possessing an excellent color and flavor in any preparation for which it is used, has little nutritive value. The fresh fruit contains about 1 per cent. of protein, 2 per cent. of acid, and about 0.2 per cent. of sugar. The flavor of roselle jelly somewhat resembles that of the cranberry but is perhaps more delicate.

MANGOSTEEN

Many writers on tropical fruits have considered the mangosteen as the most delicious of all known fruits, but this is a matter of taste. The mangosteen (*Garcinia mangostana*) is a tree of medium size native to the Federated Malay States. The leaves are large and glossy green and the tree comes into bearing at about 10 years of age. The fruit is purplish-brown, spherical in shape, and 2 or 3 inches in diameter. The rind is thick, tough, and leathery and surrounds the white edible pulp in which the seed are embedded. Each fruit contains from one to 4 or 5 seed, but often only one of these seed is fully developed. The mangosteen thrives best at low altitudes in hot moist districts. It is therefore strictly tropical in distribution. The tree which ultimately attains a height of 20 to 30 feet is of extremely slow growth. Seedling mangosteens are inferior in flavor and other qualities to grafted varieties. Most mangosteens, however, are seedlings since thus far little attention has been given to artificial methods of propagation.

The seeds are commonly planted single in pots and the seedlings are transplanted when they reach a height of about 2 feet. The mangosteen has no commercial importance.

CUSTARD APPLES
Sour Sop, Sweet Sop, Cherimoyer, and Bull's Heart

Among the various species of custard apple known in the Tropics the four just named are best known and most widely used. The sour sop (*Anona muricata*) is a native of the West Indies. It is a quick-growing shrub or tree which attains a height of 15 to 20 feet and bears ovate or reniform fruit weighing 4 to 10 pounds and covered with flexible green prickles. The pulp of the fruit is white and contains large black seeds. The sour sop has a sweet-acid flavor and is eaten either out of hand or in ices and cool drinks. The sour sop has become widely distributed throughout tropical countries.

The bull's heart (*A. reticulata*) is a bushy tree with large smooth heart-shaped fruit of a yellow and reddish-brown color. This tree is a native of the West Indies but is quite widely cultivated in the Oriental Tropics. The fruit is rather insipid.

The sweet sop (*A. squamosa*), also called custard apple or sugar apple, is a small tree native of Asia and Central America and is now widely cultivated in the Tropics and subtropics. The fruit is about the size of an apple and the rind of the fruit is formed of scales which when ripe break away from the white, sweet, granular pulp. The tree thrives best in dry localities up to an altitude of 2,500 feet. The sweet sop is propagated by seed, cuttings, or grafting. The fruit weighs about 1½ pounds but varies greatly in size in different localities. Each fruit contains from 50 to 60 seed. The sweet sop contains 1 to 2 per cent. protein and 16 to 18 per cent. sugar. The customary planting distance for this tree is about 10 by 10 feet.

The cherimoyer (*A. cherimolia*) is a small tree native of

OLIVIER VARIETY OF LOQUAT

South America and of the West Indies. It bears green round fruit 2 to 5 inches in diameter and weighs 2 or 3 pounds, with a pitted rind. The opinions expressed as to the flavor of this fruit must be purely personal since it is highly esteemed by some and detested by others. The cherimoyer is propagated by grafting. The tree appears to prefer dry hills. It is widely cultivated in Madeira, Canary Islands, and also to some extent throughout all tropical countries. It thrives best perhaps in stony soil and the planting distance is 10 by 10 feet. There is a great variation in the quality and flavor of the fruit of different varieties. The best varieties are propagated by grafting. The fruit commonly contains 1.5 per cent. protein and about 18 per cent. sugar.

Sour sop, sweet sop, cherimoyer, and other custard apples grow and fruit in Florida, but the cherimoyer does not always fruit well. It has been found that it is pollinated by insects. Crosses have been made between the sweet sop and cherimoyer, which promise to do better than either of the parent forms.

LOQUAT

The loquat (*Eriobotrya japonica*) is a small or medium-sized tree, native of China, and extensively cultivated in Japan, India, Australia, Italy, Sicily, and to some extent in Hawaii, California, Florida, Georgia, Mississippi, and Louisiana. The only commercial cultivation of loquat in the United States is in California. The loquat is an evergreen tree, rather closely branched, and much used as an ornamental as well as for its fruit. The leaves are alternate, dentate, densely tomentose beneath, and the small cream-colored flowers are borne in terminal panicles. The fruit is pear-shaped, about 1 to 1½ inches in length, and lemon-yellow or orange-red in color, with 1 to 4 or more large black seed and a small amount of pulp with acid-agreeable flavor.

The loquat is propagated by seed, cuttings, budding, or grafting. Seedling loquats are of poor quality. Cuttings are rather slow in development and uncertain. The preferred method of propagation is by budding and the quince, or seedling loquat, is most used for stock upon which to insert the bud. In California, the trees are planted about 12 by 24 feet apart. Budded trees begin bearing at the age of 4 or 5 years and reach full bearing at 10 years of age, when the yield is about 200 pounds of fruit per tree. The fruit matures in the spring. Loquats are consumed chiefly as fresh fruit but are also used in making jelly, jam, and preserves. The fruit is well adapted for this purpose, and the flavor is delicate and extremely agreeable. There are perhaps 100 or more well known varieties of loquat but the varieties most prized in California are Early Red, Thales, Champaign, Advance, and Victor. The loquat thrives within about the same temperature limits as are required by lemons. The fresh fruit contains 4 per cent. of sugar.

MALAY APPLE, SURINAM CHERRY, ROSE APPLE

These three tropical fruits are closely related botanically, and it seems desirable, therefore, to refer to them briefly in conjunction with one another.

The Malay apple (*Eugenia malaccensis*) is a handsome tree native to Malaya and attains a height of 20 to 50 feet. The tree bears dense racemes of red flowers in graceful pompons and later a profusion of bright red fruit with a white pithy pulp. In Hawaii, the fruit is called Mountain apple. Each fruit has one large seed. The tree is propagated by seed but as a matter of fact has not been widely cultivated. In some parts of Hawaii it is a common forest tree occurring in large areas. The fruit of the Malay apple is only sparingly seen on the market. The skin is unusually thin and delicate and is therefore easily injured in shipment. It can be shipped only short distances, perhaps within the limit of 24 hours. The fruit is eaten fresh, in which state it has an agreeable but not very pronounced flavor, or may be used in making vinegar. The fruit contains 6.8 per cent. of sugar.

The Surinam cherry (*Eugenia micheli*) is a small tree native of Brazil. It bears a round, ribbed fruit 1 inch in diameter, of bright red color, somewhat resembling the tomato. The pulp of the Surinam cherry is too acid to, eat fresh, but is quite extensively used in preserves. This fruit is also called the Brazil cherry. The tree bears small white flowers and is propagated by seed. The fruit contains 1 per cent. protein and 6 per cent. sugar.

The rose apple (*E. jambos*) is a tree of medium size, native of India. It bears fragrant rose-colored fruit of sweet-acid flavor, and is 1½ inches in diameter. This fruit is much used in preserves. The tree thrives in moist districts up to an altitude of 3,000 feet. It is cultivated in Ceylon and to a less extent in Hawaii and other tropical countries. The fruit is usually of inferior quality. The flowers of this tree are large and bear numerous long white stamens. The rose apple in fresh condition contains 12 per cent. sugar. It is grown in California for its foliage or ornamental flowers but does not fruit in that state.

CAPE GOOSEBERRY

The Cape gooseberry (*Physalis peruviana*) is native of Peru but is now grown everywhere, even in some of the Northern States in this country. It is a straggling, more or less upright, herbaceous plant belonging to the same family with the potato and tomato. On the mainland of the United States it usually attains a height of 10 to 18 inches, but in Hawaii and other tropical regions it reaches a height of 1½ to 5 feet, with a spread of 6 to 10 feet. The leaves are irregularly toothed and heart-shaped at the base and very pubescent. The flowers are pale yellow and about ½ inch in diameter. The fruit when ripe is greenish-yellow, spherical, and the size of large marbles.

The fruit is surrounded by a loose papery husk. It is eaten either raw or in sauce, pies, and jam. In Hawaii the Cape gooseberry is called poha and is cultivated to a considerable extent. The fruit ships well and is sent to Honolulu in large quantities from the Island of Hawaii. The fruit contains 2 per cent. protein and 8 per cent. of sugar. In a fresh condition the Cape gooseberry is decidedly laxative.

PASSION FRUIT

A number of closely related species of passion vine bear edible fruit. The water lemon (*Passiflora laurifolia*) is a climbing vine, native of the West Indies, which bears yellow fruit about the size and shape of a goose egg. The rind is tough and leathery and the numerous seed are embedded in a gelatinous pulp. This species of passion fruit is widely cultivated in Hawaii. The passion fruit so widely cultivated in India and Australia is *Passiflora edulis* and has a purple rind. The granadilla (*P. quadrangularis*) is perhaps the most vigorous grower of all the species of passion fruit. It is a climbing vine, native of tropical America, and has become quite generally distributed throughout the Tropics. The fruit is oblong and attains a large size, being often 6 to 8 inches long and 3 or 4 inches in diameter.

The water lemon carries well in cold storage and may be safely held at a temperature of 32° F. for 3 months or longer. Their fine foliage and handsome flowers make all of these species suitable for ornamental purposes.

MAMMEE APPLE

The Mammee apple (*Mammea americana*) is a native of South America and the West Indies. The tree reaches a height of 35 to 60 feet and bears white fragrant flowers and spherical, round, brown, hard-shelled fruit 3 to 5 inches in diameter, with one or more seeds and a yellow, sweet aromatic pulp. The fruit is eaten fresh, stewed, or preserved, but the flavor is not commonly well liked. The flowers of the Mammee apple yield by distillation an essential oil used in liqueurs under the name eau de creole. The tree is propagated by seed. It thrives well in Florida, where it bears fruit of the usual size and quality.

WAMPI

The wampi (*Clausena lansium*) is closely related to citrus belonging in the same family with these fruits. It is a small tree attaining a height of 18 to 20 feet with a luxuriant development of smooth pinnates leaves and small dense panicles of white fragrant flowers. The wampi is native of southern China. The fruit develops in clusters like the grape, the individual fruit being nearly spherical and the size of a large marble. The rind is rough and leathery. The fruit contains 1 to 3 seed and the juicy pulp possesses an agreeable acid aromatic flavor. The wampi is not well suited for dessert fruit but may be used preferably in preserves and for flavoring meat curries. For this purpose both the leaves and the fruit may be used. The tree is propagated either by seed or by layering.

AMATUNGULA

The amatungula or Natal plum (*Carissa grandiflora*) is a South African fruiting shrub which was introduced by the U. S. Department of Agriculture and was later received for experiment in Hawaii. This plant has become quite widely distributed as a hedge and ornamental as well as a fruit bush. The bush has a densely branching habit and bears bright green leathery leaves and numerous thorns on the small branches. The flowers somewhat resemble those of the orange, being a pure white and slightly fragrant. The fruit is egg-shaped and about the size of a plum, the color being a brilliant crimson. The flavor of the fruit is acid and slightly bitter and is considered agreeable by some and practically worthless by others as a fresh fruit. It may be eaten either out of hand or may be used in the manufacture of jams and jellies. In India and Ceylon the fruit is quite widely used for pickling and in preserves. The Natal plum contains about 12 per cent. of sugar.

STAR APPLE

The Star apple is a handsome tree, native of West Indies, with unusually fine foliage, which is dark, shiny green above and golden brown beneath. The botanical name of the tree is *Chrysophyllum cainito*. There are several varieties of the Star apple, some of which bear purplish and others green fruit. The fruit is filled with a white and rather sticky latex until ripe, when the jellylike pulp around the seed has an agreeable sweet flavor. The name is due to the radiate or starlike seed cavities which are conspicuous when the fruit is cut across. The Star apple is not only a very satisfactory ornamental but the fruit is distinctly agreeable in flavor and occupies a rather important place in the list of tropical fruits which have not attained a commercial standing. North of the Equator the fruit commonly ripens from February to April. It may be safely held in cold storage and endures shipping very well. The Star apple contains 2.3 per cent. protein and 4.5 per cent. sugar.

DURIAN

The durian (*Durio zibethinus*) is a large, handsome pyramidal tree, native of the Malay Archipelago, and commonly cultivated in the Oriental Tropics. The durian fruit is round or oval and thickly armed with prickles. It is borne on the older branches, is of a yellowish color when ripe, and of an extremely offensive odor to all except those who have acquired a taste for the fruit. The durian bears fruit twice a year.

ROSE APPLE, FLOWERS AND FRUIT

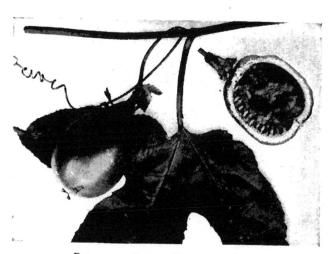

PORTION OF PASSION VINE WITH FRUIT

The spiny fruit rind when broken open exposes a five-segment fruit with a pulp of civet odor surrounding the seed. Superior varieties are propagated by layering. The durian thrives only in a hot, moist climate and the seed remain viable only a few days after removal from the fruit. The durian fruit weighs from 5 to 10 pounds. It is a conspicuous example among many which could be named of tropical fruits about which violently opposed opinions exist as to their flavor.

CERIMAN

The ceriman (*Monstera deliciosa*) is a large epiphytic creeper, native to Mexico, with large leaves 18 to 36 inches long on long petioles and with numerous elliptical perforations. The flower is large, white, and calla-like and the fruit appears as a conical spadix 5 to 8 inches long and 2 inches in diameter. It is covered with hexagonal scales which are easily removed when the fruit is ripe. In fact, the looseness of the scales is about the only external evidence of the ripeness of the fruit. After attaining nearly full size, the fruit may require 5 or 6 months in ripening. The flavor of the ceriman is not easily described. It is somewhat like that of a mixture of honey, pineapples, and bananas, and to most persons is rather sickish sweet. The plant is propagated by cuttings. It may be grown in Florida in half shade like pineapples, and in Florida the fruit ripens in 14 to 18 months after flowering. The ceriman fruit contains 1 per cent. protein and 16 per cent. sugar.

JUJUBE

The jujube (*Zizyphus jujuba*) is a slow-growing, medium-sized, thorny tree, native of New Zealand and Federated Malay States. It attains a height of 30 to 50 feet and bears ovate leaves which are tawny beneath and small flowers in axillary cymes. The white, yellow, or red fruit is 1 to 2 inches long and ½ to 1 inch in thickness. The jujube is generally propagated by seed and the fruit is borne in October or November. It is much liked by the natives in India and elsewhere, but Europeans and Americans do not acquire a liking for the fruit except as a deliberately cultivated habit. This is due to the peculiar and somewhat offensive odor of the fruit. The jujube is grown somewhat sparingly in California, Florida, and other Southern States. It is used in the preparation of sirups, confections, and lozenges. The dried fruit of *Z. vulgaris* is also an article of commerce.

SAPODILLA

The sapodilla (*Achras sapota*) is a tree 25 by 30 feet high with thick, leathery, shiny leaves and native of Central America and the West Indies. It bears two crops of fruit annually, in August and February. The gum and tannin are quite abundant in the green fruit which in appearance resembles the potato, but the ripe fruit is edible. The fruit contains in the ripe condition a brown, juicy pulp surrounding the black seeds. The sapodilla is propagated by seed or grafting and thrives up to an altitude of 3,000 feet. The tree makes a very slow growth. The latex of the fruit and stem is the source of chicle which is discussed under rubbers and gums. The sapodilla thrives in Florida as far north as Palm Beach. Fruit varies greatly in size and flavor. It appears on the markets of Florida and other Gulf States and occasionally in Washington and New York markets.

CARAMBOLA

The carambola (*Averrhoa carambola*) is a small tree, native of the Molucca Islands. It bears a pointed fruit about 4 inches long with three pronounced wings or angles. The flavor is sweet, acid, and very agreeable. The fruit is used in jelly-making and in sherbets and cool drinks or may be eaten out of hand. There is a great range of flavor among the varieties of carambola, but the two chief types are the sweet and the sour carambola. The tree may be used as an ornamental on account of its graceful habit of growth and its handsome pinnate leaves which are sensitive to the touch. The carambola contains from 3 to 5 per cent. of sugar. *A. bilimbi* is a closely related species of tree, bearing leaves with 13 to 35 leaflets and a less acutely angled fruit which is extremely acid and used for the most part only in pickles. The caramb-la grows satisfactorily in Florida. Either the carambola or bilimbi may be propagated by the shield bud method or by cuttings.

BAEL FRUIT

The bael fruit is borne on a small spiny tree (*Aegle marmelos*) which is native to India. The fruit is surrounded with a green hard woody shell about 2 to 6 inches in diameter and is composed largely of a sticky aromatic pulp which is sometimes relished for its flavor but is used chiefly for its medicinal value in dysentery. The bael fruit is propagated by seed. The tree is deciduous and endures a temperature as low as 20° F. The orange-colored transparent gummy pulp possesses an acid-sweet flavor not liked by most Europeans and Americans except when used with other fruits in sherbets. The bael fruit is under experiment in some of the Southern States.

OHELO BERRY

The ohelo berry is the most important fruit-bearing heather in Hawaii. Its botanical name is *Vaccinium reticulatum*. It is therefore in the botanical sense a Hawaiian cranberry. On the mountain slopes of the Hawaiian Islands the ohelo berry occurs on wide areas at elevations of 4,000 feet or higher. It is a low shrub with stiff crowded branches, densely covered with leaves. The leaves are oblong or ovate and leathery and the flowers are reddish-green, appearing solitary in the axils of the leaves. The ohelo berry is spherical, about ⅓ inch in diameter and of a yellow or rose color. It is used chiefly in pies and sauce. The ohelo berry contains 0.4 per cent. protein and 3.7 per cent. sugar.

JAPANESE PERSIMMON

The Japanese persimmon, native of China and Japan, is a handsome tree reaching a height of 40 feet and bearing fine foliage and yellowish-white flowers. Its botanical name is *Diospyros kaki* and the tree is therefore closely related to the common persimmon of the Southern States. In recent years the fruit has become a familiar object on the markets of most large cities. It is orange or reddish in color, variously shaped, but mostly oval and about 3 inches in diameter. There are usually 2 seeds in each fruit but some varieties are seedless. The Japanese persimmon is quite generally cultivated throughout the Tropics and to a smaller extent in California and the Southern States.

WI APPLE OR OTAHEITE APPLE

This is a large, symmetrical, and handsome tree (*Spondias dulcis*), native of the Society Islands. The fruit is spherical, yellowish, about 2 inches in diameter, with one large seed surrounded by an acid pulp. There is much fiber throughout the pulp and the flavor is not particularly attractive, although the fruit is much liked by Orientals and Polynesians. Wi apple contains about 10 per cent. of sugar.

ALMOND

Doubtless all readers are familiar with the fact that most of the common nuts of commerce are raised in northern climates. This fact becomes sufficiently apparent by the mere reference to chestnut, chinquapin, hazel nut, hickory, pecan, walnut, and butternut, all of which are grown in temperate climates.

The almond (*Prunus amygdalus*) has been grown experimentally in some of the Northern States and would perhaps yield a crop of nuts far north of the present limits of its commercial cultivation if it were not for the fact that it flowers very early in the spring. The almond is native of the Mediterranean region and the tree and flowers are much like those of the peach. There are two general types of almond, the bitter and sweet, the bitter almond being used in making flavoring extracts and prussic acid. The bitter almond is grown chiefly in Mediterranean countries. In the United States only sweet almonds of the soft-shelled group are grown and the only commercial industry of the almond is in California. There are about 1,500,000 almond trees in California, with a product of 3,000 tons of nuts per year. Among the 25 or more varieties which have been tested in California the Nonpareil, Ne Plus Ultra, and Languedoc are perhaps to be preferred. The cultural methods suitable for almond trees are the same as those which are used in peach production. The tree blooms earlier, however, and is not as hardy as the peach. The nuts are commonly bleached by sulphuring. Large quantities of almonds are produced in the Crimea, Spain, Australia, Tunis, and various other subtropical and tropical countries. In 1914 the United States imported 19,000,000 pounds of almonds.

BRAZIL NUT

This tree forms quite extensive forests along the Amazon and Orinoco, where it reaches a height of 100 to 150 feet and a diameter of 3 to 4 feet. The botanical name of the tree is *Bertholletia excelsa*. The leaves of the tree are long, with wavy edges and the round fruit is 4 to 6 inches in diameter.

This fruit is inclosed in a thick woody shell which contains about one dozen angular seeds or Brazil nuts. The tree is propagated by seed or layering. The Brazil nuts of commerce come chiefly from South America but the tree is also quite widely cultivated in the Oriental Tropics, particularly in Ceylon and the Federated Malay States.

PILI NUT

The Pili nut (*Canarium commune*) is a large and beautiful tree with an unusually extensive development of buttressing roots. The tree bears a purple plum-like fruit containing a seed or kernel of excellent flavor. The Pili nut is native of Malay and at present is quite largely exported from the Philippines. It is also cultivated in Java, where it is called the Java almond. It is an excellent avenue tree, is propagated by seed, and thrives up to an altitude of 1,000 feet.

CASHEW NUT

The Cashew nut is borne on a tree 30 to 40 feet high, native of the West Indies, and known to botanists as *Anacardium occidentale*. It is now cultivated throughout the Tropics. The parts of the fruit are rather anomalous in their structure and arrangement. The swollen stalk of the fruit is known as the Cashew apple and is used for preserves. The Cashew apple has an acid astringent flavor and is 2 to 4 inches long. The kidney-shaped nut, about 1 inch long, is borne at the tip of the Cashew apple. The nut is commonly roasted and used as a flavoring material in confectionery and for other purposes. An intoxicating drink, known as "kaju," is made by fermenting the Cashew apple. All parts of the fruit are used for medical purposes. The Cashew nut thrives in the dry districts of tropical countries and near sea level.

AMATUNGULA OR NATAL PLUM, FRUIT AND FLOWER

SAPODILLA FROM FLORIDA

PISTACHIO NUT

The Pistachio nut (*Pistacia vera*) is a native of Syria, the Canaries, and Mexico. It is also widely cultivated in various parts of the Tropics, particularly India, and has been grown with success in California, Florida, and other Southern States. The tree reaches a height of 20 feet. The leaves are alternate and trifoliate and the small flowers are borne in panicles. The nut is about 1 inch in length and is composed of a brittle shell and a greenish kernel of delicious almondlike flavor. It is extensively used in desserts and confectionery. In Syria, Mesopotamia, and Asia Minor, the tree grows up to an altitude of 3,000 feet. Perhaps the most extensive plantations of pistachio nut are in Persia, Syria, and Palestine. The tree yields a resin resembling the mastic resin of *Pistacia lentiscus*. Large quantities of pistachio nuts are shipped from Afghanistan to India, where they are used as a regular article of food, being fried in butter. As already indicated, the pistachio nut is used in confectionery and ice cream. The nut contains about 60 per cent. of oil, which is sometimes used in medicine.

QUEENSLAND NUT

The Queensland nut is a tree of medium size, native of Australia, and known to botanists as *Macadamia ternifolia*. The tree attains a height of 20 to 50 feet and bears dark green shiny leaves with spines along the edge like those of the holly leaf. The tree is propagated by seed. The nuts are ½ inch in diameter, nearly spherical, and of excellent flavor, but the shell is tough and hard to crack. The Queensland nut grows at elevations up to 2,000 feet and likes a fairly heavy rainfall. The nut contains 19 per cent. protein and 66 per cent. fat.

CHAPTER X

STARCHY FOODS

THE starchy foods in common use by the inhabitants of tropical countries include not only the majority of the familiar starchy foods of northern climates but also a number of others which are grown exclusively or chiefly in the Tropics. In most tropical countries corn, wheat, barley, oats, millets, buckwheat, and sorghum are of considerable importance. For example, there are 6,000,000 acres in India devoted to the production of corn, and India stands third or fourth in the wheat-producing countries of the world. Sorghum is widely used in some parts of the Tropics as a human food. In India, for example, sorghum seed is extensively employed in making bread. In addition to many of the leguminous food plants familiar to the inhabitants of cold climates the farmers of the Tropics also give a great amount of attention to pigeon pea, chick pea, kulthi, lablab bean, soy bean, kidney bean, cowpea, lentil, etc. Among the root crops of importance to the inhabitants of the Tropics mention may be made of potatoes, sweet potatoes, eggplant, carrot, radish, turnip, beet, etc., as well as a considerable variety of roots not grown in cold climates.

Notwithstanding the fact that nearly all the familiar starchy food plants are grown in tropical countries, the relative importance of these plants is very different in the Tropics from what it is in cold climates. A brief discussion of the more important starchy foods in general use in tropical countries is given in the following paragraphs.

RICE

Rice is the most important of the world's cereals. To more than one-half of the population of the world, rice is the chief staple food. This plant, known to botanists as *Oryza sativa*, is supposed to be a native of tropical Asia. It is now cultivated throughout the Tropics and subtropics as well as in the warmer parts of the Temperate Zones. Rice is not only the most important cereal but should probably be considered the most important food plant in the world. The world's crop of rice is about 90,000,000,000 pounds, of which 63,000,000,000 are produced in British India, 9,000,000,000 in Java, 7,000,-000,000 in Japan, 3,000,000,000 in Siam, 2,000,000,000 in Corea 1,500,000,000 in Formosa, 1,500,000,000 in the Philippines, 741,000,000 in the United States, 740,000,000 in Italy, and smaller quantities in other countries. In 1914, Louisiana produced 11,800,000 bushels, Texas 8,000,000 bushels, Arkansas 3,500,000 bushels, California 800,000 bushels, and South Carolina 179,000 bushels.

There are two general groups of rice—lowland and upland rice. Upland rice is grown without flooding or artificial irrigation in climates with a fairly abundant rainfall. Lowland rice is grown only under a flooding system or as an aquatic plant. The varieties of rice are almost innumerable. More than 4,000 varieties have been reported in Bengal alone. Thousands of varieties bear names but the synonymy of these varieties is much confused and at present it is quite impossible to conjecture the number of really distinct varieties of rice. Most of these varieties are of strictly local distribution and have been so since the dawn of history. They may therefore be geographical races. Strictly local varieties of rice are known to have been grown in Siam in the same locality since records have been kept of the civilization of that country. Some of these varieties are known also to have peculiar flavors and physical properties unlike any other varieties. The varieties of rice differ in size, shape, and color of the grain, character of straw, and fruiting panicle, chemical composition, and flavor and culinary properties. The chief varieties of rice grown in the United States are Goldseed, White rice, Japan rice, and Honduras rice.

In the Southern States rice fields are from 60 to 80 acres in extent on level lands, and 1 to 2 acres in area on sloping lands. The seed is sown broadcast or in drills from March 15 to May 1 at a rate of 1 to 3 bushels per acre. A light irrigation is given to germinate the seed. Later the water is turned on when the rice is 8 to 10 inches high. The water is then maintained at a depth of 3 to 6 inches, being withdrawn to facilitate hoeing. The final irrigation continues until a week before harvest. In small fields and in marsh soils rice is cut with a sickle, but in large fields rice is harvested with reapers.

In nearly all tropical countries the method of growing and harvesting rice is that which has been practiced for centuries by the Orientals. The Chinese method of growing rice may be briefly described as an illustration of the painstaking hand labor which this race devotes to its farming operations. Rice seed is first sprouted in bags. Within 2 or 3 days a slight sprout appears and the sprouted rice is then planted in nursery beds. The young plants are removed from nursery beds at the age of about 20 days and planted in the field at distances varying from 8 by 8 inches to 12 by 12 inches both ways. For this purpose the field is lined off in squares and three or more plants are placed in each hole. The tips of the leaves of the young plants are cut off before being transplanted. The rice is then irrigated with flowing water for about four-fifths of the time from transplanting to harvesting. Rice is harvested within 3 to 7 months from the time of seeding, depending upon the variety. The harvesting and threshing of the rice is for the most part done by hand work. The Chinese harvest their rice with a sickle. Each handful of straw is cut in two near the middle of the straw in order that the grain

DASHEEN TUBER, TRINIDAD VARIETY

heads may be laid upon the butts of the straw, thus facilitating the process of curing. The grain heads when dry are tied into bundles and shocked, after which the material is removed from the field on the backs of laborers. Threshing is accomplished largely by tramping with horses and the grain is cleaned by winnowing. The justification for all this hand labor on the part of the Chinese and other Orientals is the fact that transplanted rice gives a yield fully double that of rice planted directly in the field. The tedious method of planting, harvesting, and threshing rice according to the Chinese and Oriental custom would, of course, not appeal to the rice planters of the Southern States. The method, however, rests on a solid foundation in the countries where it is practiced. In China, for example, where the economic stress of dense population has been keenly felt for centuries, acres of land are less numerous than hungry mouths to be fed. It has become necessary, therefore, to produce more rice on a fixed number of acres.

In Ceylon, broadcasting of rice is occasionally practiced in a few localities but the Chinese method generally prevails throughout the Oriental Tropics. The yield of rice varies from 700 to 3,000 pounds per acre in tropical countries. In the United States the yield commonly ranges from 1,000 to 2,000 pounds per acre. In the Tropics two crops of rice annually are possible with certain varieties. With other slow developing varieties only one crop a year is obtained. In China and Japan, particularly in Japan, rice is grown in a continuous rotation with legumes. During the short intervals between rice crops, legumes are planted for the purpose of obtaining as much vegetable substance as possible between the harvesting of one crop of rice and the planting of the next crop. By the careful observation of this custom the fertility of the soil has been kept up unimpaired.

In fertilizer experiments with rice at the Hawaii Experiment Station, it was found that rice requires its nitrogen in the form of ammonia or inorganic nitrogen which may be ammonified and not in the form of nitrate. These experiments were continued on seven successive crops of rice in the field and were repeated in soil and sand cultures in pots. It was clearly demonstrated not only that rice requires its nitrogen in the form of ammonia rather than nitrate but that rice cannot be grown to maturity in the soil or cultures where nitrogen occurs only in the form of nitrates. In these experiments the addition of nitrate of soda depressed the yield of rice below that obtained on check plats without any fertilizer, while the application of sulphate of ammonia to the extent of 150 to 300 pounds per acre doubled the yield over that of unfertilized plats. These results are readily understood when it is remembered that rice is grown as an aquatic crop, being submerged under water 3 to 6 inches deep and that therefore nitrification cannot take place in the puddled soil. Organic nitrogen in leguminous green manuring crops, however, can be readily ammonified under these submerged conditions and from the ammonia the rice plant derives the nitrogen necessary for its development. It has also been demonstrated that practically all of the nitrogen of the rice plant is taken up from the soil by the time the plant is two-thirds grown.

Rice is too starchy a food for use as an exclusive ration by man. The organic phosphorus and the proteid in rice are largely deposited in the outer portion of the grain, which is unfortunately removed in the complete milling of rice. It is in many ways to be regretted that so strong a demand has been developed for highly polished rice and for white wheat flour, for in milling these grains to meet the market demands some of the most important food elements are removed. The general reader is doubtless familiar with the numerous scientific investigations which have connected the eating of a too exclusive diet of highly milled rice with the development of the disease of malnutrition known as beri-beri. While there may be doubt as to the universal connection of an exclusive milled rice diet with beri-beri, it has been definitely shown that the disease is one of malnutrition and that it is extremely common among the inhabitants of the Oriental Tropics who live too exclusively on milled rice. Experiments have shown that valuable organic phosphorus compounds are located in the bran and outer portion of the rice grain.

Among the by-products of the rice industry mention may be made of saké, a highly alcoholic drink made from rice, particularly by the Japanese, and also rice bran, middlings, and hulls. The Chinese also make a rice whisky called samshu. Rice bran and middlings are important feeding stuffs for domesticated animals. Rice hulls are useless for feeding purposes. In fact, they contain so much silica as to be injurious or positively dangerous when used in feeds. Complaints have occasionally been made that rice hulls have been ground by unscrupulous feed dealers and mixed with other feeding stuffs. Some experiments have been made with rice hulls in the manufacture of explosives. The hulls are also of use as packing material and for cheap insulation in the walls of icehouses.

MILLETS

A great variety of plants which may be conveniently grouped under the general head millets are used in the Tropics chiefly as human food. These plants belong to several species of cultivated grasses, including Italian millet, broom-corn millet, Japanese millet, guinea corn, pearl millet, ragi (*Eleusine coracana*), Job's tears (*Coix lachryma*), etc. These plants, roughly grouped under the term millets, may perhaps be considered as second to rice in importance as a source of human food in the Oriental Tropics. Millet seed is a staple food of about one-fourth of the world's population. In India, more than 40,000,-000 acres are devoted to the production of millets for human food. In Japan, China, and Corea also enormous quantities of millet are produced. Many of the poorer class of natives in Japan and elsewhere cannot afford to buy rice and therefore live upon millet as their staple food. Millet seed is not only used in making bread, but is cooked in various other forms and in many mixtures of other food materials.

QUINOA

When the Spanish explorers first came to South America they found the natives making common use of quinoa (*Chenopodium quinoa*) as a food. This is an annual plant native to Peru, but occurring throughout the west coast of South America and northward into Central America. The plant is closely related to the common weed lamb's quarters and yields a heavy crop of edible seeds. Quinoa has also been cultivated in Europe, California, and the Southern States, where it has been grown for its leaves, which are used like spinach.

Quinoa attains a height of 4 to 6 feet, and the leaves are thin and distinctly three-lobed. The seeds are used especially in Peru and Chile in soups, in making bread and cakes, and in brewing a kind of beer. Quinoa ash has been mixed with the leaves of cocain by the native laborers of South America in order to give the leaves more flavor for chewing purposes. There are at least three varieties of quinoa, the white, red, and black-seeded. The white-seeded variety is most esteemed in Lima and is the only one cultivated in Europe. The seeds contain 38 per cent. of starch, 5 per cent. of sugar, 19 per cent. of protein, and 5 per cent. of fat. The seed crop matures within 5 or 6 months after planting.

Quinoa has furnished food for millions of natives in South America. It has quite commonly been known as petty rice and by other names. The seeds are of about the size of a white mustard seed. Flour made from them resembles oatmeal. The red-seeded variety of quinoa contains a bitter principle which has sometimes been used in medicine. The seed of quinoa is also widely fed to poultry. This plant has not thrived well in California, where it seems to be too subject to insect attacks.

SAGO

Sago is derived from a graceful palm (*Metroxylon rumphii*), native of Malay Archipelago and somewhat resembling the coconut palm in general appearance. The tree reaches a height of 25 to 40 feet, and, like so many others of the palm family, bears long, graceful, pinnate leaves. Sago is an important source of food in southern India, Malaya, Borneo, Java, Celebes, Sumatra, Ceylon, and elsewhere. The trees grow wild in swampy land or are sometimes cultivated to a small extent. The sago palm if left to itself will live 15 to 20 years, gradually dying after the flowering period. For food purposes the tree is felled just as it begins to flower, usually at about 10 years of age.

The sago palm is commonly propagated by suckers from the old stumps. When harvested for food purposes the trunk is at once cut into 3-foot lengths which are then split lengthwise. The soft fibrous pith is removed by a process of repeated washing and straining somewhat in the manner in which cassava starch is obtained. The fiber is separated from the starch which settles out of the water and is purified by a further washing. Granulated sago is the form in which this product is commonly seen on the market. It is prepared by making a paste of the original sago meal, by mixing it with water, and pressing the paste through a sieve with meshes of the proper size. The trunk of the sago palm tree yields from 800 to 1,200 pounds of sago. Several other food products of a similar nature are used to some extent under the name sago. For example, the seeds of *Cycas circinalis* of Ceylon are of a starchy nature and are used in making a kind of sago which is eaten by the natives.

CASSAVA

Cassava, also called manioc plant, is a small shrubby perennial related to the Ceara rubber tree and occurring under two common species, the bitter cassava (*Manihot utilissima*) and sweet cassava (*M. aipi*). These plants are native of South America but are now grown throughout the tropical and subtropical world. The plants attain a height of 6 to 8 feet and bear palmately divided leaves, with 7 divisions in the bitter cassava and 5 divisions in the sweet cassava. The bitter cassava is more widely used in the Tropics than is the sweet cassava. All varieties of both species may contain prussic acid but the bitter cassava contains the highest percentage of this poison. The prussic acid in cassava is located just under the bark of the roots and is easily removed in the preparation of starch and tapioca from these roots. Cassava is an important human food product, being used by the natives of India and other tropical countries like sweet potatoes and is also extensively employed as a stock food.

Cassava is commonly propagated by stem cuttings. The mature stems are cut into sections 8 to 10 inches long and partly buried in the soil, being inserted commonly in a slanting direction at regular intervals in rows. The root or rhizomes are ready for harvest 7 to 12 months after planting. The cuttings are commonly planted in rows 4 feet apart and about 16 inches in the row. In Florida, where considerable attention has been given to cassava, the yield is about 6½ tons of roots per acre but exceptional yields of 10 to 12 tons have been obtained. The yields in tropical countries are, as a rule, higher than those obtained in Florida. The roots of a single plant sometimes weigh from 25 to 50 pounds. These roots vary greatly in shape, growing sometimes in the form of long strands 2 or 3 inches in diameter, and at other times in the form of huge conical thickened masses.

Cassava is used for a number of purposes. The milky juice of the roots is concentrated by boiling into a thick sauce which is used, after seasoning, by the natives of Guiana under the name "cassaree" as a sauce or for preserving meat. The tubers may be peeled and boiled or baked as food for man and

BREADFRUIT TREE IN FULL BEARING, HONOLULU

beast. It is in the manufacture of starch, however, that cassava finds its chief importance. In making starch the tubers are peeled and grated, the milky juice is expressed, the whole grated mass is then washed and strained until the fiber is removed, after which the starch is freed of other impurities by repeated washings and dried in the sun or in earthen ovens. Tapioca is made from cassava starch by heating the starch gently on iron plates until it flocculates into the well known tapioca granules. The United States imports of tapioca and sago in 1914 amounted to a value of $1,640,000. The world's supply of tapioca is derived largely from Brazil and the Straits Settlements. As already indicated, cassava has been grown for many years in Florida with success. Little attention, however, was given to the crop in Florida as a source of starch and tapioca. The roots are mostly used as a stock feed after cooking. It has been found that tapioca roots may be used with economy in fattening beef and pork.

ARROWROOT

The true arrowroot (*Maranta arundinacea*) is a native of tropical America belonging to the same family with ginger. The arrowroot is a perennial herb with large lanceolate leaves and white root-stocks or rhizomes 1 to 2 feet in length and 1 to 2 inches in diameter. The plant is propagated by divisions of the rhizomes in rows 3 feet apart and 1 foot apart in the row. The tubers may be harvested about 8 to 12 months from the time of planting. A good yield of arrowroot is 5 tons of tubers per acre. The tubers contain 25 per cent. starch. The yield of prepared arrowroot per acre is about 1,500 pounds. Arrowroot starch may be obtained by grating, washing, and straining the tubers by the method used with cassava. Like cassava, also, the plant seems to exhaust the soil quickly, thus making necessary a system of rotation. The best quality of arrowroot comes from Bermuda, but the largest supply is received from St. Vincent, Barbados, and Ceylon. Arrowroot starch is considered to be very easily digested and is generally recommended for invalids who have found difficulty in digesting the starch from potatoes and other plants.

Tacca (*T. pinnatifida*) is a stemless plant, native of Ceylon and the Pacific Islands, bearing 3-parted leaves on petioles 1 to 3 feet long. A scape of small greenish flowers is developed at maturity and potato-like tuberous roots which yield a starch equal to arrowroot and called pia by the Polynesians. This plant was formerly much cultivated in Hawaii. It is still cultivated to a large extent in India, Africa, and in various other tropical countries. The tubers are dug after the leaves fall and are grated, washed, and dried much like sago and cassava. The plant is propagated by the division of the roots and is commonly planted in rows 3 feet apart and 18 inches apart in the row.

SWEET POTATOES

Sweet potatoes grow everywhere throughout the Tropics and subtropics. They occur in a great number of varieties with white, yellow, and purple flowers, and with all shapes and sizes of leaves and of tubers. The tubers vary in size from a few ounces to several pounds and in color from pure white to dark purple. The flesh of the tubers of some varieties is also purple and in addition white-fleshed and yellow-fleshed forms are abundant. The sweet potato escapes from cultivation and grows almost as a weed in some tropical countries, as, for example, in Cuba. In the Tropics the sweet potato is propagated chiefly by stem cuttings. The tubers mature within 3 to 7 months after planting. The sweet potato is an extremely important food product in all tropical countries since it may be obtained the year round and bears transportation well. Sweet potatoes have been shipped from Hawaii to the mainland during the off season, particularly May to

July, when a good quality of sweet potato will bring from 4 to 8 cents per pound wholesale.

Lleren (*Calathea allouya*) is a perennial herb, native of South America, belonging with the same family as ginger and attaining a height of 2 feet. It develops long canna-like leaves and numerous potato-like tubers. Lleren is propagated by crown divisions and is planted in rows 4 feet apart and 2 feet apart in the row.' The tubers may be harvested about 10 months after planting. Lleren is much liked by the natives in the West Indies but the flavor is disagreeable to most white persons.

YAM

Many species of Dioscorea, or yams, native of East Indies and West Indies, are used for food in tropical countries. These plants are perennial, herbaceous climbers with underground tubers varying in size in different species from a few inches to 2 feet in length and from a few ounces to 40 pounds in weight Some species of yams also have aërial tubers. Yams are most extensively cultivated in the West Indies and South America, where they constitute an important source of food. They are eaten boiled or baked, like potatoes. Yams are propagated by a division of the crown and the usual planting distance is 2 by 4 feet. Pole supports are used for the vines. The tubers are harvested about 7 to 10 months after planting. The common wild yams of Hawaii are known as uhi and hoi. Yams contain 15 to 24 per cent. of starch and some of them are of fairly good flavor. In the East Indies the favorite yam is *D. globosa.* The largest yielder is *D. alata.* The common yam of the West Indies is *D. sativa.*

QUEENSLAND ARROWROOT

The Queensland arrowroot (*Canna edulis*) is a native of the West Indies but is perhaps most widely cultivated in Australia and the Pacific Islands. It is a perennial herb belonging to the family Scitamineæ and bears large broad leaves with a pronounced bronze sheen. The plant stands about 3 to 6 feet high and develops 5 to 10 purplish tubers at the base. These tubers are cooked and eaten like taro or are used in the production of the "Queensland arrowroot" of the trade. The starch grains in this product are larger and more easily soluble in water than those of the true arrowroot and the material is especially recommended for children and invalids. Queensland arrowroot is propagated by crown divisions and the planting distance is 2 to 4 feet. The crop matures within 6 to 10 months after planting. In Porto Rico an average yield is about 15 tons of roots per acre. In experiments in Queensland it has been found that about 9 tons of roots yield 1 ton of prepared arrowroot. In India it appears that the Queensland arrowroot prefers a more sandy soil than the true arrowroot. In that country the Queensland arrowroot is planted in rows 6 or 7 feet apart and 4 or 5 feet apart in the row. It has been found that roots may live in the ground for two seasons, if desired, without suffering loss. A yield of 12 to 40 tons of roots per acre has been obtained in India.

UDO

In recent years some interest has been awakened in a native Chinese plant known as udo (*Aralia cordata*). This plant has long been widely cultivated in Japan and elsewhere in the Orient. It has been introduced into California and the Southern States. Udo is a shrubby perennial suitable for ornamental purposes on account of its leaves. The plant reaches a height of 10 feet, with inconspicuous flowers in spherical umbels like those of our common sarsaparilla or ginseng. The root stalks are large and fleshy. Udo is propagated by seeds or cuttings and the planting distance is 4 by 4 feet. The young shoots are blanched by various shading devices. Shoots which

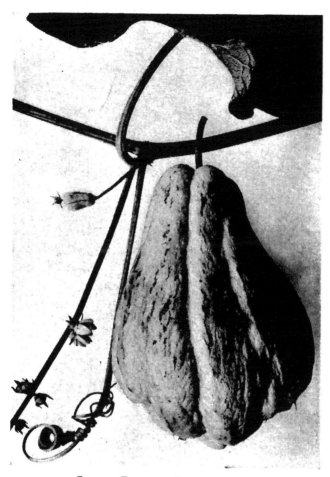

CHAYOTE, FRUIT AND PORTION OF STEM

spring from 3-year-old roots should attain a height of 12 to 18 inches and a diameter of 1 inch. The shoots must be cut into strips and soaked in water for an hour or more before boiling. They are then used in soups, salads, and on toast. Few people, however, outside of the Orient have acquired a liking for this plant. The roots are extensively used as food in Japan and China.

DASHEENS, YAUTIAS, TAROS, TANIERS

A number of related plants belonging to the family of aroids develop large starchy tubers which have long been an important source of food in tropical countries. The botanical name of dasheen is *Colocasia antiquorum esculentum.* This plant is called taro or kalo by the Hawaiians and other Polynesians. The botanical name of the yautia or tanier is Xanthosoma, of which several species have been cultivated, particularly *sagittifolium, atrovirens,* and *violaceum.* Certain varieties of yautia are commonly referred to the genus Alocasia, but since this group of plants apparently does not produce flowers its relationship is still doubtful.

In Hawaii there are 300 or more varietal names of taro and even after allowance is made for synonyms, it is probable that there are from 40 to 60 distinct varieties of taro in Hawaii. Dark taros make the best poi. This group of taro includes the varieties known as Lihua, Ele-ele, Palii, etc. The pink and white taros give the largest yields. This group includes Kuoho, Wehiwa, etc. Maña is the commonest variety of yellow taros. The taro is propagated by suckers called hulis, which develop from the top or side of the tubers. There are two main groups of taro from a cultural standpoint, the upland and irrigated taros. Upland taro, like upland rice, is grown without irrigation in climates with a reasonably high rainfall. Irrigated taros, on the other hand, are grown in precisely the same manner as rice. The areas planted to irrigated taro are surrounded by dikes just as in rice fields for holding the water at a certain depth. The water is kept flowing by constant intake and outtake.

Taro is planted at distances varying from 30 by 30 inches to 40 by 40 inches. In a study of taro growing carried on by the Hawaii Experiment Station it was found that within certain limits the wider the planting distance the larger the tubers and the higher the yield per acre. Taro tubers mature in 8 to 14 months from planting, according to the variety used. The yield varies from 6 to 18 tons of tubers per acre.

The stems of some varieties are cooked as a green vegetable. The tubers, however, are the product for which taro is raised. These tubers are eaten boiled, like potatoes, or baked in taro cakes, but chiefly in the form of poi. Poi is one of the universal and characteristic food products of the Polynesian race. It is easily prepared from taro by boiling the taro tubers and mashing them with the addition of water into a smooth sticky paste. This material is then eaten fresh or is allowed to ferment. The poi is commonly considered an easy food product to digest. Many white settlers in Hawaii acquire a liking for the product, but it cannot be said to possess an agreeable flavor or appearance. An excellent quality of flour may be prepared from taro tubers by cooking, desiccating, and grinding the material. A considerable business in the sale of taro flour was once worked up by the taro growers of Hawaii, but was later allowed to lapse. Taro tubers may also be shredded in a fresh condition and dried in strands about the size of a lead pencil. This material may then be used as a breakfast food. In that form the product has an agreeable flavor. It requires boiling for at least an hour, however, and changes from a white to a purple color as a result of boiling.

With the recent introduction of the dasheen, or taro, into Florida, some attention has been given to a method of blanching the shoots of the taro plants. It has been found that they may be readily blanched after which they can be eaten like asparagus. While the name taro is universally applied to these plants by the Polynesians, botanists have preferred the name dasheen. All the taros, dasheens, and yautias belong together in the same family with the calla lily. The flowers of the taro are large, white, and calla-like. The leaves, moreover, greatly resemble those of the calla lily, but are, of course, much larger. All of these plants are succulent and some of them, as just indicated, produce large leaves like the caladium or elephant ear. The leaf stem or petiole varies in length from 1 to 6 feet. In the yautia the leaf blade is sagittate, or arrow-shaped, with an open sinus. In the taro the leaf is peltate with the leaf stem attached about half way from the center to the basal margin. Taros have been cultivated for centuries in Japan and China and the Polynesian Islands. The areas devoted to these plants are of considerable extent in all tropical countries and the tubers therefore constitute an important article of food. The starch in the different varieties of taro ranges from 6 to 18 per cent.

BREADFRUIT

The well known breadfruit (*Artocarpus incisa*) is one of the most beautiful ornamental trees of the Tropics. It is a native of the Pacific Islands, but has gradually been distributed quite widely through other parts of the world. The tree possesses a graceful habit of growth and develops large, shiny, incised leaves and a globular fruit 4 to 6 inches in diameter. The tree attains a height of 30 to 60 feet and is highly prized as a shade tree as well as a source of an important food product. Most varieties of breadfruit have no seed. The tree is propagated by root suckers.

Breadfruit is much used in the Orient in curries. In all tropical countries where it occurs breadfruit is also eaten baked or roasted as a vegetable. In a baked form it has a very agreeable flavor which usually appeals to the new comer in the Tropics at first acquaintance. Breadfruit may also be roasted, dried, and ground into flour and is used in making poi. *A.*

nobilis of the lower parts of Ceylon is a large breadfruit tree with columnar fruit 6 to 8 inches long and 2 inches in diameter. This fruit is largely eaten by the natives with curries.

The jackfruit (*A. integrifolia*) is a huge tree native of Southern India which bears ellipsoid green fruit covered with hexagonal scales. These fruits vary in size from 10 to 60 pounds and are borne on the trunk and branches of the tree. The fruits are sometimes eaten by the natives, especially the nut-like seeds in the stringy pulp. The pulp, however, is fibrous and filled with an extremely sticky latex which coagulates into a rubber-like material.

CHAYOTE

Chayote is a common and familiar cucurbit (*Sechium edule*), native of West Indies and now cultivated generally in the Tropics. It is a perennial creeper with pear-shaped, solid, one-seeded fruits weighing 2 or 3 pounds. The fruit is cooked and eaten like a squash, which it resembles in flavor. The plant is propagated by planting the whole ripe fruit containing the seed. Supports are required for the vines which climb to great heights and long distances. The chayote bears fruit about 3 months after planting. The tuberous roots reach the size of 20 pounds and are prepared and eaten like yams. The roots contain 20 per cent. of starch and are of fairly good flavor. The chayote is also widely used as a hog feed. Chayote is quite extensively grown in Porto Rico, Mexico, tropical America, Algeria, East Indies, Hawaii, and the Philippines. Under favorable conditions one vine will bear 300 to 500 fruits a season.

LOTUS

The Chinese lotus (*Nelumbium speciosum*), native of Asia and Africa, is a water lily with a large, circular, peltate leaf, resembling those of the *Victoria regia*, and white or rose-colored flowers 5 to 8 inches in diameter. The plant bears long, moniliform or sausage-like rootstocks, and a curious receptacle

LOTUS POND IN CHINANFU, CHINA

which contains large seed. Both the seeds and rootstocks are eaten, especially by the Chinese. The rootstocks contain about 70 per cent. of starch. The cultivation of lotus in Hawaii is a rather extensive industry among the Chinese and Japanese.

SEAWEED

A large number of seaweeds are used as human food in Malaya, China, Japan, and the Polynesian Islands. The edible seaweeds include the brown, red, and blue-green species. In Hawaii, seaweeds are known as limus. Hundreds of tons of limus, or seaweeds, are annually consumed in Hawaii. No luau, or native feast, is complete without limu. More than 70 species of seaweeds are used in Hawaii as food. Formerly, the Hawaiians ate limus raw. Now they are eaten either cooked or raw. Limus contain in a fresh state 1 to 3 per cent. of protein and 10 to 14 per cent. of starch. Limus yield about 75 per cent. of their dry weight in gelatine or agar-agar.

TI

The well known ti (*Cordyline terminalis*) of Hawaii, Polynesian Islands, Malaya, and China is a short-stemmed plant with a tuft of lanceolate, leathery, shiny leaves about 2 to 4 feet long and panicles of greenish flowers. The whole plant attains a height of 5 to 15 feet. The root is a thick, starchy, saccharine structure. The roots are roasted and eaten as a delicacy. When roasted they have a sweet flavor resembling that of caramelized sugar. The roots are also fed to pigs and other stock and are quite extensively used in fermenting a strong alcoholic drink. In fact, ti roots are a common source of illicit moonshine alcohol in Hawaii. The ti leaves are generally used as plates at native feasts and for wrapping food and cut flowers. Ti leaves have also been shown to be a valuable cattle feed. In some of the Hawaiian dairies in the mountain sections ti leaves constitute an important part of the ration of cows.

CHAPTER XI

TOBACCO

Tobacco is by no means a crop which is restricted to the tropical regions of the world. In fact, it is cultivated throughout the Tropics, subtropics, and Temperate Zones. It was originally, however, a native of tropical America and the various forms, strains, and varieties of cultivated tobacco are considered as having originated from *Nicotiana tabacum* and *N. rustica.* The world's crop of tobacco is at present about 2,750,-000,000 pounds. On the contiguous mainland of the United States about 950,000,000 pounds are produced, in British India 450,000,000, in Russia 255,000,000, in Java and Sumatra 180,-000,000, in Hungary 145,000,000, in Japan 111,000,000, in the Philippines 100,000,000, in Cuba 75,000,000, in Brazil 65,000,-000, in Mexico 34,000,000, in Argentina 31,000,000, in Algeria 21,000,000, in Porto Rico 17,000,000, and smaller quantities in various other countries.

Columbus, on his first voyage of discovery, found the natives of Cuba smoking tobacco. He made some inquiry regarding the nature and properties of the weed and carried the news of the use of this plant to Europe. Tobacco was introduced into the botanic gardens of Lisbon in 1560, into France a little later, and in England about 1595. There is an enormous mass of literature relating to the discovery of the use of tobacco, its introduction into European countries, and the interesting events which were connected with its adoption by the population of the European countries. A strict government monopoly is maintained on tobacco in France, Austria, Italy, Roumania, Turkey, and a few other countries.

Tobacco is everywhere cultivated as an annual, but in the Tropics may live over for several years. The plant ranges in height from 2 to 7 feet and bears viscid leaves and stems with a heavy odor and terminal panicles of whitish, pale pink, or rose pink flowers. The seed pods are well filled with seed of such minute size that it requires about 400,000 seed to weigh an ounce. Tobacco is grown commercially on a great variety of soils and in all kinds of climates from Canada to the Equator. Both soils and climate, however, greatly affect the growth of the plant, the physical properties of leaf, the chemical composition of the leaf, and the aroma. Cuban, Philippine, Sumatra, Hawaiian, and Egyptian tobaccos would doubtless differ greatly in aroma if grown in these different countries from the same seed sample. The vuelto abajo tobacco of Pinar del Rio, Cuba, is a case in point. This famous tobacco is used as a filler, and despite numerous attempts it has not been possible to duplicate it even in other parts of Cuba. Various strains of tobacco have been introduced into Hawaii from different countries, and while these tobaccos have grown satisfactorily they have shown different physical characters and a different flavor and aroma from those which develop from the same strain in the country from which they were imported.

Tobacco seed is sown in seed beds. These beds are almost universally prepared by a special treatment of sterilization by burning. The burning of logs on the surface of the seed bed or the production of a similarly high temperature in the soil by any other means has the effect not only of sterilizing the soil with regard to fungous diseases which might attack the young plants, but improves the tilth of the seed bed so that the growth of the seedlings is more rapid as well as more vigorous. The seeds germinate in 10 to 14 days. It requires about one spoonful of seed to plant each 100 square yards of seed bed. The seedlings are transplanted at the age of 5 or 6 weeks in rows 3½ to 4 feet apart and 14 to 24 inches apart in the row. In most tobacco districts the plants are topped as soon as the flower button appears. In some localities the lower 4 or 5 leaves are removed at the same time. This process is commonly called priming. The leaves mature about 80 to 120 days from the time of transplanting.

The process of curing and fermenting tobacco has received a great amount of technical attention from chemists and biologists, and satisfactory methods have been worked out for different tobacco districts in the various tobacco producing countries of the world. The essential points in the process of curing tobacco have been thoroughly investigated by Dr. Garner of the United States Department of Agriculture, and his investigations have been utilized in the following account of tobacco curing.

In all cases the first requirement for good curing is that the tobacco be ripe when harvested. The young leaf has a rich, deep green color, and the food-manufacturing function of the leaves is about at its maximum when the flower head begins to appear and removal of this flower head stimulates the plant to a further effort to reproduce itself by sending out secondary shoots or suckers. These, however, are at once removed by the grower. Under such treatment the substance of the leaf is not carried back into the stalk, but remains in the body of the leaf. The accumulation of a surplus food supply largely in the form of starch causes the appearance of a lighter shade of green and lightish or yellowish spots on the leaf which are characteristic of the ripe leaf. The proper stage of ripeness, however, like most of the other technical details connected with the growth and curing of tobacco, can be learned only by long practical experience.

If the ripe leaf of the tobacco is quickly dried by heat it will never develop the characteristic aroma and flavor of tobacco. The development of this aroma and flavor may also be prevented by subjecting the leaf to anesthetics. The process of curing is therefore considered as consisting essentially in forcing the leaves to undergo a process of slow starvation.

Two general methods are in vogue in harvesting tobacco and managing it in the curing shed. In one of these methods the ripe leaves are picked from the stalk and threaded on strings attached to sticks which allow room for the leaves to hang without touching one another in the curing shed. By the other method the leaves are left attached to the stalks and the whole plant is removed to the barn at a stage when most of the leaves are in the best condition of ripeness. Most tobacco is cured in the air without the help of artificial heat except during wet weather. Ventilation is provided in curing barns under regulation in order to prevent the too rapid drying of the leaves. When the tobacco is first harvested the leaves contain considerable starch, but during the curing process this starch disappears. The leaf is considered as fully cured when all of the green color has disappeared and the full development of the yellow color has taken place. At this time the leaves are rather uniformly yellow or brown. The tobacco leaf loses about 75 per cent. of its weight in curing, the greater part of this loss being water. In cold or unusually wet weather artificial heat has been utilized to considerable extent, especially with wrapper tobacco. The method has been applied less to filler and binder tobacco. The heat is generated by small charcoal fires and by various other methods. In the process known as flue curing, systems of pipes are provided in the curing shed to carry off the fuel gases and the smoke does not come in contact with tobacco during the curing process, which requires only a few days. Fire curing is a term applied to the method used largely in the dark tobacco districts of Virginia, Kentucky, and Tennessee. This method consists in the use of open fires in the curing shed and the tobacco is, therefore, in contact with the smoke produced by the fires. This method is used largely in curing export tobaccos.

When tobacco leaves are cured on the stalk the resulting loss of weight is due not only to the evaporation of moisture, but also to the fact that some of the substance of the leaf is transferred to the stalk during the process of curing. It has been shown by experiment that tobacco leaves lose from 10 to 12 per cent. more if dried on the stalk than if removed from the stalk when green.

Nearly all commercial tobacco is derived from *Nicotiana tabacum*. The tobacco from this species includes the Maryland, Virginia, Paraguay, Cuban, Philippine, Seed-leaf, Latakia, Turkish, Chinese, and certain other sorts of tobacco. In this species the lobes of the corolla are pointed and the leaves are nearly sessile. *N. rustica* has distinctly petioled leaves and blunt corolla lobes. This species is the source of Hungarian, Brazilian, and certain of the Asiatic tobaccos and is always of an inferior grade. The trade terms for the commercial sorts of tobacco are numerous and the system of classification of grades of tobacco is very complicated Any thorough discussion of this classification would lie outside the field of the general reader. The terms export and manufacturing tobacco are used by tobacco dealers to indicate tobaccos used in the manufacture of smoking and chewing tobacco, cigarette tobacco, and snuff. The terms export and manufacturing are, therefore, used to distinguish these tobaccos from cigar tobacco. The tobacco which is imported into the United States consists principally of cigar filler tobacco from Cuba and cigar wrapper tobacco from Sumatra and Borneo. Importations of Turkish tobacco have also considerably increased in recent years. The yield of tobacco varies greatly according to locality and the type of tobacco. It ranges from 500 to 2,400 pounds of cured leaf per acre. There is an active competition in the production of high-grade tobaccos, particularly fillers, and it has been found that the grower must have at least a 50-acre crop in order to cure a sufficient quantity for proper fermentation. In the high-grade tobaccos this fermentation is brought about by tying the cured leaves in bunches called hands which are then piled in heaps on the floor of the fermentation house. The heaps may be 4 feet wide by 8 or 10 feet long and from 4 to 6 feet deep. The piles are torn down and rearranged from time to time in order to maintain as nearly as possible a uniform temperature throughout the mass of tobacco.

The grading of tobacco is a matter of technical skill acquired only by years of practice. Accurate grading requires a quick eye for minute differences in color. Skilled tobacco graders separate what to the uninitiated appears to be a rather uniform grade of tobacco into 15 to 20 color grades. The leaves are also graded according to size and shape. In. the system adopted in Sumatra only about 5 per cent. of a carefully cured crop is considered worthy of being classed as first-grade wrapper tobacco.

The agricultural methods adopted in the production of tobacco vary greatly in different countries. In general, tobacco is known to be a crop which rather rapidly exhausts soil for further crops of tobacco. In some of the tobacco districts of the Southern States a system of rotation has been adopted whereby tobacco appears on the same land only once in 3 or 4 years. In some of the tropical countries it is considered undesirable to plant the same land to tobacco except after an interval of 7 or 8 years. It will thus be apparent that the cultivation of tobacco is a special business requiring experience in all phases of the industry and necessitating definite plans of rotation so that the yield and quality of the crop may be maintained.

CHAPTER XII

FIBER PLANTS

A LARGE percentage of the fiber plants of the world are native of the Tropics and are cultivated to the greatest extent within the boundaries of the Tropics, although some of them, for instance the conspicuous example of cotton, are grown far outside of the limits of the Tropics. The fiber plants which are grown on a commercial scale in cold climates are not very . numerous, flax and hemp being the chief ones aside from cotton. Both flax and hemp are also grown in the Tropics, but flax has never assumed commercial importance as a tropical crop, while hemp is grown in tropical countries chiefly as a drug plant and not for its fiber. The commercial fibers of the world are derived from various botanical structures of fiber plants. The fibers are obtained mostly, however, from seed-lint, bark-bast, fruit-husks, and leaves. The fibers discussed in this chapter include those used for thread, cords, ropes, cables, fabrics, paper, brushes, mats, hats, baskets, implements, etc. Only the important ones and those which have made a place for themselves in the markets of the world or in native industries have been discussed. The number of plants from which valuable fibers could be obtained is very large. A recent account of the fiber plants of the Philippines mentions 750 such plants in the Philippines alone. An attempt to discuss all of the plants from which fibers could be obtained would make this chapter resemble a textbook of systematic botany rather than a brief account of the fibers which are really of importance in the world's commerce.

166

COTTON

Cotton, beyond question, is the most important of all known fiber plants. The original home of the cotton is uncertain, but it was probably India or Persia. Cotton has been well known in India since 800 B. C. and perhaps earlier. All wild species of cotton are tropical and perennial, but in commercial plantations the crop is grown almost universally as an annual.

While the true wild forms of cultivated cottons are not known botanically, names have been given to certain groups of commercial cottons. *Gossypium barbadense* is commonly considered as including Sea Island and Egyptian cottons. Both of these forms of cotton produce yellow flowers, smooth seed, that is without short fuzz, and a long silky lint or fiber. *G. peruvianum* includes the Peruvian, Bolivian, and Kidney cottons. These varieties of cotton develop very large leaves, yellow flowers, smooth seed, and a harsh lint of medium length. The American Upland cottons are referred by botanists to *G. hirsutum*. These forms are invariably grown strictly as annuals, the flowers are white, and the seeds fuzzy. *G. herbaceum* is a closely related species, which includes the short staple Indian and Chinese cottons. Many hybrid cottons have been produced and distributed, particularly in tropical countries with claims of unusual merit. Among these mention may be made of Caravonica and Mamara cotton. The Caravonica cotton is supposed to be a hybrid between the Sea Island and Kidney cottons, although the statements regarding its origin are somewhat at variance with one another. Three types of this cotton may appear from the same sample of seed, namely, a practically pure Kidney cotton with the seeds of each boll cemented together, a type like Sea Island, and another commonly called Caravonica wool, which appears like a true hybrid or blend between Sea Island and Kidney cottons. The Caravonica and Mamara cottons are not adapted to cold climates for the reason that a season of 7 or 8 months is required for the

production of the crop. They may, however, be pruned back
so as to produce three crops in two years under tropical conditions.

The total world production of cotton in 1915 was about 20,-
000,000 bales of 500 pounds each, of which the United States
produced 11,000,000 bales. The crop of the United States
has varied considerably in recent years, having been as high
as 16,000,000 bales in one year. The United States was the
first country to engage in the business of cotton production in
an aggressive manner, and has constantly occupied a dominant
position in this industry. As an indication of this dominant
position of the United States it may be well to quote the figures
of the cotton production for 1913. In that year the United
States produced 14,157,000 bales, British India 3,857,000,
Egypt 1,565,000, Russia 657,000, Brazil 277,000, Mexico 200,-
000, and Peru 110,000. Texas produces about 31 per cent. of
the total cotton crop of the United States. In the order of
importance in cotton production, Texas is followed by Georgia,
Mississippi, Alabama, Louisiana, Arkansas, Oklahoma, South
Carolina, North Carolina, and Tennessee. Sea Island cotton
is grown in the United States only along the coast of South
Carolina, Georgia, and Florida. Egyptian cotton is grown to
some extent in Arizona and California. All other cotton districts of the United States are occupied with Upland cotton.

The total export of cottonseed oil from cotton-producing
countries is about 45,000,000 gallons, of which the United
States exports 35,000,000 gallons. Cottonseed oil is further
discussed under oils.

Rather determined efforts are being made in various parts
of the tropical and semitropical world to increase the acreage
of cotton. Possibilities for a considerable extension of the cotton industry exist in India, Egypt, southern Russia, and in the
European colonies in Africa. Whether or not the cotton industries in these countries will be sufficiently great to take from
the United States the leadership in this industry will depend

upon various economic considerations which it would be quite futile to discuss at the present time.

JUTE

Jute is perhaps the fiber of second commercial importance. The plant is called by botanists *Corchorus olitorius* or *C. capsularis,* and is native of India, China, Formosa, Federated Malay States; etc. Jute is an annual plant with long slender stems 8 to 12 feet high and rather conspicuous yellow flowers. The seed is sown broadcast or in nursery beds from which the young seedlings are transplanted. About three months elapse between seed time and harvest. In harvesting jute the stems are cut or pulled just at flowering time. The stems are then retted in water until the trash readily separates, that is for 4 to 30 days, after which the fiber is cleaned by hand. The acre yield of jute fiber ranges from 1,200 to 3,000 pounds. Jute fiber is used for a great variety of purposes, but chiefly for gunny bags, cordage, carpets, cloth, curtains, etc. In Bengal, there are at present about 2,000,000 acres cultivated to jute and the total export of jute fiber from India is more than 15,000,-000,000 pounds annually. There are many fibers better than the jute, but the great prominence of jute fiber in manufacturing industries is due to the ease of cultivation and the lack of mechanical or technical difficulties in manipulating and spinning the fiber.

SISAL

Sisal is an agave and native of Mexico and Central America. True sisal is known as *Agave sisalana,* while henequen is known as *A. elongata,* and maguey as *A. cantala.* Sisal is ordinarily planted about 8 by 8 feet both ways. The first leaves mature at the age of 3 to 4 years and the plant sends up a tall flowering shoot or pole at the age of 7 to 9 years. Sisal is propagated either by suckers or pole plants. Suckers are young plants which develop at the base of the mother plant or grow up from the roots of the old plant at some distance away. The pole plants are the peculiarly modified structures which develop from the flowers on the branched inflorescence of the flowering pole. About 3,000 pole plants develop on each pole.

During the whole life of the sisal plant about 180 leaves are developed and these leaves yield on an average 10 pounds of fiber. The bearing period of sisal is about 5 years and the annual acre production is approximately 600 pounds of dry fiber.

Sisal is extremely drought resistant and will thrive where most cultivated crops would utterly fail. It would withstand absolute droughts of 6 months' or more duration. In fact, the young suckers may be left exposed to the sun on the surface of the soil for a period of 6 months without losing their vitality. On account of the drought-resistant properties of sisal and its general hardy nature, little or no cultivation is absolutely required. In some of the larger tropical plantations the pole plants or suckers are merely set a few inches into the soil by means of a bar or similar instrument and without any previous plowing or preparation of the soil. In this position plants are allowed to grow and produce their crops of leaves without further attention. It has been found, however, that sisal will come into bearing at least one year sooner if the ground is thoroughly plowed before planting. In Hawaii, it has been found that sisal will grow in highly manganiferous soil where pineapples and most other crops would fail utterly. Sisal thrives fairly well in a great variety of soils., Near Honolulu there is a small plantation in coral limestone and another in manganiferous soil. The sisal appears to thrive equally well in both these soils.

Various machines have been used in removing the sisal fiber from the leaves. The one which has given best satisfaction is called a raspador. In this decorticating machine the leaves are grasped by one end, while the pulp from the remainder of the leaf is crushed and carried away by a revolving wheel, after

SISAL PLANTS IN THE BAHAMAS

KAPOK TREE WITH PODS IN NASSAU

which the process is reversed to permit the removal of the pulp from the portion of the leaf first clamped by the machine. After decortication the fiber is at once dipped in water and spread out to dry. In periods of extreme drought the leaves may become so dry that the pulp is not readily removed from the fiber. In such cases decortication is assisted by a small stream of water allowed to flow upon the leaves while passing through the machine.

The fiber when dry is pressed into bales usually of 600 pounds' weight. Well-cleaned sisal fiber in the bale is an extremely attractive product. The waste pulp obtained in decorticating sisal leaves has been fed to cows in a few localities, but is extremely acid and unpalatable material. The pulp is useless as a source of alcohol for the reason that the percentage of fermentable matter in it is too low. The acid in sisal is lactic acid and the percentage increases from the base to the tip of the leaves. This acid is so corrosive that the parts of the decorticating machine which come in direct contact with the juice are made of gun metal to resist corrosion. The acid juice is also injurious to the skin and the workers are provided with rubber gloves.

The wholesale price for sisal in recent years has ranged from 4 to 8 cents, while the cost of production is about 3 cents. Since an acre yield is not above 600 pounds per year it will be seen that the acre return from sisal is very low and that the margin of profit is extremely narrow. For this reason sisal is a profitable crop only when grown in large areas.

As compared with sisal, henequen lives longer but brings a lower price on the market. The leaves have spines along the lateral edges, while sisal leaves do not, and these spines furnish some difficulty in handling and decortication. Henequen, on the other hand, gives a larger yield, sometimes as much as 1,200 pounds of fiber per acre per year.

Mexico produces 120,000 tons of henequen annually. True sisal is produced chiefly in the Bahamas, East Africa,

Hawaii, and Java. The leaves of the maguey are less rigid than henequen, but have lateral spines like the latter. Maguey is produced chiefly in the Philippines, Java, and British India. The Philippines export about 6,000 tons of maguey fiber. Attempts have sometimes been made to secure maguey and even sisal fiber by retting, but the fiber is always discolored and greatly injured by this process. All sisal fiber is therefore removed by a decorticating machine. Several other species of Agave are sometimes used locally for fiber, but hardly on a commercial scale, for example, *A. americana* and *A. decipiens*. The former produces a fiber known as pita or aloes fiber. Istle or Tampico fiber is derived from *A. heteracantha* and *A. lophanta*. These plants have thick, rigid, spiny leaves and produce a coarse fiber which is used for cordage and bagging.

Among the fiber plants related to sisal it may be well to mention cajun (*Furcræa cubensis*) and Mauritius hemp (*F. gigantea*). Mauritius hemp is indigenous to tropical America. The leaves are 5 to 8 feet long and spiny, but not so rigid as sisal leaves. The leaves contain about 2½ per cent. of fiber, which is greatly injured by retting, but is extracted without harm by scotching machines. The yield of fiber is about 1 ton per acre. Cajun, known also as silk grass, gives a fiber of superior quality, the leaves containing about 2 per cent. of fiber by weight. The cultivation of Mauritius hemp and cajun is waning. Zapupe (*Agave zapupe* and other species) recently came into some prominence in Mexico. This plant produces leaves ready for harvesting at the age of 2 years. The crop persists longer than sisal, but the commercial status of the fiber is yet to be determined.

The sisal leaves contain about 3.5 per cent. of fiber by weight and the commercial fiber varies in length from 3 to 5 feet. This fiber is second only to Manila hemp in strength. It is used chiefly for cordage. The binder twine industry requires a large amount of sisal, and sisal fiber is extensively used in making so-called Manila rope. In the cordage industry as in various other manufacturing processes a great amount of substitution and mixing is practiced. Since sisal can usually be purchased at a considerably lower price than that of Manila hemp the sisal fiber is used in cordage as a substitute for Manila hemp.

As already indicated, the commercial production of sisal is carried on chiefly in Mexico, the Bahamas, and East Africa. The United States occupies a very unimportant position in the production of this material. In Hawaii there are about 1,600 acres devoted to sisal and an annual product of 400 tons of fiber. The United States imports annually, however, 215,000 tons of sisal, 98 per cent. of which is obtained in Mexico. The quality of the Hawaiian product is excellent. The Hawaiian sisal is true sisal and is superior in value to the henequen fiber imported under the name of sisal from Mexico. In Hawaii also an improvement has been introduced in the way of modifying the decorticating machines for sisal. One of these machines will separate 1,000 pounds of sisal per day. Sisal also thrives well on the Florida Keys, but has never been produced there in commercial quantities.

MANILA HEMP

Manila hemp, or abaca, as it is called in the Philippines, is a tall species of banana with small useless fruit full of black seed and with a fiber of unusual excellence in the trunk. The botanical name of abaca is *Musa textilis*. The leaves of this plant are more decidedly tufted at the apex of the trunk than in the case of edible bananas. Abaca is indigenous to the Philippines.

The value of the fiber was demonstrated in 1656 by a Franciscan monk who devised a simple instrument which is still used by the natives for decortication. Notwithstanding numerous attempts in various tropical countries, the Philippines still enjoy a monopoly in the production of Manila hemp. The reason for the failure of Manila hemp in various other tropical countries to which it has been introduced is not apparent. A number of suckers supposed to be those of Manila hemp were imported by the Hawaii Experiment Station, but when these plants came to maturity they proved to be only a wild species of banana with small fruits full of seed and with a poor fiber weaker even than the fiber of the Chinese banana.

Manila hemp is propagated chiefly by suckers in the same manner as bananas and rarely by seed. The planting distance varies from 6 to 10 feet apart both ways. The trunk is cut down at the age of 3 or 4 years just as the plant is about to flower. It has been found that the fiber is practically ruined by allowing the plant to fruit. Such cultivation and weeding as the crop may receive during its growth are largely done by hand. For the purpose of decortication the trunk is cut into longitudinal strips and the strips are then pulled across the edge of a knife either notched like a saw or with smooth edge. The strip of the trunk is pressed against the knife edge by means of a lever operated by a second workman. A pair of laborers working in this manner will take out about 30 to 35 pounds of fiber per day. When first removed the fiber contains about 55 per cent. of moisture. After being thoroughly dried the fiber is packed in bales of about 125 pounds.

The reported yields of Manila hemp fiber range from 500 to 6,000 pounds per acre. The average yield is perhaps 750 pounds. The experience in the Philippines has shown that a plantation can be operated profitably for about 15 years before replanting becomes necessary. Manila hemp possesses a long fiber, often 6 feet in length. The lighter the color and the greater the luster of the fiber the higher the value. Abaca belongs with hard fibers and is used chiefly for cordage, particularly marine cables. It is extremely light and a given weight produces a greater length of cable than can be obtained from the same weight of most other fibers. Abaca also strongly resists the action of water, especially salt water. The fiber from the outer portion of the trunk is shortest, darkest in color, and of least value. It is used mostly in cheap bagging. Fibers from the intermediate portion of the stem are exported for cordage, while the inner part of the stem furnishes a fiber used in fine fabrics and gauzes. For many years the quality of the fiber exported from Manila was allowed to deteriorate as a result of improper sorting, cutting the trunks at the wrong stage of growth, the use of a saw tooth edge in place of a smooth knife, and packing the fiber before it was dry. Many complaints were received from manufacturers and attention was again directed to proper methods in preparing this valuable product.

About 10 per cent. of the total quantity of Manila hemp exported is best grade, 18 per cent. good current, 40 per cent. current, and 32 per cent. low. The total export of Manila hemp is about 175,000 tons. This appears to satisfy the world's demand. At any rate the market demand is apparently not larger than the supply and varies from year to year with the available supply of other fibers.

BANANA FIBER

Attempts have been made in many localities throughout the Tropics to extract a serviceable fiber from various species of edible and wild bananas. The fiber of *Musa basjoo* is of fair strength, good length and luster, and is used in Japan to some extent in the manufacture of bashofu cloth and as a substitute for wall paper. Many experiments have also been carried on with the fiber of *M. sapientum* and *M. cavendishii* and other species of bananas. Banana trunks yield about 2 per cent. of fiber which is light colored, but weak and ununiform. The natives of the West Indies have used banana fiber for making cheap bags and even garments. Companies have been organized with announcements of good prospects from the extraction of banana fiber, but this fiber is of doubtful commercial value and has never been produced in commercial quantities. If it could be obtained economically in large quantities it might be used as a cheap substitute for abaca or sisal The experiment in extracting the fiber of the Chinese banana in Hawaii indicated that this banana yielded about 2 per cent. of a fiber which gave promise of being a good material for use in paper manufacture. It is doubtful, however, whether it could be economically extracted for such purposes.

RAMIE

Ramie is a well known and much desired fiber of great merit, but suffers from the disadvantages occasioned by difficulties in extracting and cleaning the fiber. The botanical name of ramie is *Bœhmeria nivea*. It is produced chiefly in China, Formosa, Korea, Assam, Bengal, Mexico, and Caucasus. The United States imports about 4,000 tons of ramie fiber annually. The ramie plant looks like a nettle and attains a height of 6 to 12 feet. The fiber is long, exceedingly strong, and is least injured by water of all known fibers except perhaps olona.

Ramie is best propagated by root division. The plant yields two crops annually and 1,000 pounds is considered a good annual yield of fiber. The green stalks yield about 10 per cent. by weight of degummed fiber. Ramie is extracted by hand stripping, boiling in water, and special machinery devised for the purpose. The gums are then removed from the fiber by treatment with caustic alkalis or dilute acids. Ramie fiber is used in innumerable kinds of cloth, fabrics, cordage, thread, paper, etc. The wholesale price of the fiber is 12 cents or more per pound. The crop offers little difficulty from an agricultural standpoint, but the great difficulties encountered in decortication limit the large extension of the industry. Ramie has been grown experimentally in the Southern States and California. It thrives well in those States, but has not given promise of becoming a commercial industry there.

KAPOK

Kapok is the most important source of silk-cotton, or floss. The botanical name of the tree is *Eriodendron anfractuosum*. The tree is indigenous to the West Indies, Asia, and Africa. It attains a height of 30 to 60 feet, possesses a smooth bark, and horizontal whorled branches. In some countries, as for example in Cuba, the kapok tree assumes irregular and weird habits of growth. For the most part, however, it is a graceful and rather handsome tree. The leaves fall during the dry season.

The tree begins bearing at about 3 years of age. It is commonly estimated that 100 pods will produce 1 pound of floss and that about 10 pounds of floss may be obtained annually from each mature tree. The floss is used in pillows, mattresses, and recently in life belts. It has been found of unusual merit in the construction of life preservers by reason of its impermeability to water. The tree is propagated from cuttings or from seed and is planted about 20 feet apart both ways. Kapok plantations are often interplanted with coffee for shade. The pods are picked before opening and just after they turn brown. They are then dried in the sun and the seed is beaten out by bamboo brush or other hand methods. A satisfactory ginning machine for kapok is a desideratum. A few machines which are said to have given good results are now in use in the Philippines.

Floss is replacing cork for buoyant cushions and is preferred to all other fibers in upholstery on account of its great elasticity. The fiber is short, silky, and possessed of little drag or the quality of adhering together, which is so necessary for spinning purposes. The elasticity of the fiber, however, is very great and for this reason mattresses and pillows made of kapok fiber do not readily become matted.

Java produces 10,000 tons of floss annually, Ceylon 300 tons, and the Philippines 100 tons. The demand for kapok is increasing. In India, *Bombax mal ibaricum,* a plant closely related to kapok, and like kapok pi ducing large pods with black seed covered with a silky lint, is used as a substitute for kapok. The bombax fiber, however, is a reddish-brown, while the kapok is ivory white.

Kapok is often called silk-cotton, but this is a rather misleading term. The kapok pods are 3 to 5 inches long, spindle-shaped, and 2 inches in diameter at the center. Unlike true cotton the valves of the pod do not open on the tree to allow the picking of the lint, but the pods must be picked whole before the valves open, otherwise the lint would be blown away and lost. The pod is tightly packed with a soft and silky white lint very loosely attached to the small black seed.

MILKWEEDS

Several species of Asclepiadaceæ, as well as Beaumontia, Strophanthus, and certain other Apocynaceæ bear a soft fiber on the seed which has been used under the general term vegetable silk. *Calotropis gigantea,* native of China, India, and Africa, possesses a bast fiber which splits into fine silky threads which have been used for fabrics and also for cordage. Thus far this fiber has been removed entirely by hand. The yield obtained from wild areas of the tree is about 500 pounds per acre. The fiber has a high degree of resistance to moisture. The tree also yields a latex from which a low grade of rubber has been produced.

Asclepias curassavica, native of Central America and South America and now generally distributed throughout the Tropics, has sometimes been used locally as a source of fiber. *Cryptos-tegia grandiflora* yields a fine, strong fiber from bast which is sometimes used for cordage and yarn. This plant is a handsome woody climber which attains a great length, climbing from the branches and crowns of trees and bears large, pretty, rose-colored or pinkish flowers. The plant also yields a high-grade rubber.

NEW ZEALAND FLAX

New Zealand flax (*Phormium tenax*) has been widely distributed from its home in New Zealand throughout the Tropics and even into temperate climates. The plant is propagated by root division or by seed at distances of 3 by 3 feet to 6 by 6 feet. The leaves of the New Zealand flax are sword-like, 5 to 6 feet in length and contain 15 to 20 per cent. fiber. At about 3 years of age the plant sends up a flower stalk after which, as in the case of sisal and henequen, the remaining leaves are no longer useful for fiber purposes. New Zealand flax yields about 1,200 pounds of fine fiber and 800 pounds of tow per acre. The fiber is white and of silky luster and finer than hemp or linen. The native Maoris remove the fiber by hand, but decorticating machinery is used on large plantations to cheapen the product. New Zealand flax fiber is used for cordage, twine, and matting. The export from New Zealand amounts to 25,000 tons annually. The United States imports 6,000 tons of New Zealand flax per year. The plant thrives well in California as far north as San Francisco and the leaves are used to some extent by farmers as tying material, but the plant has never assumed commercial importance in the United States.

BOWSTRING HEMP

Bowstring hemp belongs to the lily family, of which several species of the genus Sansevieria have come to be known by this name. The different species of bowstring hemp are commonly found in Guinea, Ceylon, Bengal, Java, Southern China, and generally throughout the Tropics. There are about 30 well known species of bowstring hemp. They are herbaceous, stemless plants with sword-like root leaves, blotched with gray, 2 to 7 feet long or more. The leaves yield a fine white strong fiber used in mats, hammocks, bowstrings, twine, and for various other purposes. The plants are easily propagated by seed, root division, or suckers. They require little care or cultivation, spread readily by root suckers, and grow wild over large areas. Plantings rarely have to be renewed. Bowstring hemp yields its first crop at about 3 years of age. As a rule, 50 pounds of fiber may be expected per ton of leaves. The fiber may be removed by hand machines, or by a sisal decorticator. For this purpose the sisal machine merely requires special adjustment. In Porto Rico the bowstring hemp is quite an important plant for local uses. A species of bowstring hemp (*S. longiflora*), quite widely distributed in tropical America, is grown in Florida, especially on the Keys. This species produces fiber ranging from 2½ to 7 feet in length and yields about 40 pounds of fiber to a ton of leaves. It was introduced into Florida about 1890, but has never become a commercial crop.

HIBISCUS FIBERS

Nearly all species of Hibiscus, both ornamental and commercial, as well as most species of the whole mallow family, produce a strong and serviceable bast fiber in the bark. Only a few species of Hibiscus, however, have been used for the commercial production of fiber. The musk mallow (*H. abilmoschus*) has been the subject of experiment in India with reference to the value of its fiber. In these experiments 800 pounds of fiber per acre were obtained. The fiber was found to have no advantage over jute. The Deccan hemp (*H. cannabinus*), a native of the East Indies, is perhaps the most valuable member of the genus as a fiber plant. The length of the fiber of Deccan hemp is 5 to 10 feet. The fiber is inferior to true hemp and jute, but is used in India for various agricultural purposes. The stems of the plant are cut, bundled, and retted in water for about a week. The cultivation of the Deccan hemp is much like that of true hemp. The time from seed to harvest is about 3 months and the yield of fiber averages 2 tons per acre. The Cuba bast (*H. elatus*) is a tree native to the West Indies and attaining a height of 50 feet. In order to obtain fiber the tree is cut and the bark is then peeled off. From the bark a coarse bast fiber is obtained suitable for cordage and cheap bags. This fiber is also called Mountain Mahoe. Occasional mention in literature on fiber plants of *H. arboreus* perhaps refers to this species. Okra (*H. esculentus*) produces a long white smooth fiber which is not very strong. In India this fiber is used for rope, sacking, and paper. The yield is usually not greater than 180 pounds per acre. A company was once organized in Texas to extract okra fiber, but the attempt was later abandoned as impractical.

Roselle (*H. sabdariffa*), a native of the West Indies, was long cultivated in India for fiber without making use of the fruit of this plant. The fiber is obtained by retting the stems in water for 15 to 20 days. The yield is about 600 pounds per acre of dry fiber. Roselle fiber is quite extensively used for cordage and paper. Fiber is light brown in color and somewhat stronger than jute. Majagua (*H. tiliaceus*) occurs widely in Central America, South America, India, and the Pacific Islands. Among the Polynesians this straggling bush is called hau. The fiber obtained from the bast of the bark is used for rope in Trinidad and Peru. It is weaker than jute and, as ordinarily obtained, ranges in length from 4 to 6 feet.

Various other species of Hibiscus, as well as the related tree *Thespesia populnea*, called milo by the Polynesians, have been used as sources of fiber. Tronadora (*Abutilon incanum*), a native of Mexico, is a low shrub which attains a height of 8 feet. The stems are retted in water 3 to 4 days and stripped by hand. From the bast a very durable fiber is obtained, useful in manufacturing hammocks, ropes, and nets. *A. indicum* occurs quite commonly in India, Burma, Mauritius, and South Africa. The bast, which is obtained in the same manner as were the last named species, is used for cordage. *A. periploci-*

folium, a species native to tropical America, attains a height of 12 feet. Under cultivation this species yields nearly a ton of yellowish bast per acre. The bark is retted for 5 to 8 days and the fiber thus obtained is used for ropes.

PIASSAVA FIBER

From a number of palms a fiber known as piassava fiber is obtained from the margins of the leaves or leaf petioles. *Leopoldinia piassaba* of the Orinoco and Amazon regions produces on the margins of the leaf petioles long strips which split into fibers 4 to 6 feet long. This fiber is used for brooms and brushes and by the natives for ropes, baskets, hats, and other utensils. *Attalia funifera* of Brazil, known as the Bahia piassava, yields stiff, wiry, brown fiber from the fringe of the leaf petioles. This fiber is used for brushes and coarse cables. The trees begin to bear at 6 to 9 years of age. In practice it is found that one man can harvest about 100 pounds per day. The annual export from Brazil is approximately 7,000 tons.

The Palmyra palm (*Borassus flabellifer*) of India, Africa, and other tropical countries produces a fiber from the leaf sheaths resembling piassava. This fiber is used for machine brushes, ropes, twine, and fish traps. The export of Palmyra palm from Ceylon and Madras is gradually increasing. The wine palm (*Caryota urens*), common in India, Pacific Islands, and various other parts of the Tropics, yields a fiber from the leaf petiole which is quite widely used for brushes.

SUNN HEMP

The sunn hemp (*Crotalaria juncea*) is a leguminous plant native of Asia, and widely cultivated in India, Ceylon, Java, and Borneo for its fiber. The fiber is used for coarse canvas, cordage, and fish nets. Sunn hemp seed are sown broadcast and the yield of fiber per acre is 650 pounds. The stems are

DRYING SISAL FIBER IN NASSAU

cut, dried, and then retted for 4 or 5 days in water. Sunn hemp is also a valuable cover crop and is extensively grown as a green manure plant. The quantity of foliage and vegetable material produced per acre, however, is less than with several other species of Crotalaria. About 500,000 acres of sunn hemp are grown from fiber in Madras, where the fiber is produced as a substitute for jute. The fiber is really better than jute and of a lighter color.

PINEAPPLE FIBER

Pineapple fiber is produced chiefly in the Philippine Islands, Formosa, and Java. In the Philippines this fiber is used in the manufacture of the well known piña cloth, while the fiber produced in Formosa is shipped to China, where it is made into grass cloth or grass linen. For fiber, pineapple plants are spaced 4 by 4 feet. The yield is about 500 pounds of fiber per acre. Ordinarily the leaves contain 3 or 4 per cent. by weight of fiber. In the Philippines and Formosa the fiber is removed from the leaves by hand. In order to obtain the best quality of fiber it is necessary to harvest leaves at their maximum stage of growth and before they begin to wither at the tip. The Hawaii Experiment Station made a study of the possibility of utilizing pineapple leaves from commercial pineapple plantations in the production of fiber. In Hawaii, three crops of pineapples are taken before the fields are replanted. Most of the leaves of the old plants have therefore begun to wither at the tips before the three crops of fruit are harvested. A ton of these leaves was collected and put through an ordinary sisal decorticator. An excellent quality of fiber was obtained without difficulty. It was found that the leaves yielded about 3 per cent. by weight of commercial fiber. Considerable loss of fiber occurred for the reason that the sisal decorticating machine was not quite properly adjusted for pineapple leaves. Fiber obtained from old pineapple leaves under such circumstances could not be used for piña cloth, but it has good strength and seemed to be a fair substitute for sisal.

Caraguata (*Bromelia argentina*), a native of Paraguay and Argentina, yields a soft, silky fiber from the leaves 4 to 6 feet long and much resembling pineapple fiber. It is much used by the natives for making cordage and sacks. *B. pinguin* of West Indies, Central America, and South America, also called wild pineapple, yields a leaf fiber which is, however, not of much commercial value. *B. sylvestris*, native of the West Indies and Central America, has been called silk grass and "Bromelia istle." The fiber from the leaves of this plant is strong and silky and is much used by the natives for cordage and various other purposes.

OLONA

Olona (*Touchardia latifolia*) is a native Hawaiian shrub attaining a height of 3 to 10 feet. The shrub belongs to the nettle family, the flowers somewhat resembling those of the nettle. The olona occurs generally in deep ravines on all the Hawaiian islands, but is not particularly common anywhere. The fiber is highly prized by the natives for use in making fish nets and fish lines. It is extremely strong, flexible, and of great durability. Fish lines known to be 100 years old are still in prime condition. It shows a most unusual resistance to the influence of either fresh or salt water. The fiber is taken from wild plants by hand methods, the pulp of the bark being separated from the fiber. The plant has never been cultivated and the fiber is therefore not of commercial importance.

DEVIL'S COTTON

This tree, known to botanists as *Abroma augusta*, is native of India, China, Java, and the Philippines. It is a small tree cultivated to some extent in India. It yields a strong bast fiber which is white and of great strength. The fiber is fine and silky and is extensively used for cordage. It has even been recommended as a substitute for silk. The fibers are readily separated by maceration in water for 4 to 8 days. The staple of Devil's cotton is 4 to 6 feet long. The fiber is obtained from the outer dry fibrous bark of the tree, and it has been found that this bark develops so rapidly that it may be removed 2 or 3 times a year.

RAFFIA

Raffia is a well known palm 50 to 70 feet high, known to botanists as *Raphia ruffia*, and is native of Africa. The raffia palm bears pinnate leaves 25 to 50 feet long. The commercial fiber comes from both surfaces of the leaves. The epidermis and the underlying hard tissue of the leaf is easily stripped from the leaves in bands 3 or 4 feet long. The raffia is used in Madagascar for hats, mats, and plaited goods. In the United States the raffia is used principally by gardeners and nurserymen as a binding or tying material in grafting operations. It is also used in this country in wall coverings, fine grades of matting, and for basket weaving. The palm reaches maturity of its leaves at the age of 15 years and continues to yield crops of leaves for about 40 years, after which it begins to fruit. As is the case with a number of other palms the tree is of little commercial value after fruiting begins. The export of raffia from Madagascar is about 5,000 tons annually. *R. vinifera* is a West African palm, which is used for similar purposes. There are said to be about 5,000 square miles of this species near Lagos. Ultimately this area will doubtless become of great commercial value.

ESPARTO GRASS

This is a tufted grass which occurs abundantly in Tripoli and northeastern Africa generally. It is also cultivated along the northern shore of the Mediterranean, particularly in Spain. The grass is known to botanists as *Stipa tenacissima*. It requires about 3 years for the tussocks of this grass to reach a harvesting stage and the fibers obtained from the stems of the grass felt readily and yield an excellent stock for paper making, especially suitable for mixing with rags, straw, or wood pulp. The total production of this fiber is about 200,000 tons annually. The fiber is 1 to 2 feet long, fine, uniform, and strong. It has also been used in cordage, sandals, baskets, and various other utensils. Esparto grass has been grown in the Southern States, but has thus far given no commercial promise in these States.

PAPYRUS

Several species of sedge furnish valuable paper and mat-making material. The true papyrus of ancient times (*Cyperus papyrus*) was formerly cultivated by the Egyptians along the Nile. It is now found in Abyssinia, Palestine, and Sicily. The stems of the papyrus sedge are used in Egypt for making boats, mats, and baskets, but chiefly in the production of a writing paper which is manufactured from the inner bark of the stems. In preparing this material the stems are slit lengthwise, after which the stems are moistened and pressed together. As is generally well known, rolls of papyrus were interred with mummies.

The Chinese mat rush (*C. tegetiformis*) also sometimes called seaside grass, is a tall sedge with stems reaching a height of 3 to 6 feet, widely used in the manufacture of mats and hats. This sedge was formerly imported into the United States in bales for use in the manufacture of floor mattings. The leaves require splitting lengthwise into halves, and while many attempts have been made to devise machinery which would satisfactorily accomplish this operation little success has been had. The leaves are therefore split by hand. This work proved to be too expensive for American manufacturers and the enterprise was abandoned. A large percentage of the woven vegetable fiber mats used in the United States are made from this plant.

In experiments át the Hawaii Experiment Station it was found that the crop required 6 to 7 months from planting to harvest. After one cutting a rattoon crop developed within 5 months. The second crop, however, was shorter than the first crop. The yield in these experiments was about 5 tons per acre and the stems varied in length from 36 to 60 inches. Experiments with the Chinese mat rush in the Southern States showed that this crop would thrive well in the brackish marshes along the coast but, as already explained, the expense of manipulating the material by hand has discouraged the establishment of the matting industry in this country. *C. tegetum,* a closely related species, is used in the manufacture of floor matting in Calcutta and *C. unitans* furnishes material for use in coarse, cheap matting in Japan.

Bingo-i mat rush (*Juncus effusus*) is a rush extensively grown in Japan. It attains a height of 4 or 5 feet and, like the Chinese matting sedge, thrives in water along the coast, enduring even the brackish water. The rush is shorter than the Chinese mat plant; the stems are cut by hand when mature, and quickly dried. The bingo-i mat rush is not split for manufacturing purposes. In Japan it is used for making the most expensive floor mats of that country. The plant has been found to thrive in Hawaii and various other countries into which it has been introduced but no commercial industry in connection with it has been developed outside of Japan.

PLANTS USED FOR PAPER, HATS, UTENSILS, AND OTHER PURPOSES

A large number of plants in tropical countries have been found useful as a source of material for tying, for weaving baskets and various household utensils, and for the manufacture of hats and coarse garments. Most of these plants are not cultivated and the material is therefore taken from the wild plants. Few of the plants have ever become familiar to the inhabitants of northern climates.

Mitsumata (*Edgeworthia papyrifera*) is one of the three most important plants used in the paper industries of Japan. It is a small bush propagated by seed or cuttings and is cultivated on a large scale in Japan. The material comes upon the market in the form of raw stripped bast either bleached or unbleached. The strips range in length from 6 to 8 feet and are whitish or yellow in color. The yield of bast is about 600 pounds per acre. The crop comes into bearing on the second year and yields are obtained on alternate years thereafter. In manufacturing paper the material is treated somewhat in the same manner as tapa.

Rice paper plant (*Fatsia papyrifera*) is native of Formosa, where it grows extensively in the swampy forest of that island. When fully grown it is a small tree branching quite freely at the top. The stems are filled with pith of a fine texture, pure white, and this material is extensively used in making Chinese rice paper.

Ganpi (*Wikstrœmia canescens*) is native of Japan, but related species occur in various parts of the Tropics. Ganpi is a shrub which is much cultivated for paper stock in Japan. The shrub comes to bearing age at 3 to 7 years. The yield of raw bark per acre annually is about 1,000 pounds. The large proportion of the ganpi which comes into trade is obtained from wild trees. *W. viridiflora*, a native of Hawaii, yields a bast used by the Hawaiians for rope and twine.

Rice straw is extensively used in Japan for making paper. The annual produce of rice straw in Japan is about 15,000,000 tons. This material is not only used in making paper, but also to a large extent in plait work for making bags, ropes, mats, raincoats, sandals, hats, thatching, and for many purposes which appear possible only by the help of the ingenuity and patience of the Oriental. The Chinese and Japanese banana

growers of Hawaii at one time devised a method for successfully wrapping banana bunches with wisps of rice straw.

Baobab (*Adansonia digitata*) is one of the giants among
the trees. It belongs to the mallow family and is native of
Africa. The trunk of the tree attains a huge size. The inner
bark is stripped off into sheets and the bast obtained from
this bark has been found to be suitable for paper, cheap cordage, and sacking. The tree is cultivated to some extent in
Madagascar and Reunion but thus far has attained no commercial importance.

Tapa (*Broussonetia papyrifera*), or paper mulberry, is a
native of Polynesia, China, Japan, Siam, etc. Tapa is a small
bush which is widely distributed throughout the Hawaiian
Islands, as well as the other parts of the Polynesian group.
The bast obtained from the bark of this shrub is easily pulped
and is used for making paper in Japan, for the manufacture
of papier-mâché articles in Burma, and for tapa cloth in
Hawaii, Fiji, and Samoa. The bark is peeled off in strips,
after which the outer coat is scraped off with shells. The
strips are laid on a smooth log and beaten with a hardwood
mallet. The strips are then united by overlapping the edges
and beating them together. Tapa cloth varies in weight from
a muslin-like fabric to a material resembling leather. It was
used by the ancient Hawaiians for pa-u or riding garments,
for making the malo or girdle, mantles, blankets, burial cloths,
and for numerous ornamental purposes. The tapa fabrics
were colored usually yellow, red, and black in curious figures.
The finest grades of tapa are of extreme value. The manufacture of tapa, however, is a lost art in Hawaii. The material is no longer made by the natives, although tapa is
still made by the natives of Samoa. The mamake (*Pipturus
gaudichaudianus*) has also been much used in Hawaii in
making tapa cloth.

Screw pine (*Pandanus utilis*) and other species of Pandanus occur widely throughout the Tropics. They are palm-

like trees 10 to 40 feet high, with aërial straddling roots at the base of the trunk and tufted leaves usually with spiny edges. The leaves are cut, allowed to dry, and slit into strips, after which they are used for thatching and for the manufacture of baskets, mats, cordage, etc. *P. odoratissimus* is widely used in Hawaii for weaving the so-called lauhala mats. This is one of the best materials for floor matting in Hawaii. The leaves are either split in halves so as to remove the midrib or are slit into narrower strips. If split in halves, the strips are about one inch wide. These strips make a coarser matting which is not so expensive as matting made from ¼-inch strips. The lauhala mats in the moist climate of the Tropics are almost indestructible. When brought to dry climates they require moistening occasionally to prevent them from becoming brittle.

The nipa palm (*Nipa fruticans*), a native of India, Andaman Islands, etc., and generally distributed throughout the Tropics, bears leaves which are much prized as material for making hats, mattings, and various utensils. The nipa leaves are probably the most durable of all palm leaves for thatching purposes.

Bear grass (*Yucca filamentosa*) and various other species of Yucca have been used in the southwestern portion of the United States and in several tropical countries as a source of fiber suitable for coarse wrapping, sacking, fabrics and cordage. Bear grass can hardly be said to be cultivated for that purpose. For the most parts wild plants are used. The leaves are cut from the plants on the arid plains where they grow and are baled and shipped to cordage factories.

Several species of palmetto palms furnish material which is used for fiber for brushes and other purposes. *Chamærops humilis* of Algeria and other Mediterranean countries bears leaves which when shredded yield a vegetable hair or African fiber useful as a substitute for curled hair. The tree attains a height of 20 to 30 feet but is often dwarf. The leaves have a spread of 3 feet or more. The leaves of various other species of Chamærops as well as Spanish moss are used for similar purposes. The sabal palmetto, or cabbage palmetto of Florida, develops fibrous spathes upon the leaf sheaths around the "cabbage." This material is prepared by crushing and combing for use in manufacturing brushes, hats, and for other purposes. The 'saw palmetto, a dwarf trunkless palm of Florida and Georgia, yields a fiber from the leaf stems which is used to some extent as a substitute for cow hair in mortar.

The Panama hat plant (*Carludovica palmata*), a native of Central America and South America and cultivated in Ecuador, Colombia, Peru, and other countries, bears plaited, fan-like leaves 4 feet across and incised into 4 or 5 divisions. The young leaves are cut at the time of unfolding, after which they are torn into ½-inch strips and later into narrower strips or straws, bleached by sulphuring, and dried in the sun. This material brings 50 to 60 cents a pound at the point of production. The plants mature at about 3 years of age. *C. jamaicensis* is used in a similar way in making jippa-jappa hats.

The lace bark tree (*Lagetta lintearia*) of Jamaica attains a height of 25 to 30 feet. The inner bark is readily separated into sheets which when stretched form a pentagonal mesh structure like lace and much used for ornamental purposes. The bark of this tree resembles that of the paper birch. It is of a yellowish-white color and in addition to ornamental uses has been found valuable for paper cordage and even in the manufacture of cloth.

Pulu is a lustrous, golden-brown fiber which develops at the base of the leaf stalks of the large tree ferns which occur so abundantly in the mountains of Hawaii and other Pacific Islands. This material has been much used for stuffing pillows and in surgery in stanching the flow of blood. Each plant yields 2 or 3 ounces of fiber. In the eighties of the last century, Hawaii exported about 200,000 pounds of pulu annually. At present there is no industry in connection with this material. The pulu fiber was obtained chiefly from *Cibotium menziesii, C. chamissoi,* and *C. glaucum.*

Rattan is the name applied to climbing palms of numerous species belonging to the genus Calamus, especially *C. rotang.* These palms attain great length up to 300 to 400 feet, especially in India and China. The slender canes are used by the natives in making ladders, foot bridges, utensils, hats, and for other purposes. In Europe and the United States, rattan, however, is chiefly used for furniture, baskets, umbrellas, walking sticks, as a substitute for whalebone, and in numerous other ways.

Bamboo (*Bambusa arundinacea*) of India, East Indies, China, Algeria, and generally distributed throughout the Tropics is a slender tree 60 to 80 feet high, propagated by shoots and stem cuttings. There are thousands of acres covered with this species in a wild condition and it is also widely cultivated. Bamboo shoots 1 or 2 years old are much used as paper stock. For this purpose the stems are split and macerated in water 7 to 10 days. This material forms the chief paper stock in China. Bamboo is also used in China, Japan, Java, Sumatra, and elsewhere for every conceivable purpose—for sails, houses, furniture, mats, screens, utensils of all kinds, and even coarse underclothing and pipes. Various other species of bamboo are also useful but are of less commercial importance than the species just mentioned.

Sponge cucumber (*Luffa ægyptiaca*), a climbing cucurbit vine widely distributed in the Tropics, is used in India as a vegetable. When, however, the pulp is retted away in water, a fibrous interlacing network is left, suitable for use as a sponge and commonly called vegetable sponge. The plant is cultivated for this purpose, chiefly in Japan, whence 1,000,000 vegetable sponges were formerly exported annually. The industry is of much less importance at present.

CHAPTER XIII

RUBBERS AND GUMS

At the time of the discovery of America the natives of Central America and South America were found to be quite familiar with the properties of rubber and were using rubber for waterproofing garments and shoes and in making vessels and utensils of various kinds. A few years ago a mass of rubber was found in an olla, which was unburied in making some excavations in an old Indian village in Arizona. The conditions under which the rubber was found furnished quite conclusive evidence that the particular mass of rubber was not less than 300 years old. The mass of rubber had become oxidized and brittle to a depth of about ½ inch. The inner portion of the mass, however, retained apparently its full elasticity. A French explorer sent specimens of rubber from Ecuador to the French Academy of Sciences in 1736. Castilloa rubber was described in 1798, Hevea rubber in 1865, and Ceara rubber in 1874. There are a few other important dates in the development of the rubber industry. Priestley suggested the use of rubber for erasers in 1770. The process of waterproofing fabrics was invented by Macintosh in 1820. The process of vulcanization of rubber was discovered by Goodyear in 1839 and was later modified by Hancock in England. Previous to this discovery, rubber was of little commercial importance and was used only in small quantities for the few purposes to which it had been found to be adapted in its unmodified condition.

Vulcanization consists essentially in heating rubber with sulphur. A combination takes place, whether of a physical

193

or chemical nature or both. The resulting product retains its elasticity much longer and through a much greater range of temperature than is true for pure rubber. Rubber may be vulcanized by heating a mixture of rubber and sulphur, or by dipping in melted sulphur, or by treating the rubber with sulphur monochlorid. In the simple process of heating a mixture of rubber and sulphur, the rubber is ordinarily mixed with 4 to 40 per cent. of sulphur and heated to a temperature of 125° to 150° C.

Rubber is an elastic substance belonging to the hydrocarbon series and having the chemical formula $(C_{10}H_{16})x$. It is obtained by coagulating the latex of a number of plants which are native chiefly to Central and South America and Central Africa. The milky juice or latex of rubber-bearing plants is contained in the series of latex tubes and communicating structures which together constitute the latex system. The arrangement of the latex tubes is somewhat different in different species of trees. In Kickxia they are distributed chiefly just under the epidermis, immediately outside of the cambium and in the outer part of the pith bordering on the woody tissue. There are numerous strands of the latex system connecting the latex tubes in the outer and inner portions of the bark. The main latex system in Hevea or the Para rubber tree is an inner belt located about halfway between the epidermis and the cambium and no latex tubes occur in the pith. In Ficus, the latex tubes are chiefly found in the bark near the cambium. In young trees, however, they occur throughout the pith. In the Castilloa, the main latex system is in the bark and a few strands of latex tubes are located in the pith immediately underneath the wood tissue. In Ceara rubber trees, the latex tubes are found almost exclusively in the bark outside of the cambium. In order to obtain a full yield of latex, therefore, it is unnecessary to injure the cambium. The large number of connecting tubes between the main longitudinal trunks of the latex system is conspicuous in Ceara rubber trees and partly accounts for the ready flow of latex from rubber trees made in tapping wounds in any direction.

Latex is almost invariably white, resembling milk in appearance and consistency, and is essentially an emulsion containing minute globules of rubber, together with resins and proteids associated with the rubber in a watery solution. The globules of rubber vary greatly in size in different species of rubber trees. The specific gravity of latex is ordinarily a little lower than that of water. Latex contains from 48 to 75 per cent. of water, according to the species of the rubber tree, and a variable percentage of resin, proteid, and ash. These latter constituents are considered as impurities and as depreciating the value of the rubber product if they occur in too high percentages. The proportion of proteid, resin, and ash is considerably higher in young than in old mature trees. The percentage of these impurities also varies considerably according to the species of rubber tree. The lowest percentage of resin, proteid, and ash is found in the latex or rubber of mature Hevea trees.

The physical constitution of latex being that of an emulsion, the coagulation of the latex may be brought about by any chemical or physical process which will disturb the equilibrium in the emulsion and favor the segregation of the solid constituents of the latex. Coagulation of rubber latex has been accomplished by various methods. The latex of most rubber trees will undergo a spontaneous coagulation within a fairly short time. The latex may also be diluted with water and the whole mixture allowed to stand for 24 hours or more. This method may be used with Ceara rubber as well as with Castilloa rubber. After standing the rubber, being lighter than water, collects upon the water like cream, while the water remains below. Rubber may also be separated from the watery solution by centrifugal machines similar to the dairy separator. Various other chemical and physical means have been used in coagulating latex. The latex of Hevea and Landolphia may be readily coagulated by gentle heat. The same applies to the highly resinous latex of *Euphorbia lorifolia* of Hawaii. Among the chemicals which have been used in hastening the coagulation of latex we may mention acetic, citric, tannic, and formic acids, various salts of sodium and magnesium, alkaline liquids, and alcohol and acetone. The two last named reagents are used only in laboratory experiments, being too expensive for field practice.

In tapping rubber trees for obtaining the latex, almost every conceivable manner of wounding the bark of trees has been tried. The tapping systems vary somewhat, according to the species of tree, and brief mention is made of perfected methods in connection with the discussion of the important kinds of rubber trees. If all of the kinds of tapping tools were brought together they would constitute a quite formidable arsenal of instruments, including hatchet-like structures, all possible shapes and sizes of knives, shaves, paring utensils, and revolving wheel prickers. The cuts commonly made in the bark in a tapping operation also vary greatly in length and arrangement. The usual systems of tapping include long, longitudinal incisions into which short, oblique incisions may run, various lengths of V-shaped cuts, spiral and semi-spiral cuts about the trunk of the tree, the herringbone and half-herringbone system of tapping, horizontal incisions, simple shallow pricks with a revolving wheel like that in a riding spur, etc.

For many years the rubber growers have been periodically worried with the bugaboo of artificial rubber. Synthetic rubber has been produced in many laboratories in England and in Continental Europe. At a recent rubber exposition in London an automobile was exhibited with tires made entirely of artificial rubber. It was reported, however, that these tires cost about $4,000. Many patents have been taken out covering processes for manufacturing artificial rubber in the United States, England, Russia, France, and Germany. Some of these processes are strictly secret, while others have been published quite widely. Recently the Russian Government has announced a process for the manufacture of artificial rubber from vodka, and a similar process has been patented for making rubber out of alcohol in the United States. The possibility of producing artificial rubber on a real commercial basis cannot be denied *in toto,* but synthetic rubber is still in an experimental condition without commercial importance. As has been well said, synthetic rubber is heard much more than seen.

Para rubber (*Hevea brasiliensis*) is a native of the Amazon region and is now cultivated in Ceylon, Federated Malay States, and various other places in the Tropics. This tree is the source of the commercial Para rubber. In Ceylon and the Federated Malay States there are now about 680,000 acres of plantation Hevea from which the exportation of Para rubber in 1913 was 12,300 tons. The Hevea tree is usually planted at the rate of 100 to 150 per acre. It is customary to begin tapping the trees at 5 years of age and the annual yield at this age may be stated as about ½ pound per tree. At 10 years of age the yield is 2 or 3 pounds, while at 15 years it reaches 4 to 6 pounds per tree per year. The Hevea tree reaches a height of 100 feet when mature and a girth of 6 to 12 feet.

The Ceylon light crêpe rubber, obtained from plantation Hevea, was once the world's standard for rubber. At present, however, Upriver Para rubber from Brazil brings the highest price. The wild trees in Brazil are tapped daily or every other day or about 90 to 120 times during the dry season. The tappers use a small ax with 1-inch blade and attach a cup below each incision. The latex is collected and taken to the huts of the laborers, where it is coagulated in the hot smoke of burning palm nuts into balls weighing 40 to 135 pounds. On Hevea plantations, tapping begins when the trees have a girth of 20 inches 3 feet from the ground. It has been found that the flow of latex is most profuse in early morning. The most widely used system of tapping is the half-herringbone method, the trunk being divided into four vertical zones for this purpose. The phenomenon of "wound response" is much utilized in tapping Hevea. This phrase refers to the fact that within certain limits the quickly healing surface of the cut in the bark of the Hevea will yield increasing amounts by tapping it for 3 to 5 days, after which a resting period is allowed. The full herringbone system, spiral, half-spiral, and V-shaped incisions have also been used in tapping Hevea. For use in these different methods of tapping more than 50 specially devised tapping instruments have been manufactured and patented.

Para rubber contains about 95 per cent. caoutchouc, 1.5 per cent. resin, 2.5 per cent. protein, 0.5 per cent. ash, and .5 per cent. moisture.

Ceara or Maniçoba rubber (*Manihot glaziovii*) is a native of Brazil. This tree bears a 3 to 9-parted, usually 5-parted, leaf like that of cassava, instead of the 3-parted leaf as in Hevea. The bark is thin and smooth, the outer layer of bark greatly resembling that of the cherry tree. The Ceara tree reaches a height of 50 feet or more and a diameter of 2 feet or greater. The trunk commonly forks into three or more main branches. In Brazil, the Ceara rubber tree is tapped during a period of 7 or 8 weeks in the dry season. The tapping wounds are made at the base of the trunk or on the upper surface of the roots and the latex is allowed to run out on the soil, after which it is collected and washed. Ceara trunks may be tapped by slits or punctures on V-shaped cuts after stripping the outer bark. In Hawaii, a comparison was made of a large number of methods of tapping Ceara rubber trees. The best and most economic results were obtained from stripping the outer bark in narrow vertical slits and making several oblique stabs in the exposed inner bark by means of a flat chisel-like knife producing an incision about an inch in length. Results almost as satisfactory were obtained by running a wheel pricker up and down the exposed strip of bark. In tapping young trees good results were obtained from the use of long V-shaped cuts leading nearly to the base of the tree. The flow of latex has been found to be most profuse from the base of the trunk and decidedly less vigorous from the upper portion of the trunk. In Hawaii, the method adopted on Ceara plantations in preparing rubber consists merely in the use of the ordinary rubber mangler through which a continuous stream of water runs during the cleaning process. By this machine the latex is freed of dirt and much of the resin, proteid, and other impurities under the great pressure of the mangler and the dissolving influence of the water. The thick crêpe-like sheets into which it is finally rolled are then dried in the vacuum drier. Ceara rubber contains about 91.5 per cent. caoutchouc, 1.5 per cent. ash, 0.5 per cent. moisture, 3.5 per cent. resin, and 3 per cent. protein.

Other species of Manihot are also being tested in various rubber-growing districts, but commercial experience with these species is too recent for reliable opinions The species which have received most attention are *M. dichotoma, M. piauhyensis,* and *M. heptaphylla.*

The African rubber tree (*Funtumia elastica*) has been commonly referred to as the source of Lagos silk rubber. The tree bears smooth oblong leaves 5 to 10 inches long and 1 to 4 inches wide. The trunk is erect and tapering, covered with a mottled gray bark, and reaches a height of 100 feet at maturity. In Central Africa, from Sierra Leone to the East African Protectorate, the native methods of collecting Funtumia rubber were to cut down trees and then slit the bark or coagulate the latex in the bark by heat. The bark was then beaten into fragments from which the rubber was gradually collected into shreds or balls. Later the natives adopted the full herringbone system of tapping and carried the tapping wounds up the trunk to a height of 50 feet with the help of ladders and slings. Funtumia latex is rather difficult to coagulate. It coagulates spontaneously only after standing about 6 weeks.

The latex may be coagulated, however, by the gentle application of heat or by adding an infusion of the leaves of *Bauhinia reticulata* or of *Strophanthus preussii*. On plantations of Funtumia these methods and "creaming," or diluting the latex with 5 to 10 times its volume of water, are used. Chemical coagulations have also been tried. Spiral tapping and vertical cuts have given the best yield, but the yield of Funtumia rubber varies greatly and is apparently less than that of Hevea trees of the same size. Funtumia rubber contains 86.5 per cent. caoutchouc, 0.5 per cent. moisture, 6 per cent. resin, 6 per cent. protein, and 1 per cent. ash.

The Central American rubber tree (*Castilloa elastica*) is a quick-growing tree with soft rather smooth bark and large hairy leaves, 12 to 20 inches long and 5 inches wide. The temporary deciduous branches, sometimes 10 feet long, form on the young trees and later fall off. Permanent branches develop only after 3 or 4 years. The geographical range of the Castilloa rubber tree is from 22° N. in Mexico to Peru. In Mexico the tree occurs chiefly in the States of Vera Cruz, Oaxaca, Chiapas, Tabasco, and Campeche. The Castilloa rubber tree is ordinarily planted at the rate of 100 to 150 per acre. The trees are tappable at the age of 6 or 7 years. They may reach a height at maturity of 175 feet and a diameter of 4 feet. The natives of Mexico and Central America tap the Castilloa tree with a machete by the system of slanting cuts or half-herringbone method. V-cuts 8 to 12 inches apart are also much in favor. Spiral incisions and other methods of tapping have also been used by the natives. For coagulating Castilloa latex the natives use heat, ashes, soap, or an infusion of *Ipomœa bona-nox*. On plantations of Castilloa the methods employed are creaming in large vats or the use of centrifugal cream separators.

Castilloa trees are commonly tapped only three times annually. The average yield is 2½ to 3 pounds per tree per year. Some old wild trees of great size have yielded as high

Castilloa Rubber Trees Showing Method of Tapping

as 10 pounds of dry rubber in one year. The composition of Castilloa rubber varies enormously, the resin varying from 6 to 50 per cent., as prepared by different methods. The usual composition of Castilloa sheets obtained by the centrifugal method is caoutchouc 91.5 per cent., resin 7.2 per cent., protein 0.5 per cent., ash 0.3 per cent., and moisture 0.5 per cent.

The Assam rubber tree (*Ficus elastica*) is an evergreen tree with smooth elliptical leaves, attaining a height of 120 feet or more at maturity This tree is not much cultivated and tapping is done, for the most part, in vertical rows of wedge excisions made with a chisel or by means of deep V-shaped cuts. The tree is tappable at 6 years of age. The latex is coagulated by allowing it to stand for a long time or by the addition of formalin. The yield from wild trees is about 50 pounds per acre and the composition of the rubber is caoutchouc 77 per cent., resin 19.3 per cent., ash 0.5 per cent., protein 3.2 per cent., and moisture 0.5 per cent. Various other species of Ficus have been exploited to some extent as sources of rubber.

Rubber vines include species of Landolphia, Clitandra, and Cryptostegia. The species of Landolphia are woody climbers, native of Africa with simple opposite leaves, sweet-scented flowers, and large, often highly-colored edible fruit. These climbers are of very slow growth and are not tappable until they reach the age of 8 or 10 years. Some of them attain a diameter of 12 inches and a length of 300 feet or more. The rubber is collected by incising the bark and allowing the latex to coagulate in the cuts or by collecting the latex in the bark and coagulating it by heat, chemical reagents, or plant juices. Sometimes trunks of Landolphia are pulled down from the trees upon which they have been climbing, cut into short lengths, and the latex allowed to run out.

The most promising root rubbers are *Landolphia tholloni, Clitandra arnoldiana,* and *Raphionacme utilis.* Rubber is obtained from these plants by beating the separated bark or by rasping and boiling the roots. The composition of the *Landolphia heudelotii* rubber is, ordinarily, caoutchouc 91 3 per cent., resin 5.9 per cent., protein 1.4 per cent., and ash 1.4 per cent.

Guayule (*Parthenium argentatum*) is a barely shrubby plant belonging to the Composite family and native of Texas, New Mexico, and Mexico. The plant attains a height of 1 to 3 feet and is characterized by silvery gray bark and leaves, and yellow flowers which appear in September. The plants are cut, dried, and shredded and the rubber is then extracted by patented processes. Commercial attention was first called to the plant in 1876, although it must still remain doubtful whether the Indians were not familiar with the guayule plant as a source of rubber. The latex cells are in the bark and pith. The crude rubber obtained by the patented processes now in use equals 8 or 10 per cent. of the dry weight of the stems. Guayule rubber contains 20 to 30 per cent. of resin. The rubber is of fair grade and is used in the manufacture of rubber boots and for similar purposes.

The rubber-yielding plants of commercial importance belong chiefly to the botanical families of Euphorbiaceæ, Urticaceæ, and Apocynaceæ, and to a smaller extent to Asclepiadaceæ and Compositæ. More than 80 species of trees and vines have been used as a source of rubber, but only those which have been mentioned in the previous discussion have attained any real commercial importance. All commercial rubber-bearing plants, with the exception of the guayule, are confined to the Tropics. It is a well known fact that the development of latex in plants seems to occur much more commonly in the Tropics than in the cold climates. Much discussion has been had as to the function of latex in plants, but no agreement has been reached as to what this function is. The latex has been supposed to be a storage material for the nutrition of plants. It has also been suggested that it has an important function in protecting trees against attacks of insects and against injuries. The fact that the latex runs out so promptly after a slight injury of the bark and coagulates within a short time after exposure to the air has been cited as showing how effectively the latex protects the tree against wounds. As already indicated, latex commonly contains from 55 to 70 per cent. of water and a varying percentage of resin which decreases with the age of the tree in all commercial rubber plants except Hevea, in which even in young trees the latex contains only about 2½ per cent. of resin.

From many related plants the abundant latex is so low in caoutchouc and so high in resin that the dried product is used for other purposes than rubber. Some of the most important cases in point are chicle, balata, gutta-percha, and jelutong, which are discussed below.

At the present time the areas planted in rubber are in Malaya 625,000 acres, in Java 230,000 acres, in Sumatra 160,000 acres, in Burma 40,000 acres, in Borneo 25,000 acres, in East Africa 60,000 acres, in Kamerun 17,000 acres, and smaller areas in plantations in various other tropical countries. It is estimated that the total area of plantation rubber by the close of 1916 will represent 1,500,000 acres, and the estimated output of plantation rubber in 1920 will be 200,000 tons. According to the latest available statistics, the annual production of wild rubber from Brazil is 45,000 tons, from Africa 21,000 tons, from Mexico 8,000 tons, from Bolivia 3,000 tons, and from Peru 2,000 tons.

The enthusiastic stampede which characterized the development of the rubber industry during the past twenty years led to the organization of many doubtful rubber companies, the perpetration of a great many hoaxes in the sale of rubber plantations, and the sale of much worthless rubber stock. Notwithstanding these unfortunate experiences, it is the best judgment of men most familiar with the rubber industry that when rubber finally reaches the stable price of 50 to 60 cents per pound, or perhaps somewhat lower, its use will doubtless be greatly extended beyond even its present development, and reasonable profits will be insured to plantations which are managed in a businesslike way. The growth of the plantation rubber business is indicated by the simple fact that the export of rubber from Ceylon and the Federated Malay States in 1903 was 19 tons and in 1913 was 48,000 tons. Taking plantation rubber as a whole, 95 per cent. of it is Hevea. The importation of rubber into the United States in 1914 was 143,000,000 pounds. This indicates the enormous extent to which the demand now comes for the manufacture of rubber tires. The price of rubber has fluctuated quite widely since rubber became a commercial industry. The lowest London price for Para rubber was 37 cents in 1865 and the highest price was $3.12 in 1910. The present prices are greatly influenced by the European War, but it has been estimated that many of the plantations now in operation are prepared to produce rubber at a profit for 25 or 30 cents per pound.

The United States occupies a very unimportant position in rubber production. Considerable plantings of Ceara, Hevea, and Castilloa rubber have been made in the Philippines, Porto Rico, and Hawaii, but practically no rubber is now coming upon the market from these plantations. In the Philippines most of the trees are still too young. In Hawaii there are about 1,500 acres of Ceara rubber old enough for tapping. In fact, the trees have been tapped with success for 3 or 4 years. It has been found, however, that rubber cannot be produced at a profit on the Hawaiian rubber plantations when the market price of rubber is less than 55 cents a pound. Tapping has therefore been temporarily suspended until the price of rubber improves. An attempt was made on one of the Hawaiian islands to grow guayule but without success. The Hevea rubber does not thrive well in Hawaii except in protected places not exposed to the trade winds. All kinds of rubber trees which have been tried in Porto Rico do well and seem to give promise of success. Thus far, however, there is no commercial rubber industry in Porto Rico.

GUTTA-PERCHA

Gutta-percha is a product closely resembling true rubber in chemical composition but differing from it decidedly in physical properties. It is the product of a tree known as *Palaquium gutta* and of several other species of more or less related trees. These trees are native of Malaya, Cochin China, Central America, South America, Australia, and the Philippines. They are large trees of the family Sapotaceæ, with shiny leathery leaves, somewhat resembling those of certain species of rubber trees. In harvesting the gutta-percha the trees are cut down, after which the bark is removed and the latex collected by mechanical and chemical methods, or the trees are tapped by ringing or other kinds of incisions. The leaves also yield about 10 per cent. of a low grade of gutta-percha which may be extracted with toluene. The gutta-percha is collected in blocks or irregular lumps weighing 5 to 10 pounds. This mass is then put through a mangler, washed, and rolled into sheets. Gutta-percha is readily soluble in chloroform. It melts at moderate temperatures and is inelastic, differing in that respect from rubber. It is used in surgical bandages, wound coverings, like collodion, and golf balls, but chiefly for outside insulation of submarine cables. For this purpose it has long been used in large quantities. Gutta-percha has furnished a basis for the insulation of 250,-000 miles of submarine cables. At present rubber is displacing gutta-percha for most purposes, but the United States imported 1,900,000 pounds in 1914. Certain species of Sapota, Calotropis, and Euphorbia also yield gutta-percha. Gutta-percha is pliable at ordinary temperatures. It yields to pressure at 122° F., may be kneaded at 194° F., and melts at 248° F. It is decidedly resistant to hydrofluoric acid and may therefore be used in vats for etching glass.

BALATA

Balata is another product resembling rubber but differing in its physical properties from both rubber and gutta-percha. It is the product of *Minusops balata* and certain other species of trees which occur mostly in Dutch Guiana, Venezuela, and Brazil. *M. balata* is a large tree, sometimes with a diameter of 6 feet. In Venezuela the trees were cut down and the latex was removed by applying presses to the bark. In this way as much as 100 pounds of balata can be obtained from a single tree. In Surinam the trees are tapped by vertical series of jabs which are made in the tree to a height of 20 feet or more. By this method one laborer can collect 4 to 10 gallons of latex per day. From one gallon of latex about 4 pounds of balata are obtained. Balata does not readily oxidize when exposed to the air, contrasting sharply in this respect with gutta-percha and also to a less extent with rubber. It is not ductile and has, therefore, been largely used in the manufacture of machine beltings.

JELUTONG

Jelutong is a rubber-like product obtained from the latex of a tree known as *Dyera costulata,* native to Malaya, Sarawak, Borneo, and Sumatra. The tree reaches a huge size, often measuring 4 to 6 feet in diameter. The jelutong trees are tapped mostly by long V-cuts. It has been found that these trees show the wound response which is also characteristic of Hevea rubber trees. Jelutong trees are tapped about 40 times a year and yield an average of about 60 pounds of jelutong per tree. The latex is coagulated by the natives by various methods, sometimes by stirring with kerosene or powdered gypsum. The latex contains 60 to 70 per cent. of total solids and crude jelutong contains about 10 per cent. of rubber. Jelutong comes on the market in the form of white blocks weighing from 30 to 50 pounds. When the high percentage of resin is removed from the crude product the remaining rubber is of high grade. Jelutong is shipped in rather large quantities from Singapore and is used extensively in Europe and America in rubber manufacture.

The sapota tree (*Acras sapota*) of Mexico and British Honduras is a stately tree which attains a height of 20 to 30 feet, bears leathery shiny leaves, and produces a latex in the fruit, leaves, and bark, but chiefly in the bark. From the latex of the tree a gum is obtained, known as chicle, which is used as the basis of chewing gum. The wood of the sapota tree is dark purplish-red and exceedingly hard and heavy when cured. It is susceptible of a high polish and is very serviceable for cabinet purposes. The bark of the tree contains sufficient tannin to be utilized as a source of that product.

The chicle industry is most highly developed in Mexico, particularly between Tuxpan and the southern part of Yucatan. The quality of the gum obtained in Yucatan is inferior to that which comes from Tuxpan. In this center of chicle production trees are known to have been tapped for a period of 25 years. After such a long period of tapping, however, the latex yields only about 25 per cent. of gum. The tapping season begins in early September and the flow of latex is greatly stimulated by the occurrence of heavy rains. Trees which have not previously been tapped yield 15 to 25 pounds of latex. The tapping process is ordinarily accomplished by V-shaped incisions so arranged as to allow the latex to flow downward in a continuous stream. The latex is caught at the base of the trunk in leaves or other simple containers. The latex from the sapota tree is extremely sticky. It is coagulated commonly by boiling, after which the gum is kneaded to press out more of the water. If carefully prepared, the gum is quite white, but it usually has a dirty, dark gray color.

The latex from the chicle tree will coagulate spontaneously, ιand this method is often employed in the place of boiling. The gum is marketed in blocks weighing 20 to 30 pounds. Chicle was formerly used like gutta-percha in electric insulation. It is now used, however, entirely for chewing gum and exclusively in the United States. This country imported 5,896,000 pounds of chicle in 1914. The exportation of chicle from Mexico ranges from 1,800 to 2,200 tons annually.

There are many other trees which yield a product similar to chicle. For example, *Euphorbia lorifolia*, a tree native to Hawaii, yields a latex containing 42 per cent. of total solids. The solid material contains 55.9 per cent. resin, 1.5 per cent. gum, 15.8 per cent. caoutchouc, 12.6 per cent. protein, and nearly 4 per cent. of ash. A laborer can collect 40 pounds of latex per day. The latex of this tree is best coagulated by heat 80° to 90° C.

CAMPHOR

Camphor is a product of a tree known as *Cinnamomum camphora*, closely related to the cinnamon tree and a native of Formosa, Japan, and China. The tree has been introduced into Ceylon, India, East Africa, Hawaii, California, Florida, and quite generally throughout the Tropics and subtropics. The camphor tree is quite hardy and will endure climates where the winter temperatures fall as low as 15° F. Before the true camphor came into prominent commercial use, closely related products were obtained from other trees. *Dryobalanops aromatica*, a tree native of Borneo, Sumatra, and Malaya, was used perhaps before the true camphor tree, and the product obtained from it was known as Borneo camphor. *Blumea balsamifera*, a native tree of Burma, yields what has been known as Ngai camphor.

The true commercial camphor tree reaches a height of 100 feet, a diameter of 2 or 3 feet, and is densely branched. The leaves are dark green, shiny, and of leathery texture. Since 1899, the Japanese Government has tried to maintain a monopoly on camphor. Such monopoly was thought to be possible in view of the great extent of camphor forests in Formosa. It was estimated that the Japanese Camphor Bureau could put on the market about 6,500,000 pounds of crude camphor annually. About 75 per cent. of the world's supply of camphor comes from Formosa, most of the remainder being produced in Japan and China. Since the year 1900 the Japanese Government has planted about 1,000,000 camphor trees annually. The production of camphor in China has increased greatly in recent years and now amounts to about 1,600,000 pounds annually.

In Formosa, camphor is obtained from trees 50 years of age or over. The Camphor Bureau of the Japanese Government at one time prohibited the cutting of trees younger than 50 years. The percentage of camphor in the wood has been found to increase in old trees.

The world's supply of camphor is now about 5,200 tons annually, which, as already indicated, comes chiefly from Formosa. The United States imports about 2,000 tons of camphor annually. A synthetic camphor has been made from turpentine by various methods, but is inferior to the natural article and cannot compete with the latter so long as the price of natural camphor is not high. In fact, the so-called synthetic camphor is not strictly camphor, but is a product which may be used as a cheap substitute for camphor. As a result of the increasing demand for camphor, about 1,000 acres were planted of this crop in Ceylon in 1908 and further plantings have since been made in that country. The camphor tree is propagated from seed in nurseries. The seedlings are planted in the field at various distances, depending on the method of manufacture which is contemplated. In the southern United States, particularly in Florida, where leaves and small twigs of young shoots are used in the production of camphor, the seedlings are planted 6 to 10 feet apart both ways.

In the experiments which have been carried on with camphor in the United States it has already been shown that this is a promising crop, particularly for Florida. Seedling camphor trees were brought to Florida about 1870 and large plantings have been made from the seed produced by these original trees and from subsequent importations of seed. The camphor industry is growing rapidly in Florida, and it appears that the area devoted to camphor will soon exceed 8,000 acres. The center of camphor production in Florida is Satsuma, where it was reported that the Du Pont Powder Company purchased camphor plantations in January, 1916, for the sum of $6,500,000. Camphor is also grown, although less extensively, in the states of Georgia, Louisiana, Texas, and California.

Camphor is a volatile oil and is extracted by steaming the wood and leaves which have previously been ground to a fine powder. A higher percentage of camphor is obtained from leaves and young shoots than from old wood. On this account clippings from young camphor seedlings are made in Florida for use in extracting camphor. It has been found that the camphor trees can be kept trimmed back to a convenient height for working. The camphor tree was long used in the South for hedges, and these hedges are now becoming of considerable value as sources of camphor. If the trees are planted in rows 15 feet apart and 6 feet apart in the row, it has been found that within 6 years from seed the trees will form a solid hedge, which can be trimmed at intervals to secure material for the extraction of camphor. Clippings can be cut from trees at the age of 3 or 4 years, and thereafter at least 3 or 4 times a year. The twigs yield 1 to 1½ per cent. of camphor by weight, and it has been found that the yield of camphor per acre ranges from 120 to 200 pounds.

In obtaining camphor from the leaves and twigs or wood, steam distillation is carried on for about 3 hours. During this time the camphor is condensed on the walls of the distillation apparatus as a result of cooling from the surrounding water. In Ceylon the cost of producing camphor is about 27 cents a pound.

The bulk of the world's camphor is used in the manufacture of celluloid and in connection with nitro-cellulose compounds. In addition to this chief use of camphor, it is also employed to a less extent in the preparation of various medicines.

OTHER GUMS AND RESINS

All of the products which have been discussed in this chapter would be generally included under the head of gums and resins. Most of them, however, are of so great importance for specific uses that it was thought best to discuss them separately. A few brief notes seemed desirable in connection with certain other gums and resins which have some importance in the world's commerce. The chemical composition of gums and resins is not well understood. Ordinarily, gums are defined as amorphous CHO compounds which dissolve in water or take up enough water to become mucilaginous and are insoluble in alcohol. Resins, on the other hand, are CHO compounds which are insoluble in water, but soluble in alcohol, ether, and volatile oils. Balsams are a group of resins or oleoresins with a fragrant aroma or agreeable flavor. A well known example of this group of products is Canada balsam.

Copal resin is obtained either directly from living trees or as a semi-fossil product. It occurs in the East Indies, South America, New Zealand, Africa, Sumatra, Java, Philippines, and Australia. Macassar, or Singapore copal, is obtained from *Agathis loranthifolia*. South American copal comes from living trees of *Hymenæa courbaril*. Kauri copal is a fossil resin from the Kauri pine (*Dammara australis*). The dammar resin of the Federated Malay States comes chiefly from species of Balanocarpus. The copal resins are widely used in varnishes.

Gum arabic is a gummy exudation which occurs on the trunks of *Acacia senegal* and other species of wattle trees,

This gum is also known as Acacia, Turkey, Senegal, India, and Barbary gum. In obtaining gum arabic strips of bark are removed from the tree and the gum is collected from the wounds after about 60 days. Gum arabic is used extensively in pharmacies in preparing pills and for holding in suspension substances which are insoluble in water.

Gum tragacanth is a gummy exudation of *Astragalus gummifer* and other species of related plants from Syria, Armenia, Kurdistan, and Persia. In harvesting this gum the plants are incised and the gums collected in white or yellow sheets. Gum tragacanth is used for the same purpose as gum arabic, but is less soluble.

Mastic resin is obtained from a small tree (*Pistacia lenticus*) of the Mediterranean region. The gum is obtained from transverse incisions in bark and is obtained about 3 weeks after tapping. The trees are tapped 3 or 4 times during the season from June to September. The annual yield per tree is 8 to 10 pounds. The resin occurs in masses of a pale yellow color. It is brittle and melts at 108° C. Mastic was once much used in stomach debilities and for fine varnishes, but is being replaced by other resins.

Guaiacum resin is obtained from West Indian trees (*G. officinale* and *G. sanctum*). The resin occurs either as a natural exudation or is obtained by cutting the tree into sections and boring holes in the wood or by building fires under each end of the log and driving the resin out by heat. Guaiacum is widely used as a chemical indicator, being a very sensitive reagent for oxidizing substances. It is also used in medicine as a stimulant and alterative.

Tacamahaca resin is obtained from a Venezuelan tree (*Bursera tomentosa*). The resin contains considerable volatile oil. In the East Indies another kind of Tacamahaca resin is obtained from *Calophyllum inophyllum*. The resin is perhaps very similar to those of turpentine and is used in making plasters and ointments.

Candellia wax is obtained from a small Mexican spurge (*Euphorbia antisyphilitica*). A thin coat of wax occurs upon the leaves and stems of this plant. The plant is propagated by cuttings. It has been found that wax is produced only in dry districts. The wax is obtained by boiling the stems and skimming the wax on the surface of the water. Candellia wax is used in floor waxes, varnishes, shoe polish, phonograph records, and for various other purposes.

Carnauba wax is obtained from a large handsome Brazilian palm (*Copernicia cerifera*). The thin layer of wax is formed on the under side of the large leaves of this palm. The wax is scraped off and melted or the leaves are cut into pieces, boiled, and the wax skimmed from the surface of the water. Each tree produces 6 or 8 immense leaves annually. It has been found that on an average 1 pound of wax has been obtained from each 100 pounds of leaves. Brazil exports 2,000 tons of Carnauba wax annually. The wax is used chiefly in fine candles, high-grade shoe polish, and phonograph records.

CHAPTER XIV

DRUGS

No attempt is made in the present discussion to consider other than a few of the important commercial drug plants which grow primarily or exclusively in tropical countries. There are thousands of plants which have been used for the extraction of drugs. In fact, few plants have escaped the suspicion of possessing a medicinal property of one sort or another. In looking over the long list of drug plants one is reminded of the fact that a large percentage of them grow in northern climates. Some of the drug materials which it might be expected would be discussed in this chapter are referred to elsewhere. For example, castor oil and star anise oil are treated under oils.

CINCHONA

Cinchona trees, from which are obtained the alkaloid quinin and other related alkaloids, are native to South America, where they grow in abundance from a latitude of 10° N. of the Equator to about 20° S. The chief species which have been used as a commercial source of quinin are *Cinchona ledgeriana,* which yields the so-called yellow bark; *C. succirubra,* from which red quinin or red bark is obtained; *C. officinalis,* from which brown bark or pale bark is obtained; and *C. calisaya,* the source of calisaya bark. Until about 1890 practically all the cinchona bark of commerce was obtained from wild cinchona trees. Since that date the trees have been cultivated quite extensively, particularly in Java, Bengal, Ceylon, and Madagascar. Cinchona occurs as a shrub or tree reaching a height

214

of 20 to 40 feet with evergreén opposite entire leaves, and tubular rose-colored or yellow flowers in racemes. The tree endures temperatures ranging from the hottest which occur in the Tropics to about 35° F. Cinchona apparently prefers a humid climate with a rainfall of 50 to 60 inches.

In Java it is chiefly *C. ledgeriana* which is cultivated, while in Ceylon attention has been given mostly to *C. succirubra.* In recent years, however, the cultivation of cinchona in Ceylon has greatly diminished. Cinchona trees are propagated mostly from seed. The seed is planted in nurseries from which young seedlings are taken after reaching a height of about 1 foot and planted in the field at a distance of 4 feet apart. Later, during the growth of the trees, they are thinned to a distance of 12 by 12 feet. The tree may also be easily propagated by budding or grafting.

As already indicated, the chief source of quinin at present is found in the two species *C. ledgeriana* and *C. succirubra,* particularly the former. It has been found that the percentage of quinin in the bark increases gradually with age up to about 4 years. In fact, as a general rule, it is considered that the maximum percentage of quinin is found in bark from trees 6 to 9 years old. The yield of bark from cinchona trees varies greatly. In trees 9 to 10 years old an average yield of dried bark is about 22 pounds per tree, of which about 15 pounds is derived from the trunk and smaller quantities from the branches and roots. The percentage of alkaloids in the bark also varies greatly according to species and condition. In wild trees the average quantity of alkaloids in the bark is about 6 to 7 per cent., of which one-half to two-thirds is quinin, at least in the case of *C. calisaya,* but cinchonidine is the predominating alkaloid in *C. succirubra.* There are various other alkaloids in the bark of the cinchona trees.

The United States imports about 3,600,000 pounds of cinchona bark annually. This bark is obtained, as already indicated, from the trunk and roots, but the root bark is considered superior as a source of quinin. The bark is harvested by pruning and allowing the regrowth of suckers or by shaving the bark in strips, removing only a portion at one time and covering the shaved strips. The renewed bark which grows from these peeled strips is very rich in alkaloids.

The value of quinin for the treatment of malaria was discovered in 1638, and following upon this discovery the demand for bark from wild trees increased rapidly. To show the enormous interest in the cultivation of quinin it may be mentioned that in 1887 Ceylon produced 16,000,000 pounds of bark, but this country was unable to compete with Java under the low prices of quinin and the production in Ceylon has therefore fallen to about 110,000 pounds per year. Java is now one of the chief quinin-producing countries. On the cinchona plantations of Java it has been found that 2 pounds of bark per tree per year, or about 600 pounds of dried bark per acre, is a good average yield. Moreover, the cinchona planters of Java have increased the percentage of alkaloid in the bark by a long series of selections until they have obtained a strain of cinchona trees of which the bark contains 15 per cent. of alkaloids.'

Cinchona trees have been found to grow satisfactorily in the Philippines, Hawaii, and Porto Rico, but no commercial production of this material has been developed within the territory of the United States.

COCAINE

Cocaine is an alkaloid which is derived from the leaves of a shrub *Erythroxylon coca,* native to Peru and Bolivia. These countries are still the chief source of supply. The shrub attains a height of 6 to 8 feet and bears alternate, shiny, entire-margined leaves and small white flowers. The shrub is much branched and the bark of the branches and trunks is light gray in color. This shrub thrives best in the humid valleys of the Andes. It is cultivated to some extent in Bolivia, Guiana, and western Brazil, but for the most part the leaves are obtained from wild plants. The cocaine shrub is propagated from seeds. The young seedling trees, taken directly from the nursery, are planted about 4 by 4 feet. The first picking of leaves is obtained at the age of 2½ years. Thereafter the leaves may be picked several times annually. Only mature leaves are used as a source of cocaine. After picking, the leaves are quickly dried and packed in moisture and air-proof containers for shipment. On an average, 100 pounds of leaves will yield 1 pound of cocaine. The Bolivian cocaine leaves appear to yield the highest percentage of the drug cocaine. The leaves of this shrub also contain a number of other alkaloids beside cocaine. In the countries where this plant grows the natives frequently acquire the habit of chewing the leaves either alone or mixed with lime and tobacco. It is commonly believed that this habit has the effect of increasing the resistance of the laborer to fatigue, to the loss of sleep, and to the lack of food. The cocaine bush grows vigorously in Hawaii and in the Philippines, but no effort has been made to develop an industry in the growth of cocaine, largely for the reason that much hesitation has been felt toward exposing American laborers more widely than necessary to the cocaine habit.

OPIUM

The opium poppy (*Papaper somniferum*) is a native of India and Asia Minor, but has also been cultivated extensively in China, Queensland, Persia, Turkey, and various other countries. It is an annual poppy and occurs under 2 or 3 varietal forms. The best variety for medicinal use is cultivated in Asia Minor. The seed is sown in drills 2 feet apart and about 10 inches in the drill. The plant blossoms 3 months after seeding and within 10 days thereafter the seed capsules are ready to be tapped. In obtaining crude opium the green capsule is lanced at intervals of about 1-30 inch by a set of parallel blades. The lancing is commonly done during dry weather in the evening.   The latex exudes, coagulates in the cuts, and is collected the next morning.   The collections are fashioned into masses or blocks weighing up to 20 pounds and in this form the crude opium comes upon the market.   Crude opium is a black tar-like mass with a characteristic nauseating odor.

The petals are removed at the time of flowering, dried, and used as a covering for the opium blocks.   The United States imports about 450,000 pounds of crude opium annually, mostly from Turkey and Persia.   Several alkaloids are obtained from crude opium, especially morphine, codeine, narcotine, and papaverine.   Crude opium ordinarily yields from 5 to 22 per cent. of morphine and from 0.5 to 2 per cent. of codeine.   Opium obtained from Turkey has the highest percentage of morphine, while Persian opium stands next, and Indian opium has the least morphine.

The opium industry of India has given rise to a vast amount of literature on politics, anthropology, and medicine.   It is quite unnecessary for present purposes to discuss the great extent of the opium habit in India and China in former years or the political complications which arose during the development of this industry.   The value of the opium export from India in 1906 was over $30,000,000 and of this amount opium to the value of more than $24,000,000 went to the treaty ports of China.

The variety of poppy grown in India and China is largely used for smoking and eating.   At present, however, an anti-opium campaign of great intensity and extent is being maintained in China and the cultivation of the poppy has in consequence been greatly restricted.

NUX VOMICA

Nux vomica is the trade name for the seed of *Strychnos nux-vomica,* a small tree native to Ceylon and India.   This tree bears elliptical, thick, leathery leaves, and white flowers in terminal cymes. The fruit is large, round, and yellow and contains flat gray seeds from which the alkaloid strychnin is obtained. The seeds yield 1 to 2½ per cent. of strychnin and about an equal amount of the alkaloid brucine. In the Philippines it has been found that the seeds of *S. ignatii* also yield strychnine.

CUBEBS

The climbing perennial pepper (*Piper cubeba*), native of Borneo, Java, and Sumatra, bears diecious flowers in close spikes and berries on long pedicels. The unripe fruit in a dried condition is the official cubeb. The plant is propagated by cuttings and the cultural conditions required by cubebs are the same as those practiced in the cultivation of pepper. The world's supply of cubebs comes largely from Java and Sumatra. The material has frequently been adulterated with other species of *Piper*. The fruit contains from 10 to 15 per cent. of a volatile oil, which is further discussed under oils.

IPECACUANHA

The ipecac plant (*Psychotria ipecacuanha*) is a small perennial shrub, native of Brazil, with creeping stems and moniliform or variously twisted roots. From a horizontal rootstock numerous fibrous, capillary, or thick roots issue. These roots contain a white parenchyma and are covered with a brown epidermis. The leaves are smooth, entire, obovate, and pointed. The plant grows generally throughout the coast of Brazil and inland up to rather high altitudes. Most of the ipecac of commerce comes from the province of Matto Grosso. The ipecac plant is propagated largely by seed or by sprouts from pieces of roots which may be left in the soil. When the roots attain full size they are dug and dried in the sun. The dried roots are the official ipecac. Under cultivation the yield of dried roots is about 600 pounds per acre. Ipecac roots contain the three alkaloids emetine, cephaeline, and psychotrine, as well as ipecacuanhic acid. The alkaloid emetine is expectorant in action, while cephaeline is decidedly emetic. England imports about 50,000 pounds of ipecac annually and the United States a corresponding quantity.

INDIAN HEMP

Indian hemp (*Cannabis sativa*) is a common fiber plant widely cultivated in various countries for its excellent fiber. The hemp industry was formerly far more important in Kentucky and certain other Southern States than at present. On account of the fact that the drug obtained from this plant has been chiefly called Indian hemp it has often been thought that the plant from which the drug was obtained was a different species than the fiber plant. As a matter of fact, however, hemp has been cultivated in most countries for its fiber and in India, especially in Bengal, for its drug product. Hemp has long been grown for this purpose in various parts of India and Ceylon. Recently, however, its culture for this purpose in Ceylon has been prohibited.

When the plant is cultivated for the production of the drug the male flowers are removed to prevent fertilization. The drug exudes as a resin on all parts of the plant. The leaves and tips of the twigs are steeped to make hashish. For this purpose the flowering tops are compressed into masses from which the best grade of the drug is obtained. These masses contain 15 to 20 per cent. of the resin cannabin from which an intoxicating fixed oil and also an essential oil are obtained. Indian hemp is somewhat used in the United States in veterinary medicine as a powerful sedative. The effects produced by the use of hashish, or Indian hemp, are stupefying and hypnotic in nature. The natives of India and others who have become addicted to the use of hashish describe the sensations produced by this drug as in the nature of agreeable dreams followed by a sort of voluptuous stupor.

COPAIBA

Copaiba balsam is obtained from the tree *Copaifera langsdorfii,* native of Brazil, attaining a height of 50 to 60 feet with pinnate, leathery leaves and apetalous flowers. Copaiba is an oleoresin which collects in cavities in the trunk of the tree. It is also collected by artificial tapping. For this purpose grooves or cuts in other shapes are made in the trunk in the summer, and the transparent, colorless liquid is allowed to exude and dry into the resin. As much as 10 or 12 pounds of this resin may be collected from a single tapping.

PERU BALSAM

This balsam is obtained from a leguminous tree (*Myroxylon pereiræ*), native of South America, attaining a height of 50 feet, with alternate, pinnate leaves, white flowers, and one-seeded pods. The balsam naturally collects in the cavities in the bark of young twigs, where it is obtained by bark incisions or exudes from bark wounds in the trunk. A very fragrant form of the balsam is also obtained from the fruit. The tree from which the Peru balsam is obtained sometimes reaches a diameter of 2 feet, the bark is thick, the sap wood almost pure white, and the bark wood reddish-brown. The wood is extremely hard and has been used for various purposes as timber.

TOLU BALSAM

The tolu balsam tree (*M. toluiferum*) is taller than the tree from which Peru balsam is obtained, higher branching, but otherwise like the Peru balsam tree. Tolu balsam in the crude form contains 75 per cent. resin, which also yields the oil toluol used in dyes and as a volatile antiseptic.

ALOES

Aloes is a plant belonging to the lily family, native of India and Africa, but also cultivated in the West Indies for the drug and elsewhere as an ornamental. *Aloe perryi* yields Socotrine aloes, has white spines on the leaves, and spikes of orange-red flowers. *A. vera* yields the Barbados aloes, has yellow leaf spines, and yellow flowers. *A. spicata* of Africa yields the drug known in trade as Cape aloes and has white flowers. The plants resemble agaves, or century plants in habit of growth.

The drug is the dried juice of the leaves which are cut into sections, after which the juice is allowed to run out and is then concentrated by boiling, or is allowed to dry spontaneously. Socotrine aloes is yellowish and brings the highest price. Zanzibar aloes is a dark brown variety of Socotrine aloes. Both the Curaçao and Barbados aloes come from the Dutch West Indies. In fact, the main supply of aloes is now obtained from Curaçao. Aloes is used in both human and veterinary medicine as a cathartic.

CALABAR BEAN

This is a woody leguminous climber (*Physostigma venenosum*), native of Africa. It bears violet-colored flowers and a flattened, pointed pod containing 2 or 3 seeds or beans. Several alkaloids are obtained from the ripe beans, but the most important is eserine or physostigmine. Eserin is one of the most powerful alkaloids and has the specific effect of greatly stimulating the involuntary musculature of the intestines and blood vessels. The Calabar beans yield about 0.25 per cent. of eserine. The plant attains a length of 30 to 50 feet and becomes almost shrubby at the base. The beans are for the most part collected from wild vines since thus far the plant has not been extensively cultivated.

CATECHU

The drug catechu is obtained from *Acacia catechu* and also from *Uncaria gambir*. Both of these trees are native to India and the East Indies. *A. catechu* is a leguminous tree closely related to the black wattle. The astringent drug catechu is obtained by boiling the heartwood, after cutting it into chips, until the extract becomes a black tar-like mass. In this form the material is called black catechu or cutch. Pale catechu, also called gambier or terra japonica, is obtained by boiling the leaves and twigs of the climbing shrub *U. gambir*. The material is used chiefly as a brown dye and is discussed under tans and dyes.

JALAP

Jalap is a perennial twining plant (*Exogonium purga*), native of Mexico and also cultivated in Jamaica, India, and elsewhere. The plant bears cordate leaves, purple flowers, and tuberous roots. The roots are collected in the fall and carefully dried. The dried roots are the official drug. These roots contain 8 to 10 per cent. of the resin, consisting largely of a glucosid jalapurgin, which is the active principle of the plant. The jalap belongs to the morning glory family and the flowers closely resemble those of some of the cultivated varieties of morning glory. The roots occur as irregular globoid masses connected by long strands of underground root-stocks.

SARSAPARILLA

There are several kinds of sarsaparilla which have been used for medicinal purposes. The Mexican sarsaparilla has been obtained from *Smilax medica,* the Jamaica sarsaparilla from *S. officinalis,* and Para sarsaparilla from *S. papyracea.* These plants are all climbing vines provided with tendrils, shiny leaves, and spiny stems, resembling in that respect our common green brier which belongs to the same genus. The plants are indigenous to the tropical regions from Mexico to Brazil. The official drug sarsaparilla is the dried roots of the plant. These roots contain about 2 per cent. of saponin, which is the active principle. The American sarsaparilla is *Aralia nudicaulis,* an entirely different and unrelated plant.

SQUILL

This drug is obtained from a plant (*Urginia scilla*), native of the Mediterranean country. At the base of the plant an onion-like bulb is developed. The bulb scales are cut into sections and dried in the sun or in desiccators by the use of artificial heat. Squill has a diuretic and purgative action.

SENNA

The drug senna is obtained from small shrubs which are native to Egypt and Arabia. Alexandrian senna is obtained from *Cassia acutifolia* and Indian senna from *C. augustifolia.* The leaves of all the common species of Cassia are pinnate and the flowers yellow, resembling sweet pea flowers in shape. Senna is quite extensively cultivated in India. The dried leaves and the pods are used in medicine for their laxative properties. Senna is also cultivated to some extent in the Desert of Sahara.

Purging cassia (*C. fistula*), a native tree of India, is widely cultivated throughout all tropical countries as an ornamental. The tree reaches a height of 20 to 40 feet, has a smooth gray bark, and handsome racemes of large pale yellow flowers. The pods are ½ to 1 inch in diameter and often attain a length of 2½ feet. The supply of the drug from this plant comes chiefly from Central America, South America, and India. The tree begins bearing at the age of 4 years. The pulp in the pods is a thick, brown, molasses-like substance with a heavy odor. It contains 50 per cent. of sugar and also a laxative principle.

BETEL NUT PALM IN SIAM

MANGROVE JUNGLE IN FLORIDA

The tree grows chiefly throughout Ethiopia and in the Levant. In some localities this tree is called Golden Shower on account of its profusion of beautiful yellow flowers.

AWA

The Awa plant, or Kava-Kava (*Piper methysticum*) belongs to the same genus with black pepper and is native of Hawaii and other Pacific Islands. It is a small shrub 2 or 3 .feet high with a large spongy root. The roots have been collected by the Polynesian natives since prehistoric times for use in preparing an intoxicating beverage. The plant has not been generally cultivated, but for the most part the roots have been obtained from wild plants. Recently about 300 acres were planted to Awa in Hawaii. This renewed interest in Awa is due to the high price for the roots which followed upon a reputed discovery of the value of the roots for medicinal purposes. A few years ago the price of the roots was as high as $700 a ton. At present, however, the price is hardly sufficient to warrant the cultivation of the plant. It is propagated by stem cuttings. The roots are dug at the age of 3 or 4 years. Since the plant has been used for medicinal purposes the price of the roots has ranged from $50 to $700 per ton. The roots contain 50 per cent. of starch and 3 resins, one of which is an anesthetic intoxicant. The physiological effect of Awa is to produce a complete muscular paralysis.

ARECA NUT

The Areca nut, also called Betel nut, is a tall handsome palm (*Areca catechu*), 40 to 100 feet high, and native of Malaya and Ceylon. This palm bears a large cluster of yellow nuts about the size of a hen's egg. The kernel of the nut is sliced, mixed with lime and the leaves of betel pepper, and chewed by the natives. Among the natives of India the habit of chewing the Betel nut is almost as common as the chewing of gum

among Americans. The teeth are stained black as a result
of constantly chewing the Betel nut. It is considered to be a
preventive of dysentery. Areca nut is also used as a vermi-
fuge, especially in veterinary medicine, as a dentrifrice, and
also extensively in tanning. Ceylon exports about 8,000 tons
annually.

QUASSIA

The drug and insecticide material known as quassia has been
derived from two species of trees, one known as *Quassia
amara* in Surinam, and the other known as *Picrasma excelsa* of
Jamaica. The official drug quassia, used in Europe, is derived
from the first species, while in the United States the supply
comes from the second species. Surinam quassia is a shrub
5 to 15 feet high. The wood of the root and trunk is used
as the source of an extract which is employed as a bitter tonic
for medicinal purposes. This tonic is considered of unusual
value on account of the fact that it exercises few of the un-
favorable effects which are characteristic of tonics. The flowers of the Surinam quassia are of a brilliant red color.

The Jamaica quassia, on the other hand, is a handsome tree
attaining a height of 100 feet or more and a diameter of 3 feet.
This tree bears greenish flowers. The extract obtained from
the wood of this tree has been used for various purposes. It
is sometimes substituted for hops for the purpose of making
beer bitter. The wood is quite commonly used for cabinet
purposes, being of peculiar value on account of its immunity
to insect attacks.

Quassia chips have been extensively used as a source of a
bitter insecticide, especially employed in the control of aphis
or plant lice. This material has been used perhaps most widely
in controlling the hop aphis in the Western States. For this
purpose, quassia has proved to be exceedingly effective and
cheap. The insecticide quassia is commonly prepared by boiling one pound of quassia chips in one or two gallons of water,

after which the solution is diluted to make 10 gallons of spraying material. This insecticide has also proved to be an excellent repellent for ants.

STROPHANTHUS

Strophanthus is a twining shrub (*S. kombe*) of the family Apocynaceæ and native of Zambesi and eastern Africa. The shrub bears opposite leaves and showy flowers. The ripe seeds yield strophanthin, an active principle which has the effect of paralyzing the involuntary muscles. Strophanthus has been widely used by the African natives as an arrow poison.

JABORANDI

The jaborandi is a small shrub (*Pilocarpus jaborandi*), native of Brazil, with pinnate leaves and small flowers in loose spikes. The dried leaves are the official drug. The leaves contain about 1 per cent. of pilocarpin, an alkaloid used in medicine to increase perspiration and salivation.

CROTON OIL

This product is obtained from *Croton tiglium*, a shrub or small tree native of India. The tree bears alternate oblong leaves, small flowers in loose racemes, and 3-celled capsules containing seeds like castor beans. The seeds contain a fixed oil (croton oil) which is obtained by pressure. Croton oil is a well known violent and poisonous purgative.

The physic nut (*Jatropha curcas*) is a small shrub, native of Central America and South America. The seeds of this plant yield an oil resembling croton oil in its physiological properties. A similar oil is also obtained from *Euphorbia calyculata*, known as Mexican croton oil.

CHAPTER XV

TANS AND DYES

THE bark and other parts of trees and herbaceous plants in tropical countries show a much greater tendency toward the production of tannin than is the case in cold countries. This fact has led to thorough search of commercial sources of tannins, especially in tropical woods. The commercial rank which different sources of tannin occupy changes somewhat from year to year as the transportation facilities and other matters concerned with the economics of production are altered by changing circumstances. On account of the active quest for suitable sources of tannin, much attention has been given to the percentage of tannin found in crude substances collected as sources of tannin.

The dyestuffs of vegetable origin have undergone great fluctuations in value and importance since they first came into large industrial use. In recent years the markets of the world have been flooded with cheap synthetic dyes which have had the effect of greatly checking the production of natural dyestuffs. None of these artificial dyes is equal in value to the natural dyes and in view of the great disturbances in the dye market resulting from the European War it would seem desirable that attention be again given to renewing and extending the production of such natural dyestuffs as cutch, logwood, gamboge, indigo, madder, saffron, safflower, etc. These dyes are not only superior to the artificial dyes for technical purposes, but are harmless and some of them possess medicinal properties.

GAMBIER

Gambier is used both as a dye and a tanning agent. It is also frequently called cutch, terra japonica, and catechu, although these terms are not strictly synonymous. The product which comes upon the market under the name gambier is derived from *Uncaria gambir,* a climbing shrub of the madder family, largely cultivated near Singapore and in Java and also from *Acacia catechu* and *A. suma.* In preparing the tanning material the leaves and twigs of *U. gambir* and the heartwood of *A. catechu* are boiled until they yield a sirupy extract, which is then allowed to harden. Gambier comes upon the market in purple resin-like masses. It contains 25 to 50 per cent. of tannic acid. The catechu obtained from *A. catechu* is chewed by the natives of India as a gum. This plant should not be confused with *Areca catechu* or the Betel-nut palm. Gambier is also used to some extent in medicine, but chiefly as a dye-stuff for the production of browns, fawns, olives, and drabs. It gives a strictly fast color and is much used in dyeing khaki. The United States imports nearly 14,000,000 pounds annually. The leaves and spherical flower clusters of the gambier resemble somewhat those of the button bush of the United States. This plant is now extensively cultivated in Java, where much profit has been found in its production with the result that the area cultivated to gambier is increasing.

MANGROVE

Mangrove trees of several species, particularly *Rhizophora mucronata, R. mangle,* etc., are native of Ceylon and the Oriental Tropics. These trees are of medium size and exhibit a wide-spreading growth of branches. They are found in the brackish swamps and muddy lagoons, inside coral reefs, and in similar situations. The mangrove tree appears to stand on a much branched system of roots, somewhat resembling Pandanus in this respect. In harvesting the mangrove as a source of tannin the bark is stripped, dried, and packed in bales for shipment. Mangrove bark yields about 40 per cent. of tannin. The bark also yields a form of cutch. The United States imported 5,500 tons of mangrove bark in 1914. Extensive areas of swamp land in the Philippines are covered with mangrove trees, and a beginning has been made in harvesting this bark for tannin. Similar large areas of mangrove swamps occur also in Malaya.

WATTLE BARK

Wattle bark as a source of tannin is obtained from *Acacia decurrens* and various other species of the same genus native to Australia. These trees are also cultivated in India, Ceylon, Hawaii, Natal, and various other parts of the Tropics. The seeds are grown in nurseries and the young seedlings are then transplanted at distances of 6 to 12 feet apart both ways. The young trees are occasionally pruned in order to encourage the development of straight trunks. The trees may be cut and the bark stripped off at the age of 5 or 6 years, but the highest percentage of tannin in the bark is obtained at the age of 10 years or older. At this time the bark contains 40 per cent. tannin. On an average an 8-year-old tree will yield about 25 pounds of dried bark, while the yield from a fully mature tree is about 100 pounds. Wattle bark is also sometimes called mimosa bark. It is much used, especially in tanning sole leather. Wattle trees are short lived, and in order to secure the greatest harvest of bark the trees should be cut at the age of 10 to 15 years.

QUEBRACHO

Quebracho extract and bark has recently assumed unusual importance as a tanning agent. The commercial product is obtained from a large tree (*Loxopterygium lorentzii*) of South America, particularly Brazil and Argentina. The wood of the quebracho tree is unusually hard. The trees cover enormous areas in Argentina, where they occur in almost pure stands. The heartwood of quebracho contains 20 to 25 per cent. of tannin and the extract of this wood gives a reddish color to leather. In 1914 the United States imported 74,000 tons of quebracho wood and 93,000,000 pounds of extract of quebracho. It is one of the hardest known woods. The bark and sap wood are useless for tanning purposes and only the heartwood is used as a source of tannin. The quebracho logs which are shipped to the United States sometimes come from trees which were 1,000 years old or more. The quebracho extract is called a sweet tan since it does not ferment. It is used in tanning harness, belting, and sole leather. It penetrates leather rapidly and uniformly.

DIVI-DIVI

A small leguminous tree (*Cæsalpinia coriaria*), native of Central America and West Indies, produces small twisted pods which are used as a source of tannin and which bear the trade name divi-divi pods. The tree reaches a height of 20 feet and bears white flowers and flat pods about ¾ inch wide and 3 inches long. These pods yield from 30 to 50 per cent. of tannin. Divi-divi pods are used in the tanning industry as a substitute for sumac and oak gall apples. The tree is propagated by seed and planted about 16 by 16 feet apart both ways. The pods are picked when fully ripe. Mature trees yield from 40 to 75 pounds of dried pods annually.

LOGWOOD

This well known dyestuff is obtained from a small leguminous tree (*Hematoxylon campechianum*), native of Central America, but now introduced into nearly all parts of the Tropics. At present logwood is produced chiefly in Mexico, Haiti, Dominican Republic, Cuba, and other West Indian Islands. The United States imported 40,000 tons of logwood in 1914. The tree is propagated by seed, usually in nurseries, and the young seedlings are then transplanted about 15 by 15 feet apart both ways. The trees are felled at the age of 10 to 12 years. The bark and white sapwood are removed and the red heartwood is packed in bales or bundles for shipment. The wood yields a red dye known as hematoxylin.

GAMBOGE

Several species of the same genus of trees (*Garcinia cambogia, G. morella,* and *G. hanburyi*) yield the commercial product gamboge. These trees are native of the East Indies, Ceylon, Siam, and Cambodia. The gamboge belongs to the family Guttiferæ and the tree attains a height of 30 to 50 feet. A yellow viscid latex exudes from incisions made in the bark and dries into a hard mass upon exposure to the air. The best quality of gamboge comes from Siam. Crude gamboge yields about 70 per cent. of a beautiful yellow resin which is soluble in alcohol and is used by painters to give the well known gamboge yellow. Rarely, gamboge is employed in medicine as a violent cathartic.

FUSTIC WOOD

Fustic wood has long been used as a source of yellow and brown dyes for leather and wool. The importation of this wood into the United States since 1905 has ranged between 3,000 and 4,500 tons annually. On account of the present scarcity of aniline dyes the importation increased during 1915 to about 14,000 tons, and the value of the wood has also considerably increased.

Fustic wood is obtained from *Maclura tinctoria,* a tree closely related to the osage orange and native of the West Indies and tropical America. The sap wood of this tree is thin and the greater part of the thickness of the trunk is therefore heartwood, which is light yellow when fresh, gradually turning to a yellowish-brown. Europe imports fustic wood chiefly from South America, while the United States obtains its supply of the wood principally from Mexico and the British West Indies. Fustic wood is imported largely in sticks 2 to 4 feet long and 3 to 8 inches in diameter, but also in the form of chips, powder, or paste.

A number of substitutes have been used for adulterating fustic wood, among them osage orange, smoke tree (*Rhus cotinus*), southern prickly ash, espino, satinwood, yellow logwood, and other West Indian species of Xanthoxylum. For some purposes the wood of osage orange has been considered as superior to true fustic wood. The osage orange has been used successfully in conjunction with logwood and various other mordant dyes. The dye obtained from osage orange appears to be equally as fast as that of fustic wood. Both of these woods are used in producing dye for leather and many experiments along this line have already been conducted by certain tanneries. Osage orange is used chiefly for making wagon felloes and fence posts. The irregularity of the trunks, however, occasions large waste, estimated at 40,000 to 50,000 tons annually in Texas and Oklahoma.

As already indicated the osage orange is closely related to true fustic and belongs to the botanical species *Maclura pomifera*. True fustic has often been called old fustic to distinguish it from so-called young fustic, which was obtained from the wood of *Rhus cotinus*. The latter attains only a small size, seldom furnishing sticks more than 3 inches in diameter. On account of the use of the term young fustic for these sticks of wood the idea gained ground that they were small branches of the true fustic tree.

BRAZILWOOD

Several species of the leguminous genus Cæsalpinia have been used as a source of dyes. One of these trees, known as *C. brasiliensis*, has been called Brazilwood, although this term is essentially a misnomer since the tree does not occur in Brazil. Brazilwood and the related species, Pernambuco wood (*C. echinata*), both furnish a yellowish heartwood which has long been recognized as having a value for dye purposes. In the East Indies another species, *C. sappan*, commonly called Sappanwood, has been far more extensively used as a source of dye, the wood being shipped in large quantities from India to Europe. In the Pernambuco wood the sapwood is extremely thick, while the commercial heartwood constitutes only a small cylinder of the tree. Brazilwood yields a red dye known as brazilin, which is used in calico printing, especially in mixed reds and browns and also in red ink. Sappanwood yields a red dye, formerly much exported from India. Dyestuff is obtained from the wood, bark, or pods of this tree, but chiefly from the wood. The Sappan dye is especially valuable in dyeing wool and calico.

Camwood or barwood (*Baphia nitida*) comes from a large leguminous tree native of Angola and other parts of Western Africa. It yields a brilliant red dye. The United States imports only a few hundred tons of this wood annually, but it is employed much more extensively in England. Camwood dye is used mostly in calico printing.

INDIGO

The vegetable dye indigo is obtained from a number of shrubby perennial or annual legumes (*Indigofera tinctoria, I. anil, I. arrecta*, etc.). These plants attain a height of 2 to 6 feet and readily escape from cultivation, covering large areas of ground as a weed. The indigo industry was once quite widely spread, but is now confined largely to India, Siam, Java, and Natal. Since the year 1880, synthetic indigo has made the cultivation of indigo unprofitable except in favorable localities. The natural dye, however, is superior to the artificial product and is still in demand.

In propagating indigo the seeds are sown in rows about 2 feet apart. The flowers appear about 3 months from the time of seeding. The plants are then cut and steeped in water for 12 to 16 hours, after which the water is run off into another vat where it is actively agitated for 2 or 3 hours until the indigo forms by oxidation and settles to the bottom. The water is then drained off, leaving the blue precipitate which is cut into blocks and dried. In the experience of indigo planters in India it has been found that a yield of 20,000 pounds of green material per acre is satisfactory. The yield for the rattoon crops is somewhat less. From 20,000 pounds of green material about 500 pounds of indigo paste is obtained. The best grade of indigo is obtained from Java. In Java it has been demonstrated that indigo may be grown profitably in combination with tea by planting the indigo as an intercrop between the tea plants. After harvesting the indigo the plant residues may be used as a fertilizer for the tea.

The indigo plant is extremely hardy and, as already indicated, will propagate itself as a weed even if totally neglected. It has already been distributed throughout nearly all of the tropical countries. It seems more than probable that the present high prices of dyestuffs will bring about a revival of the industry of producing natural indigo.

HENNA

Henna (*Lawsonia alba*) is a much branched shrub, native of Persia, Egypt, Arabia, India, etc. The shrub bears opposite oval leaves and at maturity reaches a height of 8 to 10 feet. The dyestuff henna is obtained from the leaves and young shoots. The first clipping of young shoots with the leaves may be made at the age of 3 years and clippings may be made twice annually thereafter. The leaves are dried, ground, and made into a paste with water. This material is used by Oriental women as an orange cosmetic for the eyebrows, finger nails, and hair, and by Oriental men for finger nails, hair, and beard. Henna is used in India in coloring leather and certain fabrics. At one time it was widely used in France as a dyestuff for silk fabrics. Otherwise the material is used chiefly in the Tropics. The plant has been distributed from Persia and Egypt to various parts of the Tropics. It is hardly cultivated at present, however, except in Turkey, Persia, Egypt, and East Indies. The henna production of Egypt at one time reached the extent of 6,000,000 lbs. annually. Henna makes a fast dye, whether used on fabrics or as a cosmetic.

MADDER

Madder is a herbaceous climber (*Rubia tinctorum*) with perennial roots. The plant is cultivated in various countries from Afghanistan to Spain. It is propagated by seed or clippings. The dye is made from 3 or 4-year-old roots. These roots are prepared in the form of an infusion which yields the beautiful scarlet madder or coffee-brown color. The plant is still cultivated to a small extent in several countries, and the best grade of the dye comes from the Levant and Italy. *Rubia cordifolia*, a plant native to India, is used for the same purpose. Madder root comes on the market either whole or powdered. One of the active coloring substances in madder is alazarin. This substance has been synthesized by industrial chemists and an artificial madder dye of inferior quality is now upon the market.

ANNATTO

This well known dye, which has been used for coloring butter and cheese, is derived from *Bixa orellana*, a bush or small tree native of Central America and South America. The plant is cultivated in Guiana, Ceylon, Brazil, Guadeloupe, Zanzibar, and in other tropical countries. The bush attains a height of 7 to 10 feet and bears cordate leaves, blue flowers in terminal clusters, and ovoid, spiny, two-valved pods, containing 30 to 50 seeds. The seeds are surrounded with a scarlet tissue from which the dye is obtained. Annatto seeds are shipped with their scarlet covering or the scarlet paste is removed and shipped as such. England uses about 75 tons of annatto annually and corresponding quantities are imported into the United States. The tree is propagated from seed and begins bearing at the age of 3 years. Annatto, dye has been used in coloring lacquer, calico, and wool, but chiefly as a coloring matter for butter and cheese. The active principle of annatto is annatoin.

SAFFLOWER

Safflower (*Carthamus tinctorius*) belongs to the Composite family, resembling the thistle somewhat in general habit of growth. It attains a height of 2 to 4 feet and bears beautiful yellow or orange yellow heads of flowers. The safflower is native of India, whence it was introduced in ancient times to Egypt, the Levant, and various other tropical and subtropical countries. At the present time the chief source of safflower is in Bengal and southern France. The flowers are picked in dry weather and are immediately desiccated in an oven. During the period of drying the flowers are slowly pressed together into cakes in which form the product comes upon the market. In Bengal farmers prefer lands which are subject to overflow in growing safflower. The seed is sown broadcast in December and plants are later thinned out so as to stand 4 or 5 inches apart. The flowers are ready for picking about 100 days after the crop is sown. In India the safflower is grown both for the dye obtained from the flowers and for an oil obtained from the seed, but chiefly for the red dye. Safflower has been found to be an exhausting crop and has to be grown, therefore, in a system of rotation.

The flowers are readily injured by rain storms which may occur after they are fully opened. It has been learned that the flowers must be picked as soon as they begin to be brightly colored. Any delay may allow a fading of the dyestuff in the petals. The average yield of dry flowers is about 80 pounds per acre.

SAFFRON

The dyestuff saffron is obtained from the stigmas and tips of the styles of *Crocus sativus*. This form of Crocus was apparently native to Greece and Asia Minor. At any rate, it has been cultivated in those countries since the earliest times. The plant is a perennial with a rounded bulb and large handsome bluish or lavender flowers. Large quantities of saffron are produced in Persia and Egypt. The plant thrives in cold countries. As is well known, it is grown in the United States as an ornamental, but a good quality of saffron has been produced in Pennsylvania. The saffron crocus is a fall bloomer and a different variety from the spring blooming ornamental. The labor cost of producing saffron, however, is too high for the encouragement of this industry in the United States. As already indicated, official saffron includes the stigmas and tips of the styles of the saffron flowers. These parts are clipped off as soon as the flowers open and are dried in the sun or by the aid of artificial heat. It requires 5 pounds of fresh stigmas to make 1 pound of dried saffron. The present supply of saffron comes largely from Trieste, Spain, Greece, and Turkey. Saffron is used both as a medicine and as a dyestuff. It is readily soluble in water and therefore not suitable for use on fabrics. It is perfectly harmless, however, and has been widely used in coloring food products.

CHAPTER XVI

SPICES AND FLAVORINGS

SPICES played a very important part in the history of Europe during the Middle Ages and up to the 16th century. The first knowledge of tropical spices was perhaps brought to Europe by Arab and Jewish tradesmen. These materials brought large prices and were widely sought by the courts and aristocracy of European countries. The existence of spices in far-off, and at that time unknown tropical countries, led to great activity in the building of sailing vessels and to deep study of navigation by sailors. In fact, the geography and history of the whole world have been much modified as a result of the struggle for the possession of spices. The quest of spices took the form of a furor which affected some of the European States almost as much as the Crusades. When Vasco da Gama rounded the Cape of Good Hope and reached India, the primary result of his expedition was to lay the foundation of a colonial empire for Portugal, giving Portugal a large supply of spices. Later the Dutch activities in India and the East Indies led to an attempt to secure a monopoly of the whole spice trade, in which complete success was attained in so far as cinnamon was concerned till the year 1833. The success of the Portuguese and Dutch led to great efforts of colonization on the part of the English and to the establishment of the Straits Settlements and other English colonies in Asia.

All tropical spice plants of economic importance were native to the Asiatic tropics with the exception of vanilla, capsicum, and pimento, which come from the American tropics, and grains of Paradise and Ravensara nuts, which come from Africa.

ALLSPICE

Allspice, also commonly called pimento (*Pimenta officinalis*), is a tree native to Jamaica and other West Indies and Central America. It has sometimes been referred to as *Eugenia pimenta*. The tree attains a height of 15 to 40 feet and bears opposite shiny leaves. The leaves contain an essential oil which is used like that of *Pimenta acris* in the preparation of bay rum. The flowers of the allspice tree are small and white and the tree bears a purple one-seeded fruit about the size of a pea. In ripening the fruit loses much of its aroma. It is therefore picked before fully ripe. The fruit clusters are cut from the tree with a crook or curved knife at the end of a bamboo pole, or if more convenient the branches are pulled down with a curved stick and the fruit clusters clipped off. The fruit is dried in the sun for 3 to 12 days or in a fruit evaporator, after which the material is ready for market. Allspice is propagated by seed, the planting distance being about 20 by 20 feet. The bush begins to bear at about 8 years of age and reaches full bearing at 15 years. The average yield of mature trees is about 75 pounds of dried fruit per tree per year. At present the world's supply of allspice comes chiefly from Jamaica, which country exports about 11,000,000 pounds annually. An oil is extracted from the pimento fruit and is sold under the name pimento oil. This matter is further discussed under oils. The commercial allspice is not closely related to other plants which sometimes bear the name allspice with certain qualifying adjectives. Carolina allspice, for example, or sweet-scented shrub, bears the botanical name *Calycanthus floridus* and the wild allspice of the Northern States is *Lindera benzoin*.

CARDAMOMS

The cardamom plant is a perennial herbaceous plant (*Elettaria cardamomum*), native of Ceylon and India and belonging to the same family with ginger. The plant produces large creeping rhizomes or rootstocks and leafy stems 6 to 10 feet high in dense clumps. The leaves, somewhat resembling those of the ginger, are 1 to 3 feet long and are provided with conspicuous pinnate veins. The flowering stems are about 2 to 3 feet high and bear numerous flowers in short racemes. The fruit of the cardamom is rounded and usually somewhat 3-angled. It is 3-celled, each cell containing about 5 seeds. The fruit is picked in a green condition, dried, and bleached in the sun and usually further bleached by sulphuring. The capsules are then cream white and papery in texture, being about ½ to ¾ inch long. Cardamoms are propagated by division of the rootstocks, which are planted about 8 feet apart both ways. During the early stages of growth some shade is desirable. The cardamom plant begins to bear at the age of 3 years and comes into full bearing at 6 years. From this time on for many years a yield of 100 to 300 pounds of dried cardamoms may be expected per acre. The plant bears the year round but the best crop is obtained during the dry season. It is desirable to harvest the fruits by cutting them off with scissors. A good day's picking for one laborer is 10 to 15 pounds. The world's supply of cardamoms comes almost entirely from India, especially the Malabar coast and Ceylon. Ceylon exports about 500,000 pounds annually. Cardamoms are used as an ingredient of curry powders, for flavoring cakes and liqueurs, and in aromatic drugs and for various other purposes.

CASSIA BARK

The cassia tree of southern China (*Cinnamomum cassia*) is closely related to the true cinnamon and is said to have been used since 3000 B. C. in China as a substitute for cinnamon. The tree attains a height of 25 to 50 feet and closely resembles in appearance the true cinnamon tree. Cassia bark was used as a spice in various countries long before true cinnamon was employed for that purpose. The best grade of Chinese cassia bark, or cassia lignea, is nearly as aromatic as true cinnamon and may be used for the same purposes. Young trees are cut down at the age of 6 years and the branches harvested for their yield of bark. The bark is slipped from branches about 1 inch in diameter and flattened out, after which the epidermis is removed with a plane. The bark is then dried for a period of about 24 hours and baled.

All parts of the plant may be used for distillation of cassia oil. The dried unripe fruits, called cassia buds in trade, are much used in the place of cinnamon. The United States imports about 6,000,000 pounds of cassia bark annually. In China there are approximately 60,000 acres devoted to the cultivation of cassia. The yield averages 1½ tons per acre every 6 years. The bark of *C. iners* and *C. sintoc* of Malaya and of *C. massoia* of New Guinea is also used for the same purpose. In India the leaves of *C. tamala* and *C. obtusifolium* are almost universally used by the natives as a spice. The fallen leaves have been found to be just as aromatic as the freshly picked leaves. It is only necessary, therefore, to have a tree or two in the dooryard to furnish a continuous supply of flavoring material for home use.

CINNAMON

The true cinnamon (*Cinnamomum zeylanicum*) of Ceylon and India is a tree attaining a height of 20 to 60 feet with a densely branched compact head, dark green leathery leaves, and small yellow flowers in lateral and terminal panicles. Ceylon cinnamon is commonly considered of finer quality than that from Malabar. In the early days of the cinnamon industry, the bark was collected from wild trees. Under cultivation it has been found that the tree thrives best at an elevation of about 1,000 feet. The cinnamon tree is propagated by seed. The young seedlings are planted at distances of 6 to 12 feet apart both ways. Most planters consider that some shade for the cinnamon tree is desirable. The tree may also be propagated from cuttings. In fact, this is a quicker method than that of planting the seed. The seedlings may be cut the second or third year. Three or four shoots appear from each seedling stump and with the constant repetition of this process the plantation finally becomes a thicket. As a rule, two harvests are made each year by cutting the 2 or 3-year-old canes at a time when the bark slips readily. The twigs are at once carried to the peeling shed, where they are ringed and split longitudinally, after which the strips of bark are stripped off. These strips of bark are kept moist over night, the epidermis being scraped off next morning. In drying the strips of bark roll into quills. These quills are packed in "pipes" by selecting the larger unbroken quills and packing the smaller quills inside of them. The pipes weigh about 1 ounce and are packed together in bales of approximately 100 pounds.

About one-third of the cinnamon exported is in the form of chips and broken pieces. Cinnamon also comes from French Guiana, Brazil, and the Federated Malay States. Ceylon exports about 6,500,000 pounds annually. The yield is about 100 pounds of dried bark per acre. The chief uses of cinnamon are familiar to practically all readers. It is also employed as a medicine and as an incense. The large percentage of the cinnamon bark is used in the production of cinnamon oil, which is discussed under oils.

CHILIES

Chilies, or capsicum peppers (*Capsicum minimum, C. annuum,* and *C. frutescens*) are familiar herbs or semi-shrubby plants in almost every garden throughout the Tropics and even in temperate climates. *C. minimum,* or bird pepper, attains a height of 2 or 3 feet. The leaves are thin and narrowly lanceolate and the white flowers are about ¼ inch in diameter. The fruit is of an orange or scarlet color, oblong in shape, and ½ to ¾ inch in length. This plant is extensively cultivated in East Indies, Zanzibar, Japan, and various other tropical countries. It is the source of most of the cayenne pepper of commerce. *C. annuum* is taller and bears larger leaves and pods, 3 inches in length. This pepper is commonly called capsicum or pod pepper and is extensively cultivated in California and the Southern States. If grown as annuals, the crop is harvested in about 8 months. In the Tropics the plants may be allowed to stand for 3 years or more. It is propagated by seed and planted at distances which allow from 6,000 to 10,000 plants per acre. The ordinary yield of dried chilies per acre varies from 1,000 to 1,500 pounds annually.

The bird pepper pods are thoroughly dried in the sun and then in an oven, after which the pods are beaten to a powder. In the further preparation of the material about 15 times as much flour is added to the beaten pepper powder and the mixture is then baked and later ground to make the common red or cayenne pepper of the trade. Capsicum peppers are used in curry, in Hungarian paprika, in tabasco sauce, as red or cayenne pepper, as feed for cage birds and domestic fowls, and in medicine.

In India it appears that chilies do best on sandy loam and alluvial soils or on upland soils containing an abundance of lime. The crop is always affected favorably by a previous crop of legumes. Chilies may be allowed to grow for many years as ornamental plants or for household use. Poultry raisers quite commonly have a few of these plants in chicken yards. Most domestic fowls appear to be fond of the peppers.

CORIANDER

Coriander is an annual umbelliferous plant (*Coriandrum sativum*), 1 or 2 feet high, with pinnate leaves and small umbels of white flowers. It is a native of the Mediterranean region and is most extensively propagated in India and Southern Europe. The fruit or seed consists of two concave halves. This spice has been known since the dawn of history. It is widely used in curry powder, in confectionery, and in flavoring gin and whisky.

CAPER

Caper is a trailing shrub (*Capparis spinosa*), a native of the Mediterranean countries and now chiefly cultivated in Sicily, Italy, the southern part of France and in the Southern States. The unopened flower pods are gathered every morning and at once pickled in salt and vinegar. This material is used in flavoring meat sauces. It is slightly laxative in effect.

CURRY POWDER

Curry powder is a mixed condiment, widely used throughout the Orient to flavor rice and meats, particularly poultry. Curry powders commonly contain sago or tamarind as a basis of the paste to which are added curry leaves (*Murraya kœningii*), turmeric, fenugreek, ginger, chilies, pepper, caraway, cinnamon, etc.

CUMMIN

Cummin is an annual plant 1 to 2 feet high with seeds much like those of caraway but slightly larger. The flowers are rose-colored and borne in small umbels. The plant bears the botanical name *Cuminum cyminum*. It is a native of the Mediterranean region and is now grown chiefly in Malta, Persia, Turkey, and Punjab. Cummin seed are used chiefly as an ingredient of curry and in native medicinal preparations.

PEPPER

The source of the common black and white pepper of commerce is the plant known botanically as *Piper nigrum* of Ceylon and southern India. This plant is chiefly cultivated in Penang, Malabar, Sumatra, Ceylon, Java, Africa, and the West Indies. The pepper plant is a woody climber with alternate ovate, smooth leaves, and catkins of small flowers opposite the leaves. When mature the catkins are ½ inch in diameter and 4 to 6 inches long. Each catkin bears about 50 berries or pepper corns. The plant is strictly tropical in habitat, being cultivated about 20° north and south of the Equator. It requires a heavy rainfall. The pepper plant is commonly propagated by cuttings from the tips of the bearing vines. The cuttings should be well rooted before planting.

Pepper plants require some support during their growth. For this purpose trees are preferable to artificial support. The mango, Jack fruit, and *Erythrina lithosperma* are commonly recommended for this purpose. Pepper begins bearing at 3 years of age and reaches full bearing at 7 years. The fruiting life of the plant is from 7 to 15 years. If hardwood posts or artificial supports are used, the planting distance may be 7 feet apart both ways. At that rate the yield should be 2,000 pounds of pepper per acre. Pepper berries are red when ripe but turn black in drying.

Black pepper is the ground berries with the outer covering. If the outer covering is first removed by soaking in water and rubbing, the resulting product when ground is white pepper. In other words, white pepper is made from the ripened seeds only. In preparing white pepper the fruit is allowed to ripen more fully than for black peper. Black pepper is more pungent than white pepper but the white pepper is usually preferred in the trade. Pepper is perhaps most extensively used in the sausage-making and meat-preserving industries, while the table use of pepper is secondary from a commercial standpoint. The United States imports about 25,000,000 pounds of pepper annually.

LONG PEPPER

The long pepper plant is closely related to the common commercial pepper and bears the botanical name *Piper longum*. It is a creeping but not climbing woody vine, native to Bengal, Assam, and Ceylon. The plant bears cordate, pointed leaves and erect fruiting branches about 1 inch long. The whole spike of red drupes is marketed as long pepper. The plant is propagated by suckers which are planted at a distance of 5 feet apart both ways. Long pepper begins bearing during the first year and reaches a full yield at 3 years of age. Thereafter about 1,000 pounds of the product are produced annually per acre. Long pepper is used as a spice and in native medicine. *P. officinarum* of Java produces larger leaves and a more pungent fruit. This product is used for the same purposes as long pepper and is commonly known as Javanese long pepper. Ashantee pepper (*P. clusii*), a plant native to western Africa, has not been cultivated but the wild fruit is much used by the natives as spice.

GRAINS OF PARADISE

A herbaceous plant belonging to the same family with ginger and native of western tropical Africa yields the spice known as grains of paradise (*Amomum melegueta*). The plant attains a height of 5 or 6 feet and bears leafy stems and spikes of showy flowers on trailing shoots which rise from the rootstocks. The seeds are used as a substitute for pepper. The product is also employed in veterinary medicine and for flavoring wine, vinegar, and cordials. Grains of paradise come upon the market chiefly from the Gold Coast.

CLOVES

The search for cloves was one of the important attractive forces which drew the sailing vessels of Portugal, Holland, and other European countries to the Asiatic Tropics. Cloves are obtained from a bushy tree 12 to 40 feet high, native to the Moluccas. The tree is now chiefly cultivated in Ceylon, Zanzibar, Sumatra, Spice Islands, and West Indies. The tree bears the scientific name *Eugenia caryophyllata*. It thrives only near the sea and up to an elevation of nearly 1,500 feet. The erect branches of the tree give it a conical form. The flowers are borne at the tip of the twigs in small clusters. The cloves of commerce are the dried unopened flower buds. This product was apparently first used in China about 200 B. C. The Portuguese controlled the trade in cloves up to 1600 A. D. and the Dutch maintained control until the year 1700.

The clove tree is propagated by seed planted in nurseries under shade. The seedlings are planted 30 feet apart both ways. The tree begins to bear at 4 to 5 years of age. In the Molucca Islands two pickings a year are practiced. In harvesting cloves the flower buds are gathered by hand or are knocked off the trees by means of bamboo poles. The buds are then dried 6 to 8 days in the sun. Care is always observed in preventing dew or rain from falling on them during the drying process since moisture causes them to turn black. The buds lose about 50 per cent. in weight during the process of drying. Cloves are used as spice, as a source of clove oil, which is discussed under oils, in perfumery, soaps, toilet articles, confectionery, liqueurs, medicine, microscopy, and for various other purposes. A clove plantation at maturity yields about 10 pounds of dried cloves per tree. The world's supply comes chiefly from Zanzibar, Pemba, Penang, and Amboyna. Zanzibar alone exports 9,000 tons of cloves annually.

GINGER

The well known plant which is a source of commercial ginger (*Zingiber officinale*) is native to southern Asia, but ginger is now cultivated throughout the Tropics. It is a perennial herb belonging to the family Scitamineæ, with leafy stems 18 to 24 inches high and leaves 6 to 8 inches long and 1 inch wide. The plant bears a terminal cone of handsome curiously shaped flowers on a separate stalk or occasionally at the end of the leaf stalk. The flowers are yellowish-white, with a black and yellow spotted lip. The white, scaly, aromatic rootstock is the source of ginger. These roots are dipped in boiling water, peeled, and dried or may be merely washed and dried. In Jamaica it is customary to classify ginger as yellow or blue, referring to the color of the rootstock. Yellow ginger is preferred. A mountain variety of ginger is widely used in China in making the familiar preserved ginger.

Ginger is propagated only by short cuttings of the roots. It is planted in rows 24 inches apart and 14 inches in the row. Ginger is commonly cultivated by a system of raised beds. The roots are harvested about 10 months from the time of planting, maturity of the roots being indicated by a withering of the leaves. The yield ranges from 1,000 to 2,500 pounds of dried ginger per acre. In drying the roots lose about 70 per cent. of their weight and then contain about 10 per cent. of water. Drying is accomplished in the sun or by the use of artificial heat.

Ginger is an important crop in Malabar, Bombay, Malaya, Sierra Leone, Fiji, Barbados, and Santa Luzia, but especially in Jamaica, which exports about 2,000,000 pounds of dried ginger annually. The United States imported 3,500,000 pounds of ginger in 1914. Ginger is used as a spice, in confectionery, beverages, curry, medicine, and as preserved ginger. The essential oil, called ginger oil, from the rootstocks is used in the essence of ginger. Experiments have shown that ginger will thrive well and produce an excellent crop in Hawaii, Porto Rico, and the Philippines, but no commercial industry in producing ginger has thus far been developed in these countries.

NUTMEG

The nutmeg was sought no less eagerly than cloves by the early explorers of the Asiatic Tropics. Nutmeg is obtained from a bushy tree (*Myristica fragrans*), native to the Moluccas and Dutch East Indies. The tree attains a height of 25 to 50 feet or sometimes even 70 feet. It bears shiny, coriaceous leaves and diecious flowers. The female flowers are small and pale yellow in color. The handsome fruit is globular or pear-shaped, orange-yellow when ripe, 2½ inches long, and pendulous. The fruit is inclosed in a firm, acid, aromatic husk, ½ inch thick, containing the shiny brown seed or nutmeg which is surrounded by a beautiful scarlet lace-work or aril which is the source of the mace of commerce.

A good grade of nutmeg in the shell measures 1 inch in diameter. On ripening the husk splits into two halves. The fruit is then picked or allowed to fall, after which the nut is separated from the mace and both products are thoroughly dried. The shell is then removed from the nut. The commercial nutmeg is therefore the kernel. The nutmeg tree begins to bear at the age of 7 years and reaches its full bearing power at about 30 years of age, at which time each tree bears from 2,000 to 5,000 nuts per year. The tree lives to be 100 years old or more and bears two crops annually. It is propagated by seed sown in nurseries. When the seedlings reach a height of 10 inches they are planted at a distance of 25 feet apart both ways. Most of the male trees are cut out so as to leave one male to 10 female trees. Some shade is usually provided for the young trees. The yield of mace is usually about 1 pound per 10 pounds of nutmeg.

The chief supply of nutmeg and mace comes from Banda, Sumatra, Minahassa, Java, Amboyna, Penang, Singapore, and the West Indies. The production of nutmeg is increasing most rapidly in the West Indies. The Penang mace is most highly prized, while Banda mace is also fairly good. Mace from Batavia and Singapore, however, is inferior. Nutmegs are used in spice, seasoning sausages and other meat products, for making nutmeg butter, which is discussed under oils, and as a source of nutmeg oil which is distilled from the nut. Mace is used chiefly as a spice, being far more delicate than nutmeg and much more highly prized.

The nuts of *M. argentea* of New Guinea are sometimes used to adulterate nutmegs and are likewise largely employed in the manufacture of soap. The calabash nutmeg (*Monodora myristica*) of western Africa produces seeds with a flavor resembling that of nutmeg and sometimes used for the same purpose. Clove nutmeg (*Agathophyllum aromaticum*) from Madagascar and equatorial Africa produces nuts sometimes known as Ravensara nuts, which are used as a substitute for nutmeg.

TURMERIC

The commercial product turmeric is obtained from a perennial herb (*Curcuma longa*) belonging to the same family with ginger. The plant is a native of Cochin China but is now propagated everywhere in tropical Asia. Turmeric reaches a height of 2 or 3 feet and bears long lanceolate leaves in tufts of 6 to 10. The white or yellow flowers are borne in scaly, conical spikes. The rootstocks are thick, scaly, and ringed, and of a bright orange color. In India, about 60,000 acres are devoted to the production of turmeric, chiefly in Bengal, Madras, and Bombay. The most of the turmeric in the trade comes from Madras and Bengal.

Turmeric is propagated by division of the rhizomes, or roots, much as in the case of ginger. The plants are commonly cultivated in ridges or raised beds and the yield is about 2,000 pounds per acre.

In harvesting this crop the roots are washed, heated in earthenware pots, and then dried in the sun for a week or more. In India, turmeric roots are used fresh in the preparation of curry. Dried turmeric is used in curry powder and for coloring pickled preparations and sweet meats. Turmeric is also employed to some extent as a dyestuff. A number of other species of the same genus, *C. aromatica, C. caulina, C. angustifolia,* and *C. amada,* have been used as a source of starch, spice, condiment, dyestuff, cosmetics, and drugs.

Zedoary (*C. zedoaria*) was once quite widely used as a spice but is now employed only by the natives of East Indies in curry powder. The lesser galangal (*Alpinia officinarum*), belonging to the same family, produces red roots. This plant is cultivated only in China. It is used in Russia in medicine and for flavoring beer, vinegar, and liqueurs. The greater galangal (*A. galanga*) is cultivated in Malaya and Java. It develops a very large root with a buff flesh which is used in curries and native medicine.

VANILLA

Vanilla is one of the few important spice plants which were found indigenous in tropical America. The plant from which practically all of the commercial product is obtained is (*Vanilla planifolia*) native of Mexico and Central America. The vanilla is a large, climbing orchid, with shiny, succulent leaves 4 to 8 inches long, and racemes of large pale green flowers. The plant was first used as a spice by the Aztecs, and is now cultivated throughout the Tropics, ranging 20° north and south of the Equator. Vanilla requires a hot, moist climate and much humus in the soil about the roots. Trees, stakes, or trellises for support are distinctly required in the cultivation of this plant. Vanilla is propagated only by cuttings about 3 to 4 feet long which are planted at the base of stakes 9 feet apart both ways or at the base of nurse trees. The cuttings are first rooted in the nursery.

Vanilla plants may be pruned back at the age of 18 months in order to induce a habit of branching or they may be allowed to climb to a height of 10 to 15 feet and to become pendulous from above. Like other orchids, the flowers of the vanilla are naturally fertilized by insects, but the proper insect species are not everywhere present. Vanilla has been introduced into many countries where its natural insect visitors are not to be found. In practical vanilla growing, hand-pollination of the flowers is therefore necessary. For this purpose a pencil or splinter of bamboo is commonly used. The flower is held in the left hand and the lip pressed down so as to expose the pollen masses which are thereupon transposed to the stigma by means of the pencil or bamboo stick. Pollination is usually carried on from 7 a. m. to 3 p. m. One man after sufficient practice can fertilize 500 to 2,000 flowers per day. The period from fertilization to mature pods ranges from 4 to 9 months, varying greatly in different countries.

A good vanilla plant at full bearing may put out as many as 200 racemes of flowers bearing altogether 2,000 to 4,000 flowers. In practice, it has been found desirable to pollinate not more than 6 to 10 flowers per raceme. The vanilla pods reach a length of 4 to 6 inches and are harvested when the tip begins to turn yellow. The curing of the pods is the most important process in the vanilla industry. The pods are dipped in water at a temperature of 195° F. for 15 to 30 seconds. The pods are then put in an oven for 15 minutes, then wrapped in blankets and exposed to the sun until afternoon, and then stored in a closed room over night. This process is repeated for 6 to 10 days, at which time the pods become flexible and are of a deep chocolate-brown color. The fermentation process is then considered as being complete. The subsequent processes in curing vanilla consist largely in properly drying the pods. For this purpose the pods are exposed in a ventilated drying room for a period of 1 to 2 months. Various other processes have been adopted for sweating and fermenting the vanilla pods to develop the proper aroma.

The vanilla plant flowers once a year and begins to bear at the age of 3 years. The world's vanilla crop amounts to about 600 tons of pods annually. Vanilla-producing countries at present stand in the following order: Tahiti, Mexico, Reunion, Comores, Madagascar, Seychelles, Guadeloupe, Mauritius, and Ceylon. Vanilla is used chiefly in flavoring chocolate liqueurs, and confectionery. The artificial vanillin has been made synthetically from eugenol, the characteristic principle in oil of cloves. Artificial vanillin is much cheaper than real vanilla but has not succeeded in displacing the latter to any great extent. Vanillon (*V. pompona*) of Mexico yields a low-grade vanilla. This product is much more easily cured than the commercial vanilla and the pods do not show a tendency to split during the process of curing. The flowers are larger and the pods considerably thicker.

CHAPTER XVII

PERFUMES

As in the case of spices and flavorings, so in the discussion of perfumes it will be desirable merely to consider some of the more important perfumes which are produced largely or exclusively in the Tropics. Several hundred species of plants have been used as sources of perfume. Perfumes for the most part are essential oils and some of these oils which have been used for other purposes as well as for perfume will be discussed in the following chapter under essential oils.

Commercial perfumes in the form in which they are placed on the retail market are almost invariably of mixed composition. They contain various essential oils as a basis or body of the perfume to which a minute quantity of some expensive essential oil is added, thus giving the trade name to the oil mixture. Many synthetic products have been prepared and these products enter largely into the composition of ordinary perfumes.

YLANG-YLANG

One of the most delicate and evanescent perfumes known in the whole perfume industry is ylang-ylang, which is derived from the flowers of *Cananga odorata,* a rapid-growing tree native to the Philippine Islands, Java, and the other East Indies as well as to southern Asia. The tree is a graceful ornamental and attains a height of 60 to 75 feet. The finest ylang-ylang oil comes from Manila. Handsome greenish-yellow flowers appear every month. Petals from fully opened flowers in May and June yield the highest grade of oil. In preparing the oil the petals are carefully distilled. It has been found from experience with this material that 300 to 350 pounds of flowers will yield 1 pound of oil. Ylang-ylang oil is easily damaged to a serious extent by exposure to light and air. It is also extremely volatile and will readily escape except from very tightly-stoppered bottles. Manila exports about 4,500 pounds of ylang-ylang oil annually. The perfume which is sold under the name ylang-ylang commonly contains cologne water, essence of rose, tincture of vanilla, tincture of tolu, and oil of neroli, to which a minute quantity of ylang-ylang oil is added. An excellent quality of this oil is produced in Reunion, where the yield is reported as being frequently as high as 2 per cent. of the flower petals by weight. Good samples of ylang-ylang oil have also been received from the Comoro Islands, while the oil received from Mauritius is of inferior aroma. Madagascar has also given considerable attention to the production of this oil.

FRANKINCENSE

The term frankincense is applied to various resins which yield a strong fragrance in burning. Olibanum, a resin exuding from *Boswellia serrata* and other species of this tree in India and Africa, is also known as frankincense. Olibanum occurs as clear yellow drops of resin on the bark of these trees and is used for burning in religious celebrations and for scenting pastilles and in fumigating powders. The resins in certain species of fir and croton have also been used for the same purpose under the name frankincense.

TONKA BEAN

The tonka bean comes from a large leguminous tree (*Dipteryx odorata*) which bears handsome violet-colored flowers and long fibrous pods containing the black bean. The tree

occurs in wide distribution, in South America. Venezuela is
the source of nearly all the tonka beans of commerce. The
pods are collected and dried, after which the beans are removed
and soaked in 65 per cent. alcohol for 6 to 8 hours. The beans
are then dried again. In the process of drying the beans
become frosted or coated upon the outside by the deposition
of the crystalline volatile resin on the surface of the bean.
For the purpose of increasing the amount of frosting on
the surface of the beans sugar is added to the alcohol. Occasionally, rum is employed for partly saturating the beans
before they are finally dried for the market. The tonka bean
is used for scenting tobacco and snuff and in the preparation
of fumigating powders, perfumery, sachet powders, and in
confectionery as a substitute for vanilla. About 60,000 pounds
of tonka beans are exported annually from Venezuela.

CASSIE

Cassie is the name which has been given to the perfume
obtained from a leguminous shrub, *Acacia farnesiana,* originally native to West Indies but now occurring throughout the
Tropics. In many tropical countries the shrub becomes an annoyance or veritable pest on account of its progressive habit
of spreading. This is notably true in Hawaii and Texas. The
cassie is cultivated as a source of perfume, particularly in
France, India, and Algeria. The shrub attains a height of 4
to 20 feet and bears graceful bi-pinnate leaves and small globular heads of yellow flowers. The harvesting of the flowers is
rendered somewhat difficult by the dense branching of the
bushes and the numerous spines on the branches. In Hawaii,
this bush is known as klu. In India 2 pounds of flowers per
tree is considered a satisfactory yield. In Algeria, 1,000
pounds of flowers per acre are commonly obtained, while in
France, under cultivation, a yield of 5,000 pounds of flowers
per acre has been secured. The flowers are best when picked

in the early morning. The oil is obtained by the process of enfleurage, as is the case with many of the more delicate perfumes. This process consists essentially in dissolving the essential oil in a fixed oil like cocoabutter or coconut oil, after which the essential perfumery oil is dissolved out in alcohol. Cassie has been widely used as a basis of sachet powder. The flowers were at one time used in Hawaii to make a perfume which was sold under the name Pua Hawaii. The aroma of the essential oil of the flowers of this bush is extremely delicate, in some cases being nearly equal to that of ylang-ylang oil. The dried flowers are worth about 50 to 60 cents per pound. In France and Algeria, the wholesale price of the flowers is often not above 25 cents per pound.

MYRRH

This well known perfume of classic antiquity is obtained from *Balsamodendron myrrha,* a tree which is native to the Red Sea region. The tree exudes a gum-resin which has been widely used in the Orient as perfume and in Europe and the United States as a tooth tincture for hardening the gums. The resin also yields 2 to 10 per cent. of the essential oil of myrrh.

BENZOIN

A gum-resin known as benzoin exudes from the trunk of the tree (*Styrax benzoin*), native to Siam, Sumatra, and tropical Asia. Ordinarily, the resin is harvested by tapping the tree. In the tapping wound a resin exudes like pine resin. Benzoin comes upon the market in large yellow or brown lumps and is chiefly used in scenting toilet waters and soaps.

OIL OF NEROLI

The true oil of neroli is distilled from flowers of the bitter orange and is produced chiefly in southern France, but also to a less extent in various tropical countries, particularly Algeria, Tunis, and the West Indies, where the industry has recently become established. In France, it has been found that 500 pounds of the flowers of the bitter orange yield 1 pound of oil. The oil of neroli is chiefly used in perfume blends. The difficulty of securing sufficient labor appears to be the chief reason why the production of neroli oil in Algeria and Tunis has not been more extensive. The perfume of the flower of these countries is said to be extremely delicate. When instead of the flowers the leaves, small twigs, and young fruit of the sour orange are distilled, a perfume oil is obtained which comes upon the market under the name petit-grain oil.

FRANGIPANI

This term is ordinarily used for a compound perfume prepared according to a formula of the Marquis Frangipani and containing sandalwood oil, musk, sage, orris root, neroli oil, and various other constituents. The name has also been given to the essential oil distilled from the red, white, and yellow flowered temple trees (*Plumeria rubra* and *P. acutifolia*), which are native to Central America and the West Indies, but are now widely cultivated about Buddhist temples in Ceylon, China, and Japan, and also in Japanese cemeteries. Frangipani has also been used as the trade name for certain sachet powders prepared partly from cassie flowers.

BERGAMOT

Citrus bergamia, a well known species of the citrus tribe, yields an oil which comes upon the market under the name bergamot. This oil is produced chiefly in Italy, more especially in the province of Calabria. The oil is expressed from the fresh rind of the fruit by special machinery. For this purpose the fruit is gathered in November and December. The oil is greenish and contains some chlorophyll. It is used in scenting fine toilet soaps and in certain mixed perfumes. The essence of bergamot commonly contains 8 per cent. of the oil of bergamot per 5 quarts of alcohol. The United States imports about 65,000 pounds of bergamot oil annually.

CHAMPACA OIL

A large handsome tree (*Michelia champaca*), native of Java, India, and other parts of the Oriental Tropics, yields an oil which bears the trade name Champaca oil. The tree produces conspicuous yellow flowers and the oil is distilled from these flowers. In Java, Champaca oil is of a peculiarly delicious fragrance and of greater value even than ylang-ylang oil.

M. longifolia, a closely related species, with white flowers, also yields a perfume oil by distillation of the flowers. In Manila the flowers of this species yield about 0 2 per cent. of oil. Champaca wood oil is obtained from a different tree (*Bulnesia sarmienti*). The oil is distilled, as the term indicates, from the wood. This oil is solid at ordinary temperatures and emits an odor of tea and violets. It is quite widely used as perfumery. The chief source of the oil is Paraguay.

GERANIUM OIL

The perfume oils which are included under the term geranium oil are derived by distillation of the leaves and stems of *Pelargonium capitatum* and other species of geranium. The oil thus obtained is widely used as a substitute for the essence of rose and Palmarosa oil. The geranium has been widely cultivated as a source of oil in southern France and Spain and particularly in Algeria, where large plantations are maintained for this purpose. The plant is propagated by cuttings, which in Algeria are planted in the fall. The plants begin to yield during the following year and a plantation persists in yielding condition for 7 or 8 years. The stems of the geranium under these cultivated conditions attain a thickness of 1 inch. The yield varies greatly, according to conditions. It has been found that the first cutting of leaves yields about 1 pound of oil per 1,000 pounds of leaves, while the second cutting is nearly twice as rich in percentage of oil. The production of geranium oil in Algeria is perhaps larger than that of any other country. Algerian oil stands next to French oil in value. In Algeria the plants attain a height of 2½ feet and 3 crops of leaves are harvested annually. It appears that the oil obtained from plants grown on dry hillsides is of superior value.

VETIVER

A perennial grass known to botanists as *Vetivera zizanoides* and occurring in Mysore, Bengal, and Burma in moist, heavy soil along river banks, yields from its roots by distillation the vetiver oil which is used as a basis of perfume. The leaves of this grass are practically without odor and are used for thatching and other purposes. The roots, however, when washed and dried in the sun yield by a slow process of distillation a viscous oil less volatile than the most essential oils. It is used in perfumery largely on account of its fixing properties, since it thereby prevents other essential oils from volatilizing too rapidly.

OTTO OF ROSE

The familiar perfume known as otto of rose has been heretofore obtained largely from Bulgaria, which country seems to be best adapted to the production of high-grade roses for this specific purpose. The rose commonly cultivated in Bulgaria as a source of perfume is *Rosa damascena*. *R. alba* has also been grown for the same purpose but it yields an otto of quite inferior quality. Outside of Bulgaria otto of rose is produced in other countries of southern Europe and in Persia and Asia Minor. Otto of rose is distilled from rose petals. The ordinary still used for this purpose has a capacity of about 28 gallons. In the long continued experience which Bulgaria has had in the production of this perfume it has been found that from 2,500 to 2,600 pounds of flowers are required to produce 1 pound of the perfume. Experiments with modern steam stills seem to give less satisfactory results than the primitive stills which have long been in use in Bulgaria.

CHAPTER XVIII

OILS

THE oils of vegetable origin are obtained from seeds, nuts, and beans, as well as from the leaves, fruit, trunk, and roots of various plants. These oils are commonly classified in two groups—fixed oils and essential oils. The fixed oils do not volatilize or evaporate upon exposure to air. The group of fixed oils includes drying oils, semi-drying oils, nondrying oils, and vegetable fats. Drying oils are characterized by their power to absorb oxygen and dry into an elastic film. They are therefore well adapted for utilization in paints and varnishes. Semi-drying oils are intermediate in character between drying oils and nondrying oils. They absorb oxygen slowly and only to a limited extent. Nondrying oils do not solidify on exposure to the air at ordinary temperatures. Vegetable fats are solid at ordinary air temperatures, resembling in this respect butter or tallow. Essential oils, as contrasted with this whole group of fixed oils, are volatile or evaporate on exposure to air. They carry the characteristic flavor or aroma of the plant from which they are derived. Essential oils are obtained chiefly by distillation as contrasted with fixed oils which are commonly extracted by pressure or chemical solvents. In the preparation of essential oils the material in which they are contained is finely ground, placed in a copper still, and boiled. In the process of boiling the essential oil is carried over into a condenser along with the steam. Lemon oil and lime oil may be obtained by pricking the skin of the fruit and applying gentle pressure. Distilled lemon oil is considered to be of an inferior grade. Essential oils which are used in perfumes or for scenting toilet articles are obtained, as already indicated in discussing perfumes, by the process of enfleurage. This process consists merely in saturating the material with warm fat and dissolving out the essential oil by means of alcohol. The United States imports essential oils to the value of more than $4,000,000 per year. In the following discussion the oils are grouped together according to their physical properties under drying oils, semidrying oils, nondrying oils, vegetable fats, and essential oils.

DRYING OILS

Perhaps the most important and most widely used drying oil is Chinawood oil, which is obtained from the nuts of a number of species of Aleurites. This genus includes at least six species of trees, all of which produce oil-bearing nuts. The oil obtained from these trees has long been favorably known for use in various trades and is destined to become of still greater importance. The cultivation of Chinawood oil trees is extremely simple. They require only a moderate amount of rainfall and appear to thrive in almost any soil. In fact, it has been generally observed that these trees may be successfully grown on land which is too rough or otherwise unsuited for ordinary agriculture. The trees begin bearing from seed within 3 to 5 years.

In China, there are two distinct species of economic importance. The wood oil tree (*A. montana*) grows chiefly in the subtropical parts of southeastern China. It appears to require a warmer climate and more rainfall than the tung oil tree (*A. fordii*). The wood oil tree in size and habit of growth and general appearance resembles the tung oil tree. The flowers are smaller and less conspicuous. The amount of oil exported from this tree is much less than the export of tung oil. The tung oil tree is much more widely distributed than the wood oil tree and furnishes at least nine-tenths of the

CHINAWOOD OIL NUT

wood oil used in China and exported from China to other countries. This is the tree¹which, according to all observers, recommends itself for general cultivation in other countries. It grows rapidly, seldom attains a height of more than 30 feet, and develops a much branched, rounded head. The flowers appear before the leaves and are extremely ornamental. The fruit ordinarily ripens in September and October. Each nut contains from 2 to 5 seeds. The yield per tree varies from 1 to 5 bushels or more. Until recently there have been no cultivated plantations of this tree in China. At present a renewed interest is shown in the planting of this tree.

In China the oil from both common species of Aleurites is used for a great number of purposes. In the first place, the oil is the chief paint oil of the country and is widely employed as a varnish and water-proofing material. For this purpose it is not mixed with other materials but is used as such for oiling boats, houses, and all kinds of woodwork. The oil has been shown to possess great endurance toward the action of salt water and toward weathering. From Hankow the annual export of tung oil is 15,000 tons or more. Corresponding quantities are exported from Wuchow.

In Europe and America, tung oil is largely used by paint and varnish makers and also by artists. Tung oil dries the most quickly of all known vegetable oils. It does not, however, produce so clear, transparent, and smooth a film as linseed oil. The difficulties in the technical use of the oil, however, have been largely overcome. At present tung oil is largely employed in paint driers as well as in varnishes.

The related tree (*A. cordata*), which grows quite widely at least in Japan, furnishes an oil commonly known as Japanese wood oil which has been used locally in Japan but thus far has not entered widely into international commerce. In general appearance this tree resembles *A. montana* of China. The fruit is more nearly 3-lobed, often tapering toward the point, and contains 3 to 5 smooth, compressed seeds.

While there are differences in the physical properties of oils obtained from these trees, there has been much confusion in naming the trees and in properly labeling the oils in the past. Commonly, the term Chinawood oil, tung oil, nut oil, and various other phrases have been applied indifferently to the oil coming from any one of the three already mentioned species of Aleurites. These trees are native of China, Japan, Tonkin and Annam. They have been introduced, however, into Madagascar and the Southern States in this country. It has been found that the tung oil tree *A. fordii* will thrive in Florida, South Carolina, Alabama, Louisiana, Mississippi, Georgia, Texas, and California. It will withstand temperatures in winter as low as 14° F. and it has been found to yield in these States a satisfactory quantity of nuts which produce an oil of good quality. Since the United States imports about 5,000,-000 gallons a year of Chinawood oil, it would seem desirable to attempt the commercial growing of the wood oil tree on some of the cheap and rough lands of the Southern States.

The seeds of the tung oil tree contain about 53 per cent. of oil and yield 40 per cent. of oil by pressure. Cold pressed oil is light yellow in color, while hot pressed oil is dark brown. The specific gravity of tung oil is 0.94 and the iodin number 166.7.

The present world's production of Chinawood oil is about 30,000 tons a year. It should be remembered that China probably uses twice as much oil as is exported from that country. The trees are commonly planted 20 feet apart both ways and may be expected to bear a profitable yield at 5 years of age. In fact, in Florida, some of the trees have begun bearing at the age of 2 years.

Candlenut oil is a well known paint and varnish oil, obtained from the seeds of *A. triloba,* also known as *A. moluccana.* Candlenut oil has been known by a considerable variety of names in the trade, such as country walnut oil, kekune oil, artists' oil, Bankul oil, Eboc oil, Spanish walnut oil, Belgaum oil, and in Hawaii as ḳukui oil. The candlenut tree is generally distributed throughout Polynesia, India, the Philippines, Javá, Australia, and the Pacific Islands, including Hawaii. It has also been introduced into the West Indies, Brazil, Florida, and elsewhere. The tree has wide-spreading branches, attains a height of 40 to 60 feet and is characterized by large, irregularly lobed leaves of a pale green color and nuts about 2 inches in diameter containing 1 or 2 seeds.

Candlenut oil has been used for a variety of purposes. The Hawaiians at one time strung the nuts together on sticks and used them for lighting their houses. The natural candles thus produced gave rise to the name candlenut. Candlenut oil is suitable for use in the manufacture of soft soap, in the preparation of varnishes, paints, and linoleum, in the manufacture of oil colors and lacquers, and for other similar purposes. The oil dries as quickly as linseed oil and appears to have about an equal value. Candlenut oil has been widely used in China for oiling paper used in Chinese umbrellas and for other purposes. The oil is also a good wood preservative and has been used on the hulls of sailing vessels and on buildings. For this purpose it has been shown to remain almost intact for 15 to 20 years.

During the decade 1840 to 1850 Hawaii exported about 10,000 gallons of candlenut oil annually. The industry was later allowed to lapse. A company has recently been organized in Honolulu to produce candlenut or kukui oil on a commercial scale. The study of this oil at the Hawaii Experiment Station indicated that there are about 15,000 acres of candlenut trees in the Territory and that the annual yield of nuts is 7 to 8 tons per acre. It was found that one laborer could pick up 500 lbs. of nuts per day in an ordinary kukui forest. The average oil content of the kernel of the kukui nut is 65 per cent. Since the kernel equals 30 per cent. of the weight of the nut the oil constitutes 19.5 per cent. of the weight of the whole nut, including the shell. About 90 per cent. of the total oil content is recoverable by pressure. At this rate 100 pounds of nuts will yield 17.5 pounds of oil. These figures were later verified in a commercial test on a rather large scale.

The oil cake left as a residue from the press is a very valuable fertilizer. The material contains 53.75 per cent. protein, 2.77 per cent. potash, and 2.79 per cent. phosphoric acid. Without further treatment the press cake cannot be used as a cattle feed for the reason that it exercises a poisonous effect.

The kernel of the candlenut contains an active purgative principle and is poisonous as human food. After roasting, however, it is used by the Hawaiians as a delicacy in connection with their native feasts. Even under such conditions, however, it can be eaten only in small quantities. On account of the fact that Chinawood oil and candlenut oil, as well as other drying oils, are quite commonly mixed in order to get the best properties for use in paints and varnishes, it has been thought worth while to attempt a natural blend of the physical properties of Chinawood oil and candlenut oil through the production of hybrids between these trees. In recent hybridization experiments at the Hawaii Experiment Station, about 120 nuts were obtained by cross-pollination between the Chinawood oil and candlenut oil trees. These nuts will be planted in order to determine whether the oil produced from the hybrid trees has any advantage over either of the parent trees.

Perilla oil, obtained from *P. ocymoides,* and native of East Indies, China, and Japan, constitutes about 35 per cent. of the seed of that plant. Seeds are sown in April and the plant ripens another crop of seed in October. Perilla oil dries more slowly than linseed oil. In Japan, the oil is commonly mixed with cheap lacquer. Perilla oil has also been used in extracting Japan wax, and as an edible oil, particularly in Manchuria.

Stillingia oil is obtained from the seeds of a tree *S. sebifera,* which occurs wild in Formosa and is quite largely cultivated in China. The pulp surrounding the seeds yields Chinese vegetable tallow. The seeds contain 20 per cent. of a good drying oil which absorbs 12 per cent. of oxygen within 8 days. The oil is used for lighting purposes in China and is not exported except in small quantities.

Hemp-seed oil is obtained by pressure from the seed of the common hemp (*Cannabis sativa*). Hemp is grown for this purpose in Algeria, India, and Formosa, as well as in parts of Europe and the United States. Seeds contain 30 per cent. of oil. Hemp-seed oil is light green or greenish-yellow in color. It is chiefly used as a paint or varnish oil but also in making green soft soaps. As a drying oil it possesses fair quality. Large quantities of hemp-seed oil are produced in Europe and still larger quantities are imported from China.

Gynocardia oil is derived from the seed of a large tree (*G. odorata*), native of Assam and Sikkim. The seeds yield about 19 per cent. of a good quality of drying oil. For many years the seeds of this tree were also supposed to be the source of Chaulmoogra oil, but this oil is now known to be derived from another source.

Safflower oil is obtained from the seed of the safflower (*Carthamus tinctorius*). The safflower is still quite generally cultivated in India, Egypt, Caucasus, and Turkestan. Safflower seeds yield 17 per cent. of oil by pressure. The actual percentage of oil which can be extracted by gasoline is about 28. Safflower oil is used for culinary purposes in India and also for paint and soap manufacture and in the preservation of leather and ropes. It has been found that safflower oil boiled slowly for 4 hours makes an excellent waterproofing material. In the Bombay Presidency, safflower is the most important oil-seed crop. The area devoted to the plant has been somewhat restricted since the flowers are no longer used so much as a source of dye. The oil obtained by cold pressure is pale yellow. It has a good drying quality but cannot entirely replace linseed oil. The area planted to safflower in the Bombay Presidency is about 600,000 acres. Quite extensive plantings are also being established in Egypt, Nyasaland, and other tropical countries.

Poppy seed oil, as the name indicates, is derived from the seed of the poppy (*Papaver somniferum*). This industry is most largely developed in Egypt, south Russia, India, and Persia. The seeds yield about 45 per cent. of oil. The largest poppy seed oil mills are located in Marseilles, France. The oil is white if expressed cold, but red and of less value if expressed at higher temperatures. Poppy seed oil is used chiefly as a salad oil (sometimes mixed with sesame oil) and also as a fine artist's oil. France imports 60,000,000 pounds of poppy seed annually for oil purposes.

Manihot oil is obtained from the seeds of the Ceara rubber tree (*M. glaziovii*). The seeds yield 10 per cent. of an oil which is yellowish-green in color, of a bitter flavor, and of the odor of olive oil. The oil dries in about a week and may be used as a substitute for linseed oil.

Niger seed oil is derived from the seed of *Guizotia oleifera*, a plant native to Abyssinia and also grown in the East Indies, West Indies, and west Africa. The seeds contain 40 per cent. of oil of a yellow color and nutty flavor. It is used chiefly as an edible oil but the poorer grades are employed in the manufacture of soap and for this purpose mixed with rape-seed oil.

Para seed oil is obtained by pressure from the seeds of the Para rubber tree (*Hevea brasiliensis*). These seeds contain 25 to 40 per cent. of oil. The oil is of a yellow color and dries into a clear film. The industry may assume considerable proportions when the active demand for seed for planting purposes ceases. The oil dries less rapidly than linseed oil and is considered inferior to linseed oil for industrial purposes. The seed cake obtained as a residue from the oil press has been used as a cattle food in Europe, India, and Ceylon. For this purpose the cake appears to have considerable value.

Argemone oil is derived from the seeds of the Mexican

poppy (*A. mexicana*). This plant is quite widely grown in the East Indies, where the oil from the seed is used as a salad oil and also for illuminating and lubricating purposes. In the West Indies and Mexico it is used chiefly for the latter purpose. The seeds yield about 35 per cent. of oil of an orange color. The oil possesses an acrid flavor which apparently gives it some value as a preventive against white ants and borers in addition to its value as a paint oil and wood preservative.

SEMI-DRYING OILS

Cottonseed is one of the most important of the world's oil-bearing seeds. The cultural systems used in growing cotton, however, as well as the technical methods employed in the preparation of cottonseed oil are so familiar to the American reader and have been the subject of so many books and bulletins that it seems unnecessary to discuss the matter in this connection to an extent commensurate with the commercial importance of the product. Cottonseed oil is used largely in compound lards and butter substitutes, while the lower grades are employed in soap making and in adulterating paint oils and for numerous other purposes. The oil is not satisfactory as a lubricant. Cottonseed contains about 20 per cent. of oil and about 13 per cent. of oil remains in the cottonseed meal which is the chief by-product of cottonseed oil mills. These figures indicate sufficiently the yield of oil obtained by pressure. About 35 gallons of oil are secured from each ton of seed. Cottonseed oil is held in the other material which constitutes the seed much more firmly than is the case with many other oil seeds. A significant comparison may be had by considering the absolute content of oil and the percentage of oil recovered under commercial conditions in the case of cottonseed and the kukui nut. As just indicated, the original cottonseed contains 20 per cent. of oil and the press cake 13 per cent. of oil. In sharp contrast with these figures we have the candlenut, which contains 65 per cent. of oil, while the press cake contains only 5 to 8 per cent. of oil.

The color of cottonseed oil is lighter from fresh seed than from old seed. In the commercial manufacture of cottonseed oil, the seed are delinted, decorticated, crushed, and pressed either cold or hot, according to the purpose for which the oil is to be used. The great extent of the industry in this country is indicated by the fact that the United States exports 35,000,000 gallons of cottonseed oil annually in addition to the large amount consumed at home.

Cottonseed meal or the ground press cake which remains after the oil has been pressed has long been an important stock feed. Its greatest and most effective use has been found in feeding dairy cows and in fattening steers. As a feed for chickens, pigs, and sheep, it has been less extensively used. It has long been known that cottonseed meal, when fed continuously in large rations, exercises a poisonous effect on pigs. Much attention has been given to the study of this matter and several theories have been proposed as to the cause of the toxicity of cottonseed meal. It was once suspected that the toxic action of the meal was due to the presence of pyrophosphoric acid under certain conditions. This theory, however, was later discredited. In practice it has been found that if fed in small rations in combination with certain mineral salts and an abundance of green feed the danger from poisoning is largely eliminated. Recently the North Carolina Experiment Station has isolated from cottonseed an active principle known as gossypol. It was shown that this substance has a pronounced toxic effect and that the toxicity of the meal could be overcome by subjecting the meal to any process which would oxidize the gossypol.

Soy bean oil is becoming a more and more important commercial product. The soy bean (*Glycine hispida*) is a familiar legume, native of China, Indo-China, and Japan and now cultivated throughout the world except in extremely cold climates. The most extensive plantings of soy beans are in Japan, Korea, and Manchuria, but recently the plant has assumed much greater importance in various tropical countries. Soy beans contain from 15 to 22 per cent. of oil and yield 10 to 13 per cent. of oil by the ordinary commercial methods of extraction. The oil is used in the Orient for food and light. It is imported into the United States largely for use in soap manufacture. The soy bean industry has assumed enormous proportions in China and Japan on account of the oil, meal cake, and soya sauce and other products. There are more than 12,000 soya sauce factories in Japan alone and the soya sauce factory follows the Japanese wherever they go. About one-tenth of the arable land of Japan is devoted to the cultivation of soy beans. There are a great many varieties of soy beans producing black, brown, yellow, mottled, and green seeds and varying greatly in oil content.

In the Orient, soy bean oil is largely used for human food and has become an extremely important food product. It is also employed in China for illuminating purposes and as a substitute for linseed oil in paints. The use of soy bean oil in manufacturing soap and as a machine lubricant is also important. Recently the oil has entered quite widely into the manufacture of margarine.

Soy bean meal, or the ground cake obtained as a residue from the oil factories, is well known to be an extremely valuable cattle food. Near the centers of production it is much cheaper than cottonseed meal. A few cases have occurred where poisonous effects were apparently produced from excessive feeding with soy bean meal but the matter still remains somewhat uncertain. In Japan, a number of other products are prepared from soy beans. A product known as soy-bean milk is made by soaking beans in water for 12 hours and then pressing them between mill stones, after which the powder is boiled with three times its bulk in water and filtered through cloth. The product resembles milk in appearance and is considered a valuable source of nourishment for children. The milk may be further treated with magnesium chlorid to precipitate the proteids, which are then collected by filtration, pressed, and dried into a product known as soy bean cheese. Soya sauce or shoyu sauce is a much more important product of the soy bean. This material is prepared from a mixture of boiled and pulverized soy beans, and roasted, pulverized wheat with salt and water. The whole mass is fermented with rice wine ferment in large vats for from 1 to 5 years, being stirred at frequent intervals. The product is a dark brown or almost black sauce, resembling beef extract in appearance but of a more pungent quality. Soya sauce is widely used in this form by the Japanese and serves also as the basis for Worcestershire sauce and other meat sauces used in Europe and America. The moist cake residue obtained in the manufacture of soya sauce is of very different composition from the soy-bean meal derived from oil factories. The residue which comes from the soy factories contains 15 per cent. moisture, 24.5 per cent. ash (nearly all of which is common salt), 17.25 per cent. protein, 18 per cent. fat, and 24 per cent. carbohydrates. This material may be used as a stock feed after washing out the salt in water. The soy bean crop matures in from 85 to 130 days after seeding and the yield varies from 25 to 40 bushels of beans per acre.

Kapok oil is obtained from the seeds of kapok (*Eriodendron anfractuosum*), a tree native to the East Indies, West Indies, Malaya, Central America, and Africa. The hull of the kapok seed is easily removed from the kernel. The seed yield about 18 per cent. of oil of a greenish-yellow color and agreeable flavor. This oil is used in the Tropics for food purposes. Large quantities of the seed are imported into Holland, where the oil is expressed for use in soap and as a substitute for cottonseed oil. If the seed is not thoroughly decorticated before grinding and pressing, the oil has a reddish color.- Its properties are very similar to those of cottonseed oil.

Sesame oil, also called gingelly oil and by other names, is obtained from the seed of *Sesamum indicum*. The crop is cultivated chiefly in India, Java, Siam, China, Japan, and the Levant. Sesame is an annual plant attaining a height of 2 or 3 feet. The seed are sown broadcast and the crop matures in 4 months from the time of seeding. The yield is commonly about 20 bushels of seed per acre, from which 60 gallons of oil are obtained. The seed contains from 50 to 57 per cent. of oil.

Marseilles is the great mill town for sesame seed, importing about 100,000,000 pounds of seed annually. Sesame press cake is widely and favorably known as a cattle feed. The oil is extensively used as human food and for anointing the body in India, while in Europe it serves widely as a salad oil and for use in the manufacture of soap. A particularly fine quality of seed for oil purposes comes from Palestine.

Sesame seed are dried, ground, and pressed for 1½ hours. The yield by commercial methods is 32 to 35 per cent. of oil under the system of cold pressure. After this first extraction 5 per cent. of water is added and the mass is again pressed at a temperature of 50° C. A third application of pressure is then made, yielding about 10 per cent. of oil additional to that obtained from the first two pressures. The oil secured by the first pressure is not of strong flavor and is clear, that obtained from the second and third pressure is darker, of a decided flavor, and with a tendency to become acid.

The best grade of sesame oil is used as a substitute for olive oil in salads and in medicine and also in margarine and vegetable butters. For this purpose northern Europe imports 32,000 tons of sesame seed annually. Sesame cake contains 5 to 13 per cent. of fat and 24 to 40 per cent. of protein. The cake is much used as a cattle feed in rations of 2 to 4 pounds per day.

Sesame oil is one of the important vegetable oils of India. The oil obtained from the first press keeps for a long time without becoming rancid. The area devoted to sesame in India is about 4,500,000 acres and the annual yield is approximately 200,000 tons.

Rape-seed oil is imported into Europe in greatest quantities from Bombay. The seed contains from 33 to 40 per cent. of oil. The cold pressed oil is used for eating purposes in India and Europe. In the United States, rape-seed oil is much used as a "bread oil" to grease the ends of the loaves of bread. Rape-seed oil, extracted by chemicals, is used for illuminating and lubricating purposes as well as the manufacture of soap. Europe imports 280,000,000 pounds of rape seed annually from India. The area devoted to the production of rape in India is about 3,500,000 acres.

NONDRYING OILS

Olive oil is produced chiefly in the Mediterranean countries, Syria, California, South Africa, and Australia. The pulp of the fruit yields 10 to 50 per cent. of oil according to variety and locality. The yield per acre varies from 500 to 2,000 gallons of oil. The largest yield of oil is obtained from completely ripe fruit, but the highest grade of oil comes from fruit which is not fully ripe. In ordinary practice the fruit is crushed entire, but a better quality of oil is obtained from the pulp or marc alone, in which case the oil is marketed under the name of olive kernel oil.

In California the percentage of oil in olives is comparatively low. It has been found that the fruit should be pressed as soon as possible after picking, but methods have been devised for holding the fruit a long time without deterioration. The first expression from the fresh olive pulp yields "Provence oil," "Nice oil," "Riviera oils," and other high grades of olive oil. After the first expression water is added to the pulp and pressure again applied. From the second expression, salad oil or common table oil of second grade is obtained. The pulp is then removed from the press, mixed with hot water, and pressed a third time, yielding an oil for lubricating or soap-making purposes. The stearin and other material is allowed to settle out, after which the oil is decanted from the top and filtered to render it clear. Large quantities of olive oil are used for table purposes. The United States alone imports nearly 7,000,000 gallons of olive oil annually in addition to the considerable quantities produced in California. Low grades of the oil are used in textile soaps, in calico printing, in medicinal soaps, and for various other purposes.

Castor oil is derived from the familiar castor bean (*Ricinus communis*), a plant native to Africa, but now cultivated everywhere in the Tropics and subtropics. The castor bean has been grown for the bean as far north as Kentucky in the United States and as an ornamental even in Canada. The plant is cultivated chiefly as an annual, but in the Tropics some varieties reach a height of 40 feet as a perennial. There are many varieties of castor bean, differing in color and marking of the seed and in habit of growth.

The chief sources of castor bean are India, Java, Persia, China, Japan, Mediterranean countries, Mexico, and the United States. The yield of beans varies from 12 to 30 bushels per acre. The United States imports 900,000 bushels of castor beans annually, while India exports 3,000,000 bushels of beans and 2,000,000 gallons of castor oil per year.

The castor bean yields from 25 to 40 per cent. of oil by pressure. The bean also contains a poisonous alkaloid known as ricin. Ricin does not pass into the oil if pressed cold. The first cold expression yields a medicinal oil of high grade. Subsequent expressions yield low-grade oils used for lubricating and manufacturing purposes. Low-grade or damaged castor beans are commonly treated directly with chemical solvents for the complete extraction of the oil to be used for manufacturing purposes.

In Oklahoma, castor beans are planted 15 to 18 inches

apart in rows 4 feet apart, but in tropical countries the planting distance is 5 or 6 feet both ways. The castor oil industry in India is a very important one. The oil is highly valued for use in lubricating machinery, for dressing hides and skins, for illuminating purposes, in the manufacture of soap and candles, and as a medicine. Cold pressed oil gives a more brilliant light than oil obtained from boiled or roasted beans. The press cake obtained from castor oil mills is widely used as a fertilizer for rice, potatoes, and sugar cane. In India the beans are picked from the seventh to ninth month after planting. The yield ranges from 500 to 900 pounds of beans per acre.

Peanuts are grown as a commercial crop chiefly in the East Indies, Java, Mozambique, United States, Togo, southern Nigeria and the West Indies. Senegal exports 200,000,000 pounds of peanuts annually to Europe. In the commercial preparation of peanut oil it has been found that the first cold expression yields the best oil. This oil is used as a salad oil. A second grade of peanut oil is also used for salad purposes, being sold at a lower price. The third grade of oil is employed largely in the manufacture of soap. High-grade peanut oil is quite widely used as an adulterant of olive oil and in preserving sardines and for other culinary purposes. Peanuts yield 32 per cent. of oil by the ordinary commercial methods. The oil cake which is thus obtained as a residue contains 8 to 9 per cent. of oil and is an excellent cattle feed. The chief tropical producing countries export nearly 700,000 tons of peanuts annually for use as a source of oil.

Rice oil, obtained from rice bran and meal, has come to be a commercial product of considerable importance. Unmilled rice contains 2 or 3 per cent. of oil. Most of this oil is located in the outer portion of the grain and is therefore removed in milling. In the rice mills of Rangoon it has been found that the bran contains as high as 20 per cent. of oil. Rice oil commonly shows a rather high acidity. It is extracted by commercial solvents and is chiefly used in the manufacture of soap.

The almond oil of commerce is chiefly expressed from bitter almonds in the Mediterranean countries and Persia. The seeds yield from 20 to 45 per cent. of oil. In trade the oil is much adulterated with oil from peach or apricot kernels. Almond oil is used almost exclusively for pharmaceutical purposes. By distilling the seeds an essential oil of bitter almonds is obtained for use in perfumery, confectionery, and medicine.

Tea oil is obtained chiefly from the seeds of *Camellia cleifera* and other species of this genus, including the commercial tea plant. The production of tea seeds for oil is confined largely to China, Tonkin, Assam, and Japan. For this purpose the seeds are gathered in the fall. The seeds yield 15 per cent. of oil by pressure. This oil is sometimes used as a food oil in China, but in Japan it is employed chiefly as an expensive hair oil and for lubricating delicate machinery. Tea oil is light yellow in color, closely resembling olive oil in its general character, but possessing a somewhat acrid taste. It serves fairly well as an illuminating oil and gives excellent results in the manufacture of hard white soap. The press cake obtained as a residue in the manufacture of tea oil is poisonous and therefore of no value as a cattle feed. Its fertilizing value is also rather low.

Ben oil is obtained from the seeds of *Moringa pterygosperma,* a tree native to India, Syria, Arabia, Nigeria, Jamaica, and other countries. The seeds of this tree yield about 36 per cent. of oil. Ben oil is composed of 60 per cent. liquid oil and 40 per cent. white solid fat. The oil has a yellowish color. It is used in the Orient as a cosmetic oil and also in the enfleurage process of extracting perfumes from flowers.

Sterculia oil is derived from the seed of a moderate-sized tree (*S. fœtida*), native to the East Indies, Indo-China, and Malaya. The seeds of this tree yield 30 per cent. of oil, which is commonly used in Java and other Oriental countries as a cooking oil and for illuminating purposes.

Canari oil is obtained from the pili nut tree (*Carnarium*

commune), indigenous to Malabar and the Molucca Islands, and cultivated also in various other parts of the Tropics. The nuts of this tree yield 56 per cent. of oil by pressure. The oil is of a yellow color and very agreeable flavor. It is used exclusively as a food oil.

VEGETABLE FATS

The most important of the oils which come under this group is palm oil, obtained from the nuts of *Elæis guineensis*, native of west Africa, where it occurs in enormous areas. The oil palm is also cultivated in various tropical regions, particularly in Nigeria. It is a handsome tree 40 to 60 feet high, with large, graceful, pinnate leaves. The oil palm begins bearing at the age of 5 or 6 years and comes into full bearing at 15 years of age, after which it continues its productive life for 60 to 70 years. Each tree bears about 10 bunches of 200 nuts each per year. About 70,000 tons of palm oil and 175,000 tons of kernels are annually exported from west Africa. The United States imports 25,000 tons of palm oil per year.

The bunches of ripe nuts are cut off with a machete and allowed to fall to the ground. The fruit pulp yields a yellowish oil which is widely used in the soap and candle industries. The kernels yield a white fat which is much employed as a vegetable butter. The kernel oil is obtained by hydraulic pressure in the oil mills of Europe. A high-grade pulp oil is secured by the natives through the use of hand presses and a low-grade oil by boiling. The yield averages about 1 to 3 gallons of oil per tree annually. This yield could be much increased by improvement in the methods of handling the nuts. The present native methods are very wasteful. It has been estimated that these careless methods cause an unnecessary loss of about one-third the possible oil yield.

From 1 ton of the palm kernels 900 pounds of oil are obtained. This oil is a white, solid mass at ordinary temperatures. It is used in the manufacture of soap and candles and in constantly increasing amounts in margarine and cooking fats. About 35,000 tons of the kernel oil are used annually in northern Europe in the manufacture of margarine. Palm kernel cake contains 6 per cent. fat and 18 per cent. protein. This product is widely and favorably known as a cattle feed, being used for this purpose not only by the natives but also in Europe, where the material is shipped in large quantities.

Cocoa butter constitutes about 50 to 55 per cent. by weight of the cacao beans. It is obtained as a by-product in the manufacture of cocoa as indicated in the discussion of cocoa under Beverages. Cocoa butter is yellowish when fresh but turns white with age. It possesses a chocolate flavor and is very firm at ordinary temperatures. Cocoa butter is used in pharmacy, confectionery, and in the preparation of perfumes. Large quantities of the material are ordinarily to be had for this purpose.

Chinese vegetable tallow is a firm fat which occurs as a coating on the seeds of *Stillingia sebifera*, a tree native to China and Indo-China. Each fruit of this tree has 3 seeds. The tree begins bearing at 5 years of age and produces 50 pounds of seeds per tree per year or about 15 pounds of fat. Hankow is the center of production, which amounts to 10,000 tons a year. About 5,000 tons of the material are sent to Europe and the United States. It is extensively used in China and elsewhere in the manufacture of candles. The seed kernels yield Stillingia oil, which is discussed elsewhere in this chapter.

Chaulmoogra oil is a vegetable fat obtained by expression from the seeds of the tree *Taraktogenos kurzii*, native to Burma and Assam. Under pressure the seeds yield a yellowish oil possessing the consistency of butter. The oil is much used in the Orient and in Europe in treating skin diseases, and is sometimes used internally in the treatment of tuberculosis. In the Orient, Chaulmoogra oil has been much used in treating the superficial lesions of leprosy.

Hydnocarpus oil is a yellowish, semi-solid vegetable fat obtained from the seeds of (*H. wightiana*), a tree native to India. Under pressure the seeds yield 32 per cent. of the oil, which is used as a substitute for Chaulmoogra oil. The seeds of *H. anthelmintica* also yield by pressure about 16 per cent. of an oil called lukrabo oil, which is similar in odor and consistency to Chaulmoogra oil.

Pongam oil is derived from the beans produced by *Pongamia glabra,* a tree native to India, Ceylon, and Malacca. The beans yield by pressure about 25 per cent. of yellow oil, which is much used in medicine and for illuminating purposes in India.

Carapa oil is produced by the seeds of *C. guianensis,* a handsome tree native to French Guiana. This tree reaches a height of 75 feet and bears pinnate leaves. The natives obtain the oil by boiling the seeds in water and allowing the oil to drain from the mass. The seeds yield about 40 per cent. of oil by pressure. This oil is employed by the natives in Guiana, Brazil, etc., as an ointment to protect the skin against the attacks of insects.

Shea butter is a vegetable fat obtained from the nuts of *Butyrospermum parkii,* a tree native to the west coast of Africa and the Sudan. The tree grows to a height of 40 feet or more. The nuts are pounded and boiled in water, after which the fat is skimmed off. The oil has found quite a wide use in the manufacture of soap and candles.

Nutmeg butter is derived from the nutmeg kernel by pressure. Only a small part of the 1,500 tons of nutmegs annually produced in the world is used as a source of nutmeg butter. The seeds yield 40 per cent. of fat of a yellow color, nutmeg flavor, and of the consistency of tallow. Most of the nutmegs of Europe come from the Banda Islands. Mace butter is made both from the mace of the commercial species of nutmeg and also from *Myristica argentea,* a tree of common occurrence in New Guinea. Nutmeg butter is largely used in medicine in the preparation of ointments.

Kokune butter, also called mangosteen oil, is obtained from the seeds of the mangosteen which yield about 20 per cent. of fat of a white color and not unpleasant flavor. Kokune butter is prepared especially on the west coast of India where it is widely used as a food fat.

Cohune oil is obtained from nuts of the palm *Attalea cohune*, native to Central America, especially Mexico, British Honduras, and Guatemala. The nuts are about the size of nutmegs and contain 40 per cent. of the firm yellow fat. The nuts offer much difficulty in grinding, and suitable machinery for crushing them has not yet been devised. The cohune palm is estimated to occupy nearly 2,000,000 acres in British Honduras, or approximately two-fifths of the total area of the colony. The nuts are borne in large bunches and the yield of each tree is 1,000 to 2,000 nuts per year, or about 200 pounds of nuts. The kernels of the nuts are about 1 inch in diameter. Occasionally, however, they attain a greater size. The fat obtained from the kernels is solid white, of a crystalline structure, and resembles coconut oil in appearance and smell. The kernels yield about 65 per cent. by weight of fat.

Coconut oil has long been one of the most important of the vegetable fats, and its importance is increasing constantly with the improvement in methods of refining and purifying it. This oil is discussed in the chapter on coconuts.

Japan wax is derived from the berries of *Rhus succedanea*, a sumac bush native of Japan, China, and Tonkin. By pressure the berries yield 20 per cent. of a greenish wax.

The most important refineries for this material are located in Kobi and Osaka. The total production of Japan wax is about 2,400 tons annually, and of this quantity about 250 tons are exported to Europe and America.

Mowra fat is produced by *Bassia latifolia* and *B. longifolia* which are native nut-bearing trees in India. For the most part the nuts are collected from wild trees but the cultivation of these trees is increasing in recent years. Mowra fat is widely used in India and is also exported to the extent of 66,000,000 pounds annually. The oil content of the nut kernels is 55 to 65 per cent. Mowra fat is soft and yellow. It is used in India as a cooking fat particularly for mixing with ghi, or clarified butter, and for tallow. In Europe, mowra fat is employed in the manufacture of margarine and also as a chocolate fat. In soap-making, mowra fat is of equal value with palm oil. Mowra cake contains a poisonous saponin and is therefore not suitable for use as a cattle feed. The material, however, makes a good fertilizer, containing 17 per cent. protein and 7.5 per cent. ash.

The same material is obtained from Mauritius under the name illipe oil. In Mauritius it appears that 100 kilograms of shelled nuts are required to yield 16.5 liters of pure oil. While this oil is used in considerable quantities in India as a cooking oil, it seems not likely to assume any importance in that regard in Europe or America.

ESSENTIAL OILS

Citronella grass oil is obtained by distillation from the leaves of the grass *Andropogon nardus* which is cultivated especially in Ceylon and Java. In Ceylon about 40,000 acres are devoted to the production of this crop. Two cuttings a year are obtained and the yield of oil per acre is 40 pounds per year. The oil is used chiefly in perfuming toilet soaps of the cheaper quality. There appear to be several grades of this oil in Ceylon and apparently two or more varieties of citronella grass are used as a source of the oil. A planting of citronella grass persists for 15 years or more before the plants become exhausted.

Lemon grass oil is obtained from the leaves of a closely related grass, *A. citratus*, native to India and Ceylon. The yield obtained from this grass averages 20 pounds of oil per acre with a value of about $500. The oil is used in scenting fine toilet soaps and for various other purposes. Lemon grass oil is also called verbena oil. Several other species of Andropogon yield oils which have been used for similar purposes. This is particularly true of *A. muricatus, A. odoratus, A. laniger,* and *A. martini.* From the latter species Palmarosa oil or Indian geranium oil is derived. The United States imports about 890,000 pounds of citronella and lemon grass oils annually. Recently the cultivation of lemon grass for the production of oil has reached large proportions in Uganda. The oil obtained from Uganda, however, is thus far inferior to the East Indian product.

Eucalyptus oil is derived chiefly from *E. globulus* and *E. citriodora.* These trees are native to Australia but are now widely cultivated throughout the Tropics and subtropics, including California and the Southern States. Oil has been produced from more than 100 species of eucalyptus and the oil from these different sources has been found upon examination to differ somewhat according to the species from which it is derived. Blue gum (*E. globulus*) is, however, the chief commercial source of eucalyptus oil and is taken as a standard. The fresh leaves from this tree yield about 1 per cent. of oil which is rich in eucalyptol, the active medicinal principle of the oil. Eucalyptus oil is widely used for medical purposes, especially as a nasal oil spray. The oil from certain other species of eucalyptus has been used to some extent in scenting soaps and other toilet articles. This is particularly true of *E. citriodora,* the leaves of which yield a pale yellow oil with the strong odor characteristic of citronella grass. Eucalyptus oil is in all cases obtained by distillation of the leaves.

Sandalwood oil is derived from the wood of *Santalum album,* the true sandalwood tree, native of India, especially in Mysore, Coimbatore, and Malabar. Upon distillation the wood yellow color and of a thick molasses-like consistency. It is yields 1.5 to 6 per cent. of oil. Sandalwood oil is of a pale used in medicine and perfumery, especially in the Orient. Sandalwood oil is also obtained from various other species of Santalum, including *S. freycinetianum, S. pyrularium,* and *S. haleakalæ* of Hawaii, and also from *S. cygnorum* and *S. preissianum* of Australia. In Mysore, sandalwood plantations belong to the government. Large quantities of wood are shipped from that region to Europe where the wood is used chiefly for distillation to obtain sandalwood oil.

The trade in sandalwood was at one time an important industry in Hawaii. This material was largely shipped to the Orient where it was used in the preparation of chests and fancy boxes, and also for the preparation of the oil and its subsequent use in perfumes. The tree has been practically exterminated in Hawaii as a result of the indiscriminate methods of harvesting.

Cinnamon oil, as the name indicates, is obtained from the chips or waste and broken pieces of cinnamon. Large quantities of this waste material accumulate during the preparation of the cinnamon quills. Cinnamon oil has been much adulterated with the essential oil of the cinnamon leaves. Cassia oil is derived from cassia bark and is of a much ranker odor and of a correspondingly lower value. The cultivation of the cassia tree as a source of oil is carried on chiefly in southern China. The oil is obtained principally from the leaves. A similar oil is derived from the bark, flowers, and twigs, but the process of distillation of the leaves is cheaper. Cassia oil has been found to be much adulterated with resin. The true cinnamon chips yield ½ to 1 per cent. of oil. This oil.is extensively used in perfumery and in medicine. The United States imports 125,000 pounds of cassia and cinnamon oils annually.

Gurjun balsam oil is derived from a balsam which exudes from the stem of a tall tree (*Dipterocarpus turbinatus*), native of India. This balsam is quite largely used to adulterate copaiba balsam.

Lemon oil is obtained from the rind of the lemon. The oil is produced in small quantities in nearly all tropical and subtropical countries, but chiefly near Messina, Sicily. The United States imports about 450,000 pounds annually. Lemon oil is also produced in other Mediterranean countries, New South Wales, Jamaica, Florida, and California. Several methods have been developed for obtaining the oil, but the method chiefly used in Sicily consists of pricking the rind with a needle brush and catching the oil with a sponge by hand pressure on the rind. Lemon oil is chiefly used as a flavoring material.

Orange oil is derived mostly from the sweet and sour orange rind, particularly in Sicily and Italy. The oil is expressed by the method just mentioned in connection with lemon oil. Orange oil is used in scenting soaps and toilet waters and in perfumes. The United States imports 80,000 pounds annually.

Lime oil is produced in Italy from the rind of the lime in the same manner as lemon oil. In the West Indies the lime oil is obtained as a by-product by distillation in concentrating lime juice.

Oil of cloves is derived from the familiar spice *Eugenia caryophyllata,* native of the Molucca Islands, where it is still most widely cultivated as a spice. Clove oil is now produced chiefly in Zanzibar and the Pemba Islands. The oil is obtained by distillation of the cloves or dried unexpanded flower buds. Cloves yield 15 per cent. of clove oil by the process of distillation. The oil is clear at first but soon becomes yellowish in color. It has a high specific gravity, being heavier than water. Clove oil is used in medicine, as an antiseptic, in microscopy and in flavoring.

Ginger oil is obtained chiefly from the West Indies and East Indies. The oil is distilled from the roots of Jamaica ginger. These roots or rhizomes yield about 2 or 3 per cent. oil of a yellow color which is chiefly used in flavoring liqueurs.

Cardamom oil is now obtained principally from India and Ceylon. The oil is distilled from the commercial cardamom seeds. The Ceylon seeds yield 3 to 6 per cent. of oil. The chief use of cardamom oil is for flavoring purposes.

Oil of cubebs is obtained mostly from Java. The dried cubeb fruits yield 10 to 15 per cent. of a greenish oil by the process of distillation. Cubeb oil is used in medicine and in flavoring liqueurs.

Camphor oil really belongs in the same series with camphor, the oil being the liquid portion and camphor the solid portion of the product of distillation of camphor wood and leaves. The oil is separated from the camphor by pressure or draining.

Cascarilla oil is derived by distillation from the bark of *Croton eleutheria*, a shrub native to the Bahamas. The bark of this shrub yields 1 to 3 per cent. of an oil which is very aromatic and is used in fumigating pastilles.

Patchouli oil comes largely from Penang, Malacca, Java and Mauritius. It is obtained by distillation from the leaves of a perennial herb (*Pogostemon patchouli*) belonging to the mint family. This herb grows to a height of about 2 feet. The dried leaves yield by distillation 2 to 4 per cent. of oil, which is chiefly used in scenting soaps and perfumery. The patchouli leaves are fermented in heaps before being distilled. The plant has long been cultivated in the Straits Settlements and in the islands of the Indian Ocean. The Chinese seem to be particularly adept at making a success of this crop. The plants attain their full height within 6 months after seeding, at which time the first crop of leaves is taken. Two other crops of leaves may be obtained at intervals of about 6 months, after which the crop is replanted.

Cummin oil is produced chiefly in Sicily, Malta, and India. The fruit of the cummin yields 2 to 4 per cent. of a yellow oil by distillation. Cummin oil is not extensively used.

Pimento oil comes into the trade chiefly from the West Indies. Pimento oil is also commonly known as allspice oil

HARVESTING OLIVES IN TEBOURBA, TUNIS

BAMBOO PLANTATION IN LOUISIANA

and is derived by distillation of the dried unripe allspice berries. The dried berries yield 3 to 4 per cent. of a reddish oil which is much used for flavoring purposes.

Oil of bay is derived from a tree (*Pimenta acris*), closely related to the allspice bush. It is a small, handsome tree suitable for use in ornamenting gardens and grounds. The leaves yield by distillation 1 to 3 per cent. of oil which is chiefly used in the preparation of bay rum. The best grade of the oil comes from St. Thomas. The tree begins bearing oil-yielding leaves at 3 years of age. The average yield of oil is 50 pounds per acre annually.

Cajuput oil is obtained from a shrub (*Melaleuca cajuputi*), native of Bouru and Banda Islands. The shrub belongs to the family Myrtaceæ. The oil is obtained by distillation of the leaves and is of greenish color. Cajuput oil is used in medicine chiefly for external application. The United States imports 10,000 pounds of this oil annually.

Lignaloe oil comes upon the market chiefly from Mexico. It is derived by distillation of the wood of *Bursera delpechiana* and *B. aloexylon*. Oil of the same name also comes from South America, where it is obtained from *Ocotea caudata*. The Mexican trees yield the best oil when 40 to 60 years old. On young trees, however, strips of bark are removed to hasten the maturity of the wood. In order to obtain the oil the wood is cut into chips and distilled. It yields 7 to 10 per cent. of the oil. Lignaloe oil is an important Mexican export product.

Star anise oil is derived by distillation from the fresh fruits of star anise (*Illicium verum*), native to China and Tonkin. It is also widely cultivated in various parts of the Tropics and subtropics. The plant is propagated by seed and the seedlings are taken from the nurseries for planting at the age of 1 year. The tree is pyramidal in shape and attains a height of 25 to 50 feet. The tree begins bearing at 10 years of age. Upon distillation the fruits yield 1.5 per cent. of oil which is much used in flavoring liqueurs. The tree fruits twice annually.

CHAPTER XIX

TIMBERS AND WOODS

For the most part the general character of tropical forests is very different from that of forests in cold climates. One becomes accustomed to forests made up of one or two predominating species of trees with only an occasional bush or tree of another species scattered here and there through the otherwise almost pure stand. Some of the familiar combinations of trees are oak and chestnut, beech and maple, pine and hemlock, etc. Besides these mixed stands of only two predominant species we have the immense areas of white pine, fir, spruce, and other soft woods in which almost no other species of tree occurs. Tropical forests present a very different appearance. Most of these forests consist of a mixture of many species of trees. In some cases the forest is composed of several hundred species of trees, with no one species covering any part of the forest exclusively. The mixed nature of tropical forests has offered a considerable economic disadvantage to lumbermen in that they can not harvest areas continuously but must seek here and there for specimens of the particular kind of tree which they desire. Not all tropical forests, however, are of such a mixed nature. There are quite pure stands in large areas of teak, eucalyptus, Albizzia, wattle, candlenut, algaroba, oil palm, quebracho, ohia, etc.

So much has been written of the extremely hard and heavy woods which occur in tropical countries that a misconception as to the relative importance of heavy woods in the Tropics has taken root. It is quite absurd to suppose that all of the important tropical timbers are heavier than water, although

290

several of them will sink in water even after cured and many more are heavier than water in a green condition. To assume, however, that mahogany, ebony, and lignum vitæ are the really important timbers of the Tropics would be as ridiculous as to assert that black walnut, quartered oak, and curly maple are the most important timbers of the United States. Tropical timbers and woods are of great variety and of great importance. The few species which are imported to Europe and the United States give only the faintest idea of the extent and variety of tropical timbers.

At the outset it may be well to state that in the Tropics, just as in northern climates, soft-woods are of vastly wider extent and importance than hard woods.

The family Dipterocarpaceæ furnishes the most important timbers, especially in the Oriental Tropics. It is a large family with numerous species of trees which are universally used in tropical countries for general construction purposes. The sal tree (*Shorea robusta*) occurs in immense areas of almost pure stand in India. This tree is called guijo in the Philippines. It furnishes a hard and moderately heavy wood, used in ship building, houses, planks, carriages, and for numerous miscellaneous purposes. The eng tree (*Dipterocarpus grandiflorus*) of the Philippines, Borneo, and Malaya Peninsula, and called apitong in the Philippines, furnishes a fairly hard and heavy wood, used in heavy structural work, planks, railroad ties, and many other purposes. The sal and eng are only two examples chosen from the important trees of this family. There are more than 100 species of Dipterocarpaceæ which are used commercially in the Oriental Tropics.

The legume family is next in importance as a source of timber and wood and stands first in the production of woods for furniture and ornamental purposes. These woods are often highly colored and of good grain, and many of them are widely used for building purposes and for structural work. For example, *Acacia catechu*, besides yielding a cutch from the wood, is also used in farm implements and for railroad ties. Various species of Albizzia furnish excellent wood for houses, boat building, furniture, tea boxes, farm implements, bridges, etc. Golden shower (*Cassia fistula*), a smooth-bark tree, with drooping racemes of beautiful yellow flowers, furnishes a hard, heavy wood, gray or red in color, and brittle, but more durable in the soil than even teak. It is extensively used for fence posts, boat spars, carts, etc.

Rosewood (*Dalbergia latifolia*) is one of the famous leguminous trees of India. The wood is extremely hard and heavy. The heartwood is of a purple color with black streaks and with a rose-like odor. This tree furnishes the Indian rosewood or blackwood. Among the other Indian trees which produce rosewood, mention may be made of *D. sissoo* and *Pterocarpus indicus*. The Seychelles rosewood comes from *Thespesia populnea*, which is called "milo" in Hawaii. Brazil supplies a large part of the rosewood of commerce from the tree *D. nigra*. The grades of rosewood known as violet wood and king wood come from other related species of trees in South America and Madagascar. In fact, the rosewood of commerce is derived from more than 25 species of trees, of which *D. latifolia* is the best Indian species for cabinet and furniture purposes.

Andaman redwood, named from its origin in the Andaman Islands, is derived from *Pterocarpus dalbergioides*. This tree produces a red heartwood streaked with black and brown. The wood is extensively employed in the manufacture of furniture, door frames, balustrades, finishings of Pullman cars, and for other purposes.

The family Ebenaceæ is chiefly noted for furnishing the ebony of commerce. There are about 30 species in this family which produce ebony, the best grade coming from species of Diospyros, to which our common persimmon belongs. Ebony is very heavy, extremely hard, and of a black or dark greenish color streaked with black. Coramandel wood is a rare, variegated sort of ebony obtained from the tree *D. quæsita*. Ebony is used for canes, inlaying, fine cabinets and furniture, piano keys, violin keyboards, rulers, and other similar purposes. The wood is very fine-grained and does not warp. The ebony of commerce comes largely from India, Ceylon, Malaya, Java, the Philippines, Africa, and Mauritius.

Lignum vitæ (*Guaiacum officinale*) is a tree native to South America and the West Indies. This tree furnishes perhaps the heaviest of all woods. The fibers are much twisted and the color of the wood is dark brown with black streaks. It is extremely tough and is therefore used in the manufacture of bowling balls, rollers, propeller bushing, and for similar purposes. Lignum vitæ is becoming scarce and substitutes for it are much sought. Perhaps the best substitute for this wood is mancono (*Xanthostemon verdugonianus*) of the Philippines. Mancono wood is of about the same specific gravity and toughness as lignum vitæ and is even harder. Many other woods are also used as substitutes for lignum vitæ, especially *Calophyllum inophyllum* and *Dodonæa viscosa*.

Mahogany (*Swietenia mahogani*) is a tree native to Central America and South America. The tree was first brought to Europe by Spanish explorers. This and related species have been introduced into India and the Philippines, where they are cultivated to some extent. Mahogany is becoming so scarce that about 25 substitutes are in use to replace it. Mahogany is the most highly prized of cabinet woods. It is used for fine cabinet purposes, furniture, and piano cases, now mostly as a veneer. In the Philippines *Pterocarpus indicus* yields a wood which is called Philippine mahogany. This wood varies from straw color to blood red. The trees reach such size that planks 25 feet long and 6 feet wide have been obtained. It takes a high polish. Philippine mahogany is used extensively for cigar boxes.

Kauri pine (*Agathis robusta*), of New Zealand and Queensland, is a stately conifer 150 feet high, often with a fine bole

100 feet long. The tree is peculiarly free from defects of any kind. The kauri pine is the most important timber tree in New Zealand. The tree often reaches a diameter of 15 feet at the base. The lumber is extensively exported to Europe and is used for all kinds of building purposes, flooring, siding, paneling, doors, etc.

Karri (*Eucalyptus versicolor*) and jarrah (*E. marginata*), both native of Western Australia, attain such great size that huge planks of unusual width can be obtained from them. The wood is dark red, heavy, and hard. It is resistant to teredo and hence has been much used as piling. Karri and jarrah woods are also employed for paving blocks and heavy structural work. The Australian Government made a large exhibit of these woods at the Portland Exposition for the purpose of calling attention to their value and usefulness for various purposes.

Eucalyptus has been extensively planted in California where it was introduced in 1856. These trees are native of Australia, about 150 species being known. Of this number 75 species or more have been grown in California, but 90 per cent. of the eucalyptus in that State is blue gum (*Eucalyptus globulus*). Eucalyptus wood is used in California for fuel, piling, poles, railroad crossties, mine timbers, paving blocks, furniture, cooperage, tool handles, and for many other purposes. The strength and durability of the wood are quite satisfactory. The chief disadvantage of eucalyptus wood is that it warps and checks badly in the seasoning.

Sandalwood is obtained from *Santalum album* of India and Malaya and from related species which occur in Fiji, Hawaii, and elsewhere. These trees furnish the yellow or white sandalwood of commerce. In the early days of the Hawaiian Monarchy, the demand for this wood was so great that the tree was practically exterminated in the Territory. The sandalwood now has to be obtained from other sources in India and Malaya. It is used in inlaid work and for boxes, chests, fans, and for various other ornamental purposes. Sandalwood chests are greatly prized on account of their reputed immunity to insect attacks, and also on account of their aromatic and agreeable odor. Sandalwood is also used as a source of sandalwood oil (which is discussed under oils) and is burned for incense. For this purpose it is ground and mixed in a paste-like material used by the Chinese in the form of fumigating sticks. Various species of trees have been used as substitutes for the sandalwood, particularly *Exocarpus latifolia*, in the Philippines, *Erythroxylon monogymnum* in India, and *Ximenia americana* in South America.

Koa (*Acacia koa*), of Hawaii, is a tall leguminous tree with spreading crown and irregular, frequently conical trunk. The trunk of the koa tree is often 6 to 8 feet in diameter at the base but may taper rapidly to a relatively small diameter at the height of 20 feet. Koa is much sought for use in making furniture, cabinet cases, house finishing, canes, fancy boxes, and calabashes. It is exported to some extent to England and the United States but the trees are becoming scarce and the supply will hereafter be greatly limited unless efforts are made to cultivate the tree.

Satinwood (*Chloroxylon swietenia*) is a tree native to India and Ceylon, which furnishes a hard, very heavy, and durable wood of a pale yellow color, and with a decided sheen when smoothed. Satinwood is much used for general construction work and even for railroad ties in India. In Europe and the United States, however, satinwood is much sought for inlaying, borders, scrolls, backs of brushes, veneer in fine furniture and railway cars, and for similar uses. Another form of satinwood is obtained in the West Indies from species of Xanthoxylum.

West Indian cedar (*Cedrela odorata*), of the West Indies and South America, is a tall, handsome tree of the family Meliaceæ, with pinnate, opposite leaves and greenish-white flowers. The wood is of a brick red, blood red, or purple-red color. It is quite immune to attacks from insects. West Indian cedar is soft, fragrant, and easily worked. It is most extensively used for making cigar boxes, canoes, and paneling.

Ohia (*Metrosideros polymorpha*), of Hawaii, is a tall tree which occurs in pure stands on the mountain slopes of Hawaii. The trunks are angular and twisted, furnishing much difficulty in the saw mill and occasioning a large amount of waste in sawing up the logs for lumber. Ohia forests are particularly abundant in the Puna district of Hawaii and on the windward side of Maui. A serious disease of unknown origin caused the destruction of several thousand acres of ohia on Maui. On the Island of Hawaii large areas of ohia have been cut for the manufacture of flooring, paving blocks, and railroad ties. Experiments by one of the western railroads indicated that ohia ties were very satisfactory and 2,000,000 railroad ties were ordered on the strength of this experiment.

Teak wood is obtained from the well known tree *Tectona grandis*, native of Malabar, Java, Burma, Siam, the Philippines, and neighboring regions. This tree belongs to the verbena family. It bears large, ovate leaves and racemes of small white flowers. The heartwood is of a golden yellow color, turning brown, and finally black with age. Teak is the world's standard of ship-building timber. It is moderately hard and extremely useful for all kinds of purposes. Teak is the chief export of Burma and India, being used chiefly for decks of steamers, backing of armor plates, house building, and general carpentry work. The best teak is obtained from Malabar, that obtained from Java, Burma, and Siam being slightly inferior and lighter in color and weight. Teak wood is of medium hardness and possesses a characteristic scent which depends upon an oil in the wood. On account of the enormous demand from all parts of the world for teak wood, it has been found profitable to cultivate this tree as a forest crop. It adapts itself readily to cultivation and makes an excellent growth even on relatively poor soils.

Several species of trees yield a soft wood of peculiar physical properties resembling cork. Chief among these trees is kapok, *Bombax malabarica, Alstonia scholaris, Erythrina indica,* and species of Anona, Hibiscus, and Dyera. Cork obtained from the pith of so-called corkwood trees should be distinguished from true cork, as the term is ordinarily used, which is derived from the bark of the cork oak (*Quercus suber*). This tree occurs in largest areas in Portugal, Spain, and France. Various other tropical trees possess a bark which is suitable for use as cork. The world's cork production amounts to 2,500,000 pounds annually. Practically all of this material comes from Portugal, Spain, France, Italy, Tunis, Algeria, and Morocco. The commercial demand for cork is increasing.

An immense and rapidly increasing industry is developing in the utilization of vegetable ivory in manufacturing buttons. In discussing tropical agriculture we may therefore refer to the button crop as one of great importance. Vegetable ivory is obtained from a considerable number of palms, particularly the tagua palm (*Phytelaphus macrocarpa*) and about 20 other species belonging to the same genus. In addition to this group of tagua palms, a number of other species furnish a vegetable ivory of considerable value. Among these species is *Metroxylon vitiense*, a palm native to Fiji. The nuts from this tree furnish a vegetable ivory which comes on the market under the name Australian corozo. About 500,000 pounds of these nuts go to Europe annually. The nuts of *M. amicarum* are also used for the same purpose. Another palm, known as *Hyphœna thebaica,* yields Abyssinian corozo. This palm abounds in Nubia, Abyssinia, and desert parts of Africa and Asia Minor. It is sometimes called the king of the desert. The tree bears nuts 2 inches long and 1 inch broad from which good buttons are prepared, but the material is not so hard as the nuts of the other species mentioned above. In addition to these palms we may mention *Borassus flabelliformis, Raphia vinifera, Attalea funifera,* and *Corypha umbraculifera* as sources of vegetable ivory suitable for use in making buttons.

The use of the nuts of the tagua, or vegetable ivory palm, for the manufacture of buttons, dates back about 50 years, when this material first came into notice from nuts shipped out of Ecuador. After a few experiments with the hard kernel of these nuts, vegetable ivory sprang into great favor as a button material. The industry has rapidly increased in Ecuador until at present about 20,000 tons of vegetable ivory nuts are exported annually from Ecuador alone. Constantly increasing quantities are also being shipped from Colombia, Panama, and Central America. The tagua palm occurs chiefly near the sea coast from Panama to Peru, but is also found at elevations as high as 2,500 feet. The palm grows slowly, finally attaining a height of 10 to 20 feet or rarely 30 feet. The leaves resemble somewhat those of the coconut palm. The first flowers appear at the age of 3 or 4 years, the male and female inflorescence differing greatly in appearance. The male flowers appear in a cylindrical spike about 4 feet long, while the female flowers are grouped in a shorter cluster. The tagua palm bears the year round, flowers, immature, and mature fruits occurring on the plant at the same time. The fruit resulting from the female inflorescence is in the form of a large, spiny, spherical mass, containing 60 to 90 nuts in clusters of 5 or 6. The spiny burr-like covering of the fruit opens at the bottom when mature, allowing the nuts to fall out.

The kernel of the nut does not reach its maximum of hardness until the nut is completely mature. As a rule, therefore, the nuts are gathered from the ground, since, if the whole fruit were removed, some of the nuts would be found to be immature. The vegetable ivory palm begins bearing at 6 years of age and continues to bear merchantable nuts for 50 to 100 years. The ordinary price paid to the laborer who gathers the nuts is 50 cents per 100 pounds.

The United States occupies an important place in the manufacture of buttons from vegetable ivory. Of the 50,000,000 pounds of vegetable ivory nuts exported from South America annually, more than 27,000,000 pounds come to the United States. There are reported to be 23 button factories using this material in this country, the chief centers being Rochester, Brooklyn, Newark, and Springfield, Massachusetts.

The vegetable ivory nuts are somewhat flattened and about 2 inches in the longest, diameter. The vegetable ivory nut contains a small cavity and the tissue immediately surrounding the cavity is softer and more likely to show defects than the outer portion of the nut. A chip to be used for making buttons is sawed from either side of the nut and the rest of the material becomes waste. From vegetable ivory nuts, buttons are prepared varying in size from ¼ to 1¼ inches in diameter. The process of sawing, shaping, polishing and dyeing vegetable ivory buttons has been carefully developed in the button factories of the United States and the industry is constantly growing.

In the technical utilization of vegetable ivory for button manufacture it has been found that there is a shrinkage of 650 pounds per ton in drying the nuts and removing the shells. In sawing out the chips for use in button manufacture there is a waste from sawdust and cores of another 400 pounds. A ton of nuts, therefore, yields approximately 950 pounds of material available for making buttons. Recently efforts have been made to find a use for this waste material. Vegetable ivory sawdust has been used in Germany as an adulterant of coffee along with ground date seeds and other material. An analysis of vegetable ivory sawdust shows that it contains 10.6 per cent. of water, 1.95 per cent. ash, 0.96 per cent. fat, 3.28 per cent. protein, and 83.21 per cent. fiber and nitrogen-free extract. A test of this material as cattle feed at the Massachusetts Experiment Station indicated that it is fairly digestible and possesses some value as a feed.

This brief discussion of tropical timbers and woods has taken account merely of a few of the most important and interesting ones, particularly from the viewpoint of their utilization in the United States. As already indicated, the Tropics produce a very large number of trees of commercial importance. The Philippine forests alone contain more than 2,500 species of trees, of which at least 400 are used for economic purposes in Manila and elsewhere in the islands. Only 6 or 8 of these species, however, are really of great importance as commercial sources of timber and wood. The timber resources of our other tropical possessions are of much less importance. In Hawaii, practically the only export timber is obtained from ohia and koa, the sandalwood tree being practically exterminated.

CHAPTER XX

LEGUMES AND OTHER FORAGE PLANTS

LEGUMES occupy as important a place in the ration of the inhabitants and live stock of the Tropics and in the fertility of the tropical soils as is filled by these plants in northern climates. Many of the familiar legumes of the United States are found growing to some extent in most tropical countries, but the list of leading legumes in the Tropics is quite different from that of the United States. In tropical countries there is much greater predominance of leguminous trees and shrubs. Many of the large forest and ornamental trees are leguminous. One need only mention tamarind, Poinciana, algaroba, and the numerous species of Acacia, Cassia, Albizzia, and Pterocarpus, as well as the numerous shrubby and half-shrubby legumes of lesser economic importance.

A great variety of native grasses are used for various economic purposes in the Tropics. There are certain species of grasses, however, which have become of almost world-wide distribution, at least in tropical countries, and attention is given in this chapter chiefly to these important species of almost universal distribution rather than to the innumerable native species of grass which are locally utilized for grazing or forage purposes.

There is also a rather large list of miscellaneous forage plants and products which merit some attention. In the Oriental Tropics nothing is wasted. The American farmer has little conception of the painstaking economy of the Oriental. The strictest economy practiced by the most up-to-date American farmer would appear to the Oriental to be little less than sheer wanton wastefulness. No part or portion of any forage plant is allowed to go to waste in the Oriental Tropics. All this material is utilized either for human food, as feed for stock, or for some technical purpose, and ultimately every scrap of the by-product is returned to the soil as a source of fertility. All kinds of oil cakes, particularly those obtained from oil palm, coconut, peanut, soy bean, Para rubber, etc., are utilized for feed and for other purposes to the fullest extent. Moreover, such unpromising materials as sisal waste, obtained in the decortication of sisal fibers add to the list of forage materials. Then, too, there is the wide use of ti leaves, banana trunks and leaves, fern trunks, and even the trunks of the papaya tree. All of these materials furnish more or less valuable additions to the list of forage products.

LEGUMES

Of the various leguminous trees which have been utilized for commercial purposes in the Tropics, the algaroba is perhaps the most important. This tree, in the form in which it occurs in Hawaii, is commonly referred by botanists to *Prosopis juliflora*. Much difference in opinion prevails, however, as to the correct botanical name for the tree, and until this point is settled it may as well be known by the scientific name just mentioned. Algaroba is native to Central America and South America, and related forms are of wide occurrence in Arizona, New Mexico, and Texas, where at least two species are known under the common names mesquite and screw bean.

It is in Hawaii, however, that the representative tree of this group, known as algaroba, has attained its greatest significance. The tree reaches a height of 15 to 50 feet and a trunk diameter up to 30 inches. The cream-colored or pale yellow flowers are borne in slender axillary spikes or catkins. The leaves are bi-pinnate and the pods are linear or curved, 4 to 9 inches long, somewhat flattened but thick, and slightly constricted between the seeds. Both spiny and spineless forms of this tree occur and some indication has been obtained in Hawaii that the spineless condition is to a large extent hereditary.

Some idea of the ease with which this tree may be distributed may be gained by a brief consideration of its history in Hawaii. The tree was first brought to Hawaii in 1828 and the original tree still stands in the city of Honolulu. It has been propagated almost entirely by seed and for the most part without any attention to artificial distribution. The pods are a favorite food of all kinds of live stock and the seeds have been for the most part distributed through the agency of live stock. The pods possess a firm, fibrous covering which incloses a sugary pulp of molasses-like consistency in the center of which is embedded a row of seeds, each seed being inclosed in an extremely hard case. These seed cases are not digested by live stock but are merely softened somewhat by the digestive juices. The seeds, therefore, pass through cattle, horses, and pigs in excellent condition for germination. In fact, it has been found that the best method of planting algaroba seed consists in feeding the whole pods to cattle or horses and then planting the manure of these animals in places where it is desired to extend the distribution of the tree. In Hawaii, this tree shows by its distribution how effective a method of planting trees may be found in the natural wandering of live stock upon the range.

The tree thrives best at sea level in dry regions. Thus far it has not borne crops at altitudes above 2,000 feet. Moreover, the algaroba does not do well on the windward or rainy sides of the Pacific Islands. It will endure unusual droughts of long extent. It is not uncommon to see prickly pears and other drought-resistant plants wilt under the stress of severe drought, while algaroba maintains its foliage in good condition and appears not to be greatly affected. Most of the roots of this tree are shallow but a few of them run to great depths, sometimes 40 or 50 feet. The tree has been quite widely distributed in Australia, India, and the Philippines, but it has nowhere been so keenly appreciated as in Hawaii. For many years difficulties were experienced in grinding the algaroba pods. All kinds of special mills and drug mills were tested for this purpose without success. The sugary pulp surrounding the seeds sooner or later causes the accumulation of a hard gum upon the machinery and renders the operation of the machine impossible. The Hawaii Experiment Station gave considerable attention to this matter in the hope of finding a way by which the seed could be ground and thus make available the chief source of protein in the pods. Finally a very simple solution of the problem was found. If the pods be kiln-dried they can be readily ground by the ordinary alfalfa meal machine. If, on the other hand, a very fine spray of water is allowed to play upon the rollers during the operation of the machine, the algaroba beans can be readily ground without gumming the machinery. In the natural condition the molasses-like pulp is extremely sticky. When slightly moistened, however, or partly dried, the material offers little difficulty in grinding.

In Hawaii the algaroba occupies an area of 50,000 acres or more, occurring on all the islands of the Territory. As soon as methods for grinding the beans were devised a large industry sprang up in preparing this feed. The industry now amounts to about $400,000 annually. The two companies which are preparing algaroba feed offer about $10 a ton for the algaroba beans in the pod, picked and delivered by the roadside. This makes a considerable source of revenue to men, women, and children of the poorer classes. The ground algaroba feed gives excellent results in rations for cows, horses, mules, pigs, or chickens.

Recently some experiments have been carried on in using the ground material as a substitute for coffee. When the algaroba bean (and this term always means the whole pod, including the bean) is ground and roasted, the sugary pulp is caramelized and the material makes a fine and readily soluble substance of good flavor which can be used as a substitute for coffee. A company has recently been organized to put this material on the market.

Carob bean (*Ceratonia siliqua*) is another leguminous tree of much importance in tropical countries. It is a native of the Mediterranean region. Ordinarily it does not attain as great a size as the algaroba. The tree bears leathery pods 4 to 9 inches long and 1 inch wide. The dark green leaves are simply pinnate. The tree is extremely long-lived. From the age of 20 to 60 years each tree may be expected to bear 200 to 300 pounds of pods annually. The pulp of the pod contains 50 to 60 per cent. of sugar and this material is much used as a stock feed by the Arabs. It has long been imported into England under the name locust bean or St. John's bread. The pulp has also been used from the earliest antiquity as a human food and to some extent is made into a jam like tamarind. The carob bean has been introduced into California, where it appears to thrive well.

The pigeon pea, also sometimes called Porto Rican pea, on account of its wide use as human food among the Porto Ricans, is an erect and much branched legume which, if allowed to grow for several years, becomes semi-shrubby. Its botanical name is *Cajanus indicus* and the plant is native of India. It is now extensively cultivated throughout the Tropics. The green peas are used as human food in place of garden peas and in India the ripe peas are also used as human food. The ripe peas are favorite feed for chickens. For this purpose it is merely necessary to plant the chicken yard to this crop. The plants live as perennials and bear pods the year round which shed their peas so as to make an almost constant supply of feed for chickens. The plant is also useful at the same time as shade for poultry. Pigeon pea is also extensively used as a windbreak and as a green manure. The plant has been quite widely grown in Hawaii for the past 12 years. Exceptionally, it is allowed to grow for 8 to 10 years. It may attain a diameter of 8 inches, becoming almost a small tree. If not pruned back the plants readily reach a height of 10 feet within 2 years. It yields its first crop about 7 or 8 months from the time of planting. The pods are 2 or 3 inches long and ½ inch wide and contain 4 to 6 seeds. Many varieties of pigeon peas are known, varying in color from light yellow to black and many of them variously speckled. As a low hedge plant the pigeon pea is extremely valuable in tropical countries. When planted about gardens and pruned, it develops into a dense hedge somewhat resembling the privet hedge in general appearance. In this form it is useful chiefly in protecting young seedlings and delicate plants from the effects of the constant trade winds. It is possible to obtain a dense pigeon-pea hedge 2 or 3 feet in thickness and 3 to 6 feet in height. As a green manure plant it gives excellent results. For this purpose it is perhaps best planted broadcast or by drill, using about 2 bushels of seed per acre. The plants are readily plowed under after they attain a height of 2 or 3 feet and the vegetable substance promptly decays into a form available as plant food. The pigeon pea is fairly free from serious insect pests except the small blue butterfly, the caterpillars of which live in the pods.

Chick pea (*Cicer arietinum*), also native of India, is much more widely cultivated in the Tropics than in northern climates. It is commonly called garbanzo by the Porto Ricans and Mexicans who are particularly fond of the peas. In India, the chick pea is cultivated in large areas, especially for its seed, which is used as a stock feed and to some extent for adulterating coffee. The chick pea is an annual, attaining the height of 12 to 18 inches. The fuzzy pods contain only 1 or 2 peas.

The soy bean (*Glycine hispida*), a legume native to China and Japan, is a familiar crop in most of the Southern and Central States. The soy bean shows a great variety of form and habit of growth. Some varieties are raised exclusively for the bean, and these forms shed the most of their foliage before the beans are mature. Some of these dwarf forms do not stand higher than 8 to 10 inches. Other varieties are better adapted as forage plants and attain a height of 2 or 3 feet, some of them showing a trailing habit. In tropical countries the soy bean is raised chiefly for the production of soy-bean oil and soya sauce. The crop is widely cultivated by the Japanese in Hawaii, but the great local demand for soy beans by the soya sauce factories makes it necessary to import an additional 2,500,000 pounds of the beans annually. The dwarf early-maturing varieties produce from 600 to 1,000 pounds of beans per acre and the yield of the late, tall varieties is nearly twice as great.

The velvet bean is one of the favorite leguminous crops of the Tropics, several varieties being used particularly as a green manure crop. The velvet bean is now referred to the genus Stizolobium. In Hawaii a number of varieties of the velvet bean have proved to be satisfactory, particularly the Florida velvet bean, the Mauritius or Bengal bean, and the Lyon velvet bean. The last named variety comes from the Philippines, where the beans are much used as human food. They resemble Lima beans in appearance and flavor. As a green manuring crop the Lyon velvet bean has given perhaps the best results. It matures in about 165 days from planting and yields an immense crop of green material for plowing under. The crop is also used as a green feed or hay for cattle. It is little affected by serious insect pests.

In tropical countries, as in northern climates, alfalfa is one of the most important herbaceous legumes. It occupies a peculiarly important place in agriculture in the Tropics for the reason that the ordinary clovers, such as white, red, and alsike clovers, do not thrive well in tropical countries except at high altitudes. All the well known varieties of alfalfa have been grown in the Tropics. In general, Turkestan and Arabian alfalfa have given better results in point of yield and in quick growth after cutting than the common alfalfa. Alfalfa may be depended upon in tropical climates to yield a crop each month the year round. It is therefore not so necessary to cure the crop for hay as in cold climates, since it is possible to secure a continuous supply of green feed from a plantation of alfalfa. Under favorable conditions 13 crops have been obtained in 12 months.

It is particularly desirable in planting alfalfa in the Tropics to avoid infestation with dodder as far as possible. Dodder, like the alfalfa, of course, grows the year round and spreads with sufficient rapidity to be a very serious pest if once introduced into a field of alfalfa. While it is customary to harvest 10 to 13 crops of alfalfa per year in tropical climates, the total annual acre yield is not higher than is obtained in favorable localities in Arizona, New Mexico, and California.

If it were not for the unusually serious attacks of plant lice, to which cowpeas seem to be particularly susceptible, this crop would be perhaps the most valuable leguminous crop for forage and green manuring in most tropical countries. In some localities, however, the planting of cowpeas is a hazard on account of the frightful scourge of plant lice. A fine crop of cowpeas may be entirely destroyed in the course of 10 days. In some instances, the whole surface of the plants, stems, and leaves are completely covered with plant lice. Lady birds and parasitic insects multiply with great rapidity, but these natural enemies of the plant lice seldom succeed in destroying them before the cowpea crop is ruined.

In general, it has been found that the drier and warmer regions and seasons are best adapted to this crop and it should preferably be grown without irrigation. The largest yields of seed and forage are obtained when the crop is drilled in rows and well cultivated between the rows.

Jack bean (*Canavalia ensiformis*) is an annual, bushy legume, native to the West Indies and attaining a height of 2 to 5 feet. It bears handsome, purple flowers and sword-like pods 9 to 15 inches long and an inch or more wide, with about 12 large pure white beans in each pod. The beans bear a brown hilum. The jack bean is cultivated in the West Indies, southern United States, Java, Hawaii, and quite generally throughout the Tropics, chiefly as a green manuring crop. The jack bean is particularly well favored for growth in tropical countries on account of its hardiness and relative immunity to insect attacks. Plant lice seldom appear in injurious numbers on the jack bean. The plant yields from 16 to 20 tons of green forage per acre and about 1,200 pounds of seed. Usually only one crop is obtained from a single planting. In fact, the plant is considered an annual. Occasionally, however, a good rattoon crop has been obtained, particularly if the first cutting is made before the plants are mature. Jack bean is particularly valuable as a green manure crop for planting between rows of sugar cane, coffee, rubber, and sisal, where it can be plowed under as a source of plant food. The plant is quite strongly resistant to drought but is not equal to velvet beans in this regard. Perhaps the largest yields are obtained by planting the beans in rows 18 inches apart and 6 to 10 inches apart in the individual row.

The sword bean (*C. gladiata*) has often been grouped together with the jack bean, which it closely resembles. This plant is widely cultivated in tropical Asia, Africa, Hawaii, and generally in the Tropics. The plant closely resembles the jack bean, but the pods are somewhat shorter and wider and the beans are either red, gray, or white. The sword bean is somewhat used as a vegetable, the young, green pods and beans being employed for this purpose, especially in India, Ceylon, Burma, Japan, and Mauritius. Otherwise, the sword bean is chiefly used as a cover crop and as forage for cattle. For the latter purpose it is superior to the jack bean, which often possesses a bitter flavor.

Crotalaria, under various specific forms, occurs everywhere in the Tropics. One of these species is sunn hemp (*C. juncea*), which is discussed under fiber plants but is also much used as a cover crop. This is a slender, erect species, with conspicuous yellow flowers. One of the most important forms of Crotalaria for use as a green manure in Hawaii is *C. saltiana*, which has in recent years given a good account of itself for this purpose. This form of Crotalaria is unusually hardy. It thrives either in wet or dry districts. It will make a fairly good crop under a rainfall of 20 inches and thrives abundantly under a rainfall of 200 inches. The seed will germinate promptly without attention after scattering broadcast upon the soil. This Crotalaria is not useful for feed but is an exceptionally good green manuring crop. It is not attacked by insects, except the blue butterfly, which merely reduces the number of pods. The seed of the plant can be readily obtained by offering children 10 cents a pound for it. This species of Crotalaria has been recently used with pronounced success as a green manuring crop in Hawaii and elsewhere.

The kudzu bean (*Pueraria thunbergiana*) of Japan and China is quite hardy outside of the Tropics. It is a perennial legume with large starchy roots. The plants grow only a few feet during the first season, but may reach a length of 40 to 75 feet during the second year. It is propagated in Florida by cuttings or seed and is used as a cattle pasture and as an arbor vine. Moreover, in Japan a fine grade of starch is extracted from the roots for special use in confectionery. Kudzu bean yields a heavy crop of hay which contains about 17 per cent. of protein and 30 per cent. of carbohydrates.

The adzuki bean (*Phaseolus angularis*) of southeastern Asia is widely grown for human food in China, Japan, and

India. It is often cultivated in rotation between crops of rice. The adzuki bean is an erect, bushy legume 1 to 3 feet high. The yield averages 30 to 40 bushels of beans per acre.

Guar (*Cyamopsis tetragonoloba*) of the East Indies is an erect, single-stemmed or branching annual legume. It is used in India chiefly as a green feed for cattle, but the dry beans are also used in fattening cattle and the green beans as human food, especially in curries. Guar is extremely resistant to drought. It grows 3 to 6 feet high. This plant is cultivated to some extent in Oklahoma, Texas, California, and other Southern States.

Bonavist bean, also called lablab bean (*Dolichos lablab*), of India, is a vigorous, perennial, woody, climbing legume, with white, purple, or red flowers, flat pods, and white or black beans with a conspicuous hilum. The pods, together with the beans, are consumed as human food by the Orientals, especially during the young and tender stages. Lablab bean gives some promise as a hay and forage crop in Texas, Florida, and Cuba.

Kulthi (*D. biflorus*) of India is an annual running vine cultivated in India chiefly as human food and also for cattle. The dried beans are used as human food, while the hay is fed to cattle. As a forage crop this plant has given good results in Texas. In Hawaii the yield averages about 1,400 pounds of seed per acre.

Moth bean (*Phaseolus aconitifolius*) of India is an annual, densely branching legume about 18 inches tall, with a spread of 2 or 3 feet. The moth bean is grown in India for the dried beans which are used as human food. In the Panhandle district of Texas, this bean yields 2 tons of hay per acre, which, in most respects, has proved to be superior to cowpea hay.

The winged bean (*Psophocarpus tetragonolobus*) of Malaya is a vigorous, perennial climber with showy blue flowers and curious square pods 4 to 9 inches long. The green pods and beans are highly relished as human food in India. The plant is also cultivated in Burma for its large starchy roots.

Mungo bean (*Phaseolus mungo*) is a small, herbaceous legume native to India. It is now quite generally cultivated in tropical countries. There are many varieties of mungo, the seeds varying in color from red to yellow or green. The seeds are extremely small and are borne in slender pods. The plant is. erect or semi-erect in habit, attaining a height of 1 to 2 feet. Mungo beans are used in rotation between rice crops in Japan, where the seeds are also used in preparing a fondant for fine confectionery. The bean is also extensively used as human food in India. Moreover, in Hawaii, the mungo bean appears to be a promising crop.

A closely related species (*P. semierectus*) is coming into use in Hawaii as a green manure. This plant is a much branched creeper, bearing handsome dark purple flowers and long, slender, terete pods containing minute beans. Under favorable conditions it produces a large amount of vegetable substance and seems to have much value as a green manure crop.

GRASSES

Among the numerous grasses cultivated in tropical countries, a prominent place must be given to Para grass (*Panicum barbinode*), a native of South America. This species is commonly called Panicum grass in Hawaii, where it was introduced from Fiji in 1902, after which it became rapidly distributed over the Territory. Para grass is a coarse, long-stemmed grass which readily roots at the joints. It is widely cultivated throughout the Tropics as a forage grass and for this purpose is extremely valuable. After a planting has once been established it requires little or no attention, except to cut a crop at frequent intervals. It is not drought resistant, and therefore does not yield heavily in dry regions unless irrigation water is applied. The Para grass does not seed profusely and in many localities the seed seems to be sterile. For this reason it is almost universally propagated by sections of the long, jointed stems which strike root readily when planted in the soil. Para grass is not only valuable for green forage and hay but has recently been employed in Hawaii as a green manure crop. The pineapple growers have found that if segments of the stems of Para grass are scattered broadcast over a field of pineapples after the second rattoon crop of fruit has been removed, it is possible to cut up the pineapple leaves and plant the Para grass simultaneously by running over the field with a disk harrow heavily loaded. For forage purposes Para grass is commonly propagated by planting the sections of the stem a few inches apart in rows 1 to 2 feet apart.

The Guinea grass (*P. maximum*) is a related species, native to Africa, but of quite different habit of growth. This grass has become widely distributed throughout the West Indies and various other parts of the Tropics. It is readily propagated by seed or by division of the roots. The Guinea grass has an upright habit of growth and sometimes attains a height of 6 to 10 feet. Such coarse growth is run through a feed cutter before being used as a forage for cattle or horses. From 4 to 8 cuttings annually may be obtained. In propagating this grass by other methods than by seed it is customary to plant root divisions in rows 5 feet apart and about 2 feet apart in the row. The Guinea grass has the habit of a bunch grass.

Rhodes grass (*Chloris gayana*), of South Africa, is an extremely valuable hay grass in tropical and semi-tropical regions. For this purpose it is largely used not only in Africa but also in Australia, Hawaii, and various other tropical regions. A planting of Rhodes grass will yield satisfactory crops of hay for a period of 7 to 10 years, after which the planting must be renewed. Rhodes grass is extremely resistant to drought. It has an upright habit of growth, reaching a height of 2 to 5 feet. In newly planted fields the plants put out horizontal runners which may extend 6 to 8 feet from the parent plants. These runners root at the joints and thus aid the rapid extension of the plant. The stems of Rhodes grass are fine and the quality of hay appears to be excellent. The seed may be sown broadcast or preferably by drill. About 2 pounds of seed are required for an acre.

Natal red-top (*Tricholæna rosea*) is an erect, perennial grass with graceful, rose-pink, flowering panicles. When in full flowering it is one of the most beautiful of grass crops. Natal red-top is primarily a hay grass and does not withstand overgrazing. The grass will reach a height of 2 feet about 3 months from the time of seeding. The young growth is tender but old stems become tough and wiry. Unless the season is unusually dry, from 4 to 6 crops may be expected annually. On the Island of Kauai, Natal red-top has been found to be a very valuable grass when planted together with water grass.

Water grass (*Paspalum dilatatum*), a native of tropical America, is one of the most valuable and important grasses in tropical countries. It was introduced from Australia into Hawaii about 30 years ago, where it has become a favorite grazing grass on the cattle ranches. At sea level, especially on the leeward coasts of the islands in the trade-wind belt, water grass makes a good growth only during and following the rainy season. The best results are obtained from this grass in regions where the rainfall ranges from 60 to 120 inches annually. As a grazing grass it has given an excellent account of itself wherever it has been used. On the Island of Kauai, it has been found that water grass, planted at distances of 6 to 10 feet apart both ways in dense areas of the worthless Hilo grass (*P. conjugatum*), will crowd out and entirely displace the Hilo grass within 2 or 3 years.

The seed of the water grass is often of poor quality. In some tests only 25 per cent. or even less is capable of germination. For this reason it is necessary to use 6 to 10 pounds in seeding an acre. Moreover, a reasonable amount of moisture is necessary for the successful germination of the seed.

Bermuda grass is an extremely hardy, vigorous, and useful grass in tropical countries. In Hawaii, it was introduced in 1835 and now covers a larger area in the Territory than any other single species of grass. In Hawaii, the Bermuda grass is commonly known as manienie, from the Spaniard Marin, who is supposed to have introduced it. It is not valuable as a hay grass. In fact, it seldom reaches a height suitable for cutting. Thousands of acres of grazing land, however, would be practically barren if it were not for the Bermuda grass. Moreover, Bermuda grass is the only grass which has proved satisfactory for lawn purposes. It remains green the year round and is extremely sturdy in contesting the ground with weeds. On the Island of Lanai, 5,000 acres of wind-eroded soil was saved by planting Bermuda grass. This experiment was interesting as showing the great resistance of Bermuda grass to drought. The 5,000 acres of land had been eroded to a depth of several feet by the action of the fierce trade winds which continuously blow through the channel between Maui and Molokai. As a last resort, Bermuda grass was tried as a possible means of preventing further erosion. Sections of the stem of this grass were planted at distances of 8 feet apart both ways over the whole area. The rainfall in this region is extremely low and for a period of 2 years it was still doubtful whether the grass would grow. The whole area, however, is now completely covered with a dense mat of Bermuda grass serving as good grazing ground for cattle and sheep.

A large form of Bermuda grass which has been called giant Bermuda grass was recently found in Mississippi, and has been distributed from there to various tropical and subtropical countries. It is propagated in the same way as the ordinary form of Bermula grass, namely, by stem cuttings. Some stems of the giant Bermuda grass were received by the Hawaii Station and planted in a dry locality on the station grounds. The plant made an astonishingly rapid growth, throwing out runners 10 feet long within a period of 2 months. From this plat material was sent to several ranchers, who reported good results in both dry and wet districts.

Sudan grass during the past few years has become familiar to all readers of agricultural literature on account of the great promise which it has given, especially in the Southern States. This grass, as is generally known, is essentially a variety of Johnson grass but without its underground rootstock. It is native of Africa. The grass was made the subject of experiment at the Hawaii Experiment Station, where it grew to a height of 5 feet and began flowering within 55 days from seeding. The seed has been distributed to all of the islands and favorable reports have been received regarding it from all localities except those at considerable altitudes. Neither the Sudan grass nor the closely related Tunis grass appear to thrive well at high altitudes. The Sudan grass rattoons readily provided a reasonable amount of moisture is furnished. One of the difficulties of growing the grass for seed in the Tropics is the extreme fondness which birds show for this seed. Sudan grass grows to a height of 6 to 11 feet, but even the coarse stems of the rankest forms of the grass appear to be highly palatable to horses and cattle. The Tunis grass is a closely related variety, very similar to the Sudan grass, but it has a long narrow panicle.

MISCELLANEOUS FORAGE PLANTS

Mention has already been made at the beginning of this chapter of some of the miscellaneous plants and materials used for forage purposes in tropical countries. It might be well to give details regarding a few of these miscellaneous plants which are of special significance in certain tropical regions.

The prickly pear is familiar to all persons who have traveled in the southwestern part of the United States. The ordinary prickly form of this plant is not considered satisfactory as a cattle food until the spines have been burned off. Various methods have been devised in Arizona and elsewhere for economically burning off the spines. Several species of Opuntia, or prickly pear, occur in large areas in tropical countries. In parts of Australia the plant has become a veritable scourge and large rewards have been offered for a satisfactory means of eradicating it.

In Hawaii the prickly pear bears two forms of fruit—red and white. These fruit are of a rather agreeable flavor and are somewhat used as human food. It requires extreme care in preparing them for use, however, on account of the danger of getting the minute spines mixed with the fruit. The prickly pear is one of the important forage crops on some of the cattle ranches in Hawaii. There are about 3,000 acres of this plant on the Island of Maui, and 10,000 acres or more on the leeward side of Hawaii. Cattle and horses eat this cactus chiefly during the dry season when other feed is wanting. It is considered an emergency feed, but during the past 15 years two or three droughts have occurred in which cattle were maintained for several months almost exclusively on the prickly pear. All tender parts of the plants within reach of the cattle were eaten by them and it became necessary for the cowboys to cut off higher branches in order to save the cattle. The prickly pear in Hawaii is extremely spiny, but cattle and horses have learned to eat the plants apparently without harm.

Recently attention has been given to a smaller and almost spineless prickly pear which was introduced into Hawaii by Marin. This species attains a height of 6 to 8 feet and is densely branched. The slabs commonly have a length of 8 to

10 inches and a width of 3 to 4 inches. The species appears to be more resistant than the common spiny form of prickly pear. In a comparative test of Marin cactus, ordinary spiny prickly pear, and various varieties of Burbank spineless cactus on the Island of Kahoolawe, the Marin cactus was the only one which successfully established itself. Moreover, the Marin cactus, under ordinary conditions, grows 3 or 4 times as fast as the common forms of spineless cactus.

Honohono is the Hawaiian name for *Commelina nudiflora,* a succulent plant closely related to the common Tradescantia or wandering-jew. It grows as a weed in practically all of the rainy districts of the Territory. In fact, on some of the sugar plantations it has been found impossible to control or eradicate it by any other method than the use of a spray of arsenite of soda. Honohono has been found to be an extremely valuable feed for dairy cows. For this purpose it is perhaps most extensively utilized in the region about Glenwood on the Island of Hawaii. There are several thousand acres covered with honohono in that region. It has been found that the plant rattoons very promptly after cutting and that the yield is readily maintained, particularly if a light dressing of manure is applied immediately after cutting. In some experiments recently conducted in that section, it was found that 12 crops per year could be obtained, totaling a yield of 200 tons of green material per acre. Judged by its chemical composition, honohono is not particularly nutritious since it contains about 90 per cent. of water. It is an extremely valuable forage plant, however, in the section where it is used chiefly as a dairy feed, for the reason that most grasses, except perhaps Para grass, do not thrive well in the heavy rainfall of that district. The average rainfall of the district in question is about 250 inches per year. *C. benghalensis* is much used for the same purposes in Ceylon.

Rainy districts in the Tropics are noted for the immense and graceful tree ferns which develop under such conditions.

These ferns reach a height of 6 to 20 feet or more, rarely 50 feet, and a trunk diameter of 6 to 12 inches. These immense trunks are filled with a soft starchy pulp. An analysis of the common tree fern of Hawaii (*Cibotium chamissoi*) shows that the trunk contains 69.38 per cent. moisture, 1.12 per cent. protein, 4.23 per cent. sugar, and 20.9 per cent. starch.

In the region about the volcano Kilauea large forests of these tree ferns occur and in this region a rather novel use has been made of the trunks, particularly in feeding pigs. It was well known that the trunks were not particularly palatable in an uncooked condition. Large cooking vats were constructed and put in use for preparing this material as a hog feed. For a distance of 3 or 4 miles about the living crater of the volcano there are numerous cracks from which live steam issues constantly. It was soon found that by preparing a grill and placing it across one of these cracks the immense fern trunks could be placed upon the grill and allowed to remain until they were thoroughly cooked in live steam The value of fern roots as a pig feed is well understood in Oregon and Washington, where pigs are pastured on the large areas of cut-over lands in which the bracken fern grows profusely.

In all sugar-cane districts, cane tops or cane trash are an important source of forage. When the sticks of cane are cut and cleaned for the mill, the leaves and tips of the stems are cut off. This material contains 74.47 per cent. of water, 1.54 per cent. of protein, 0.42 per cent. of fat, 14.71 per cent. of nitrogen-free extract, 7.31 per cent. of fiber, and 1.55 per cent. of ash. The ratio of the weight of cane tops and cane trash to the weight of the sticks of cane has never been very accurately determined, and under different conditions varies considerably. It may be fairly estimated, however, that with a yield of 50 tons of cane per acre there are from 10 to 25 tons of cane tops and leaves. This indicates at once the enormous amount of forage material which is available in the neighborhood of sugar-cane plantations.

As already indicated in the chapter on sugar cane, all this material has been burned on many plantations, particularly in Hawaii. It is only recently that the frightful wastefulness of this practice has been realized. Cane tops and trash are now largely plowed under, but a vast amount of material is still available as stock feed. Cane tops or even the whole plant may be ensiled as easily as corn or any other common silage material. No difficulty is experienced in fermentation or spoiling if the material is handled properly in satisfactory silos. Cane silage develops no higher percentage of acid than corn silage. The material when properly fermented has a sweet-acid, and very agreeable flavor. The odor is not so unpleasant as that of corn silage. Cane tops or the whole cane may be made into silage by itself, or mixed with Para grass or other available materials. In Florida considerable attention has been given to this matter, and particularly with Japanese cane, a variety grown in Florida almost exclusively for forage purposes. Japanese cane is well adapted for use as a forage crop in all of the Gulf States. It has been found to furnish also satisfactory pasturage if stock are not allowed to remain in the field too late in the spring. In Florida, Japanese cane has proved to be one of the cheapest sources of silage. It may also be harvested and cured like corn fodder. It is most nutritious if allowed to stand until the danger of frost appears. The yield of Japanese cane in Florida has varied from 5 to 27 tons per acre.

Silos did not come into much use in the Tropics until quite recently. Their importance, however, is gradually increasing. In Hawaii, for example, many silos have been built the past 5 years. These silos are of various types, some of them being constructed of reënforced concrete, while others are in the form of pit silos. A great variety of material has been used for silage, including alfalfa, cowpeas, sorghum, corn, sweet potato vines, Para grass, various other grasses, and even prickly pear. On the Island of Lanai some success has been had in making a mixed silage composed of prickly pear and wild grasses. The slabs of the prickly pear furnished moisture and obviated the necessity of using water which would have been required if wild grasses had been used alone. During the process of fermentation it was found that the spines on the prickly pear softened and became flexible and leathery.

CHAPTER XXI

LIVE STOCK AND ANIMAL PRODUCTS IN THE TROPICS

THE live-stock industry of tropical countries differs in many respects from the same industry in cold climates. In general, live stock is of less commercial importance in tropical countries as compared with the values of plant products. While nearly all tropical countries abound in animals which are suitable for various domestic purposes, there has never been, until recently, any great organized effort to develop the various phases of live stock along commercial lines. Travelers who are familiar with the various improved breeds of live stock are ordinarily impressed rather unfavorably with the appearance of the domestic animals which they find in the Tropics. Many newcomers from cold climates believe that a great reform should be started in this matter and that this reform should at once involve the importation of superior sires of our improved breeds of stock for the improvement and breeding up of tropical live stock. Enthusiasm of this form, however, should not be allowed to carry one away to extreme measures, for the reason that the breeds of live stock now found in the Tropics have come about as a natural adjustment to tropical climates and are likely to withstand the climate and give a better account of themselves than would the improved breeds imported from cold climates. Numerous blunders have been made in the attempt at the wholesale and sudden reformation of the live stock industry of the Tropics. These blunders have invariably been expensive and discouraging. The common breeds of live stock when transported to tropical climates fall a prey to various diseases to

322

which they are highly susceptible, or are unable to thrive and yield a profit to the owners under the conditions of feed and pasturage which prevail in most tropical countries. In the improvement of animal industry in the Tropics, therefore, it is perhaps wise to proceed very slowly and to admit that perhaps one important reason for the existence of the present tropical breeds of cattle is their superior adaptability to the conditions under which they must live.

DAIRYING

It may be well to take Hawaii as an example of the conditions which must be met in carrying on the dairy industry in tropical climates. There are certain obvious advantages in such climates over cold climates. Green feed, for example, can be grown the year round. Alfalfa will mature a crop every month, and in unusually favorable years 13 crops may be grown per year. This furnishes, of course, an abundance of excellent green material for milk production. Alfalfa is by no means the only crop which may be grown for green feeding to dairy cows. Sorghums, Para grass, corn, and a great variety of forage grasses may be grown as soiling crops for dairy cows. In many localities it appears not to be necessary to produce hay in order to get fairly satisfactory results in milk yield.

In the neighborhood of sugar plantations, endless quantities of cane tops are available for green feed at the cutting season. At higher altitudes some of the smaller varieties of sugar cane, particularly the Japanese cane, may be grown specifically as a cattle feed. Sugar cane may be readily used as a silage crop and makes an excellent and palatable silage.

In the matter, therefore, of green fodder the advantage lies all with the Tropics as compared with cold climates. In almost every other respect, however, the Tropics are at a disadvantage in the matter of milk production. Cows give less milk in tropical climates. It is rare that cows of the best breeding give more than 5,000 pounds of milk per year in a tropical climate. The yield is more likely to be from 4 to 7 quarts per day. Moreover, all grains are higher in price than in cold climates and cultivation of the soil and the production of green crops are more expensive than is the case in any of the well known dairy districts of the United States. The prevalence of insect pests, particularly the horn fly, is another large disadvantage of the Tropics. The horn fly prevails in many tropical countries in numbers unheard of in the dairy sections of the mainland, and the constant annoyance of these pests helps to reduce the condition and the milk yields of dairy cows. In consequence of these various disadvantages, the cost of producing milk in the Tropics is considerably higher than in cold climates. The same tendency may be observed on the mainland of the United States, milk costing more and more as one proceeds from the North to the South. In Honolulu, for example, it is questionable whether the dairyman can make a reasonable profit on sanitary milk delivered to the consumer at a lower price than 15 cents per quart.

It must be remembered, however, that tropical countries do not depend for their milk upon the dairy breeds of cattle with which we are familiar. In fact, most of the milk used by the inhabitants of the Tropics does not come from the ordinary humpless, taurine cattle with which we are familiar. In India, Asia Minor, and Africa, milk is obtained from the zebu, the water buffalo, sheep, goat, and mare. The water buffalo, or carabao, as it is known in the Philippines, gives a large yield of milk of a fairly high fat content. In a number of localities, some effort has been made to improve the milking qualities of the buffalo by the ordinary methods of selective breeding. Considerable success has been achieved in this work. In Poona, India, for example, a strain of buffalo was obtained which yielded 40 quarts of milk per day of high fat content. Even with this enormous milk yield, however, the animals were not considered economic for commercial dairy purposes. Their feeding capacity was found to be far greater than their milk-yielding capacity and the cost of maintaining the animals on rations which would allow the continued production of high milk yield proved to be prohibitive.

The zebu yield, for the most part, 2 to 10 quarts of milk daily with a fat content of about 4.5 per cent. Hybrids between the zebu and taurine cattle sometimes give even less milk. In Egypt and quite generally in tropical Africa, the zebu is used as a work and draft animal and the milk which may be obtained is only a secondary consideration. Under such conditions, it would be unreasonable to expect any high milk yield. Little or no effort has ever been made to improve the milk-yielding capacity of the zebu for the reason, as just indicated, that this animal is everywhere considered of prime importance as a work animal. Throughout Egypt and tropical Africa also, goats' milk is widely used. Under tropical conditions, the milch goat yields from 3 to 5 quarts of milk per day. Goat milk is also extensively used in Cuba, Porto Rico, Central America, South America, Malta, Cyprus, southern Europe, Asia Minor, and quite generally throughout the Tropics. As is well known also, these animals are driven along the streets of the towns and milked before the door of the customer. The customer is thus assured of a perfectly fresh milk supply, but this method of delivering milk does not lend itself to the development of any large commercial dairy industry. In fact, there seems to be no such insistent demand for commercial dairying in the Tropics as in the colder climates; the per capita consumption of milk is less, and the modern extensive development of the condensed milk industry offers a fairly satisfactory milk supply at prices with which the dairymen in the Tropics could not compete.

BEEF CATTLE

The term cattle has been rather widely and loosely used by various writers in referring to the development of animal industry in the Tropics. The term is here used to mean the collective group of familiar breeds of beef cattle which form the basis of the commercial beef industry in the great beef-producing countries of America and Europe. The term cattle, as used in India, refers, of course, to the zebu or Brahmin cattle.

The almost universal presence of the zebu and buffalo in the Tropics and their great resistance to tropical diseases has made it seem unnecessary in many of the tropical countries to experiment with the breeds of humpless cattle with which we are familiar. Nevertheless, certain tropical countries have offered unusually favorable conditions for the commercial development of a beef cattle industry based upon the common beef breeds, such as Hereford, Shorthorn, Angus, Devon, etc. The cattle industry of Hawaii, for example, is fairly well developed. The largest ranch in the Territory is devoted chiefly to the production of Herefords, the manager of which has become a rather noted breeder. Another ranch has found greatest profit in raising Devons and has gradually built up a herd of pure-bred Devons of somewhat unusual merit. One or two other ranches have preferred to devote their energies to Shorthorns and have succeeded excellently well with this breed. According to the most recent statistics, the number of cattle in Brazil is about 9,000,000; in Mexico, 5,000,000; and in Uruguay, 8,000,000. Neither the zebu nor hybrid zebus have ever acquired any great importance in the cattle industry of South America. Fairly good representatives of the ordinary beef breeds of cattle are to be found throughout Central America, South America, and the West Indies. In the West Indies, however, most cattle contain some trace of zebu blood. From India, the zebu spread eastward through Siam and Cochin China to southern China and the Malay States and neighboring islands. It was also carried westward through Persia, Arabia, and all of tropical Africa. There are, therefore, very few taurine or humpless cattle in any of these countries. Apparent mixtures of the zebu and taurine cattle are found throughout tropical countries and these hybrid strains are probably of great antiquity. There have been frequent importations of taurine cattle also, particularly in recent years, into all parts of the Tropics and these animals have been used to some extent in crossing with the native races of zebus or hybrid zebus.

In the Belgian Congo, satisfactory results have recently been obtained from the introduction of Belgian and Brittany cattle. These animals were used for crossing on the native cattle and the hybrids show not only a remarkable degree of resistance to tropical diseases but a rather better form and milk-yielding capacity than those of the native cattle. Similar importations are being made into nearly all tropical countries in the attempt to improve the native strains of cattle. It should be remembered in connection with any discussion of the cattle industry of the Tropics that the inhabitants of the Tropics look upon cattle as work animals more than as a source of meat or milk. For this reason the demand for beef and milk in the tropical countries is immeasurably lower in proportion to the number of inhabitants than in cold climates. The Buddhist and Brahmin population are almost strictly vegetarian and consider their cattle as sacred. In India, therefore, aside from the British or other temporary residents, the Mohammedans are the chief meat eaters and they eat zebu, buffalo, camel, and other food animals.

ZEBU (*Bos Indicus*)

The zebu is readily distinguished from taurine cattle by the possession of a hump on the withers, usually drooping ears, and commonly a white ring around the fetlock. The zebu is also called Indian cattle, Indian ox, Brahmin cattle, sacred cattle of India, and by other names. The color of the zebu may be white, brindle, tawny, spotted with brown or black, dark with a bluish tinge, and of numerous other shades. There are all possible horn variations, even the condition of hornlessness. The zebu weighs up to 1,500 pounds. The milk yield in all cases is low. The zebu is readily crossed with taurine cattle and the hybrids are fertile.

The zebu and even hybrids, with no more than an eighth of zebu blood, have commonly been found to be immune to Texas fever. The hide is thick, the hair rather sparse, and cattle ticks do not readily attach themselves. For this reason importations of Brahmin cattle have been made in Texas, Florida, and elsewhere in the United States for the purpose of developing a strain of cattle immune to Texas fever. The zebu probably does not occur anywhere as a wild species. It has spread, however, throughout the Tropics in a bewildering variety of races—small, large, with large hump, almost without hump, and in almost endless color patterns. Many of these forms, as already indicated, are probably hybrids between the zebu and taurine cattle. The immense importance of the zebu in British India may be gathered from the fact that according to admittedly imperfect census returns there are at least 95,000,000 of these cattle in that country.

A pure strain of zebu was recently introduced into the Belgian Congo, where it was acclimatized without difficulty. In Persia, most "cattle" are zebus, although there are a few European cattle and hybrids to be seen occasionally. Arabian cattle are all zebus. In a strain of zebu near Aden, an unusually high milk yield has been developed. In India, there are very few cattle without humps. The zebus or Brahmin cattle are used for oxen in teams, as pack and riding animals, and for milk. In Ceylon, the zebu is used on freight wagons and farm implements. The zebu is also commonly used for

the same purpose in Burma, Sumatra, and Java. In Porto
Rico, nearly all cattle have some zebu blood and the same
should be said for Central America and West Indies, including
Cuba.

Throughout tropical Africa, from the Cape to Cairo, the
zebu prevails in a great variety of forms but is largely replaced by European cattle in Cape Colony. Some of these
forms are practically without hump, particularly the Egyptian cattle. In Madagascar, there are at least two well recognized races of zebu. In the French colonies of West Africa,
there are about 1,500,000 zebus and this animal is considered
of fundamental importance as a source of power for agricultural development. As a work animal the zebu has everywhere shown his superiority over taurine cattle, at least in
tropical countries. This is due not only to his greater resistance to tropical diseases but to a generally more perfect adaptation to tropical conditions. The zebu ox will keep in good
condition where the taurine ox will be miserably poor. The
zebu appears to be less nervous and stronger and more enduring, at least under tropical conditions. In Cuba, for example,
a special effort is being made at present to improve the size
and excellence of the work oxen of the country. Practically all heavy hauling, plowing, and other farm operations are
done by oxen. These oxen are crosses between the zebu and
Jerseys or other breeds of cattle. Their ability to do hard
work under varying tropical conditions is sufficiently attested
by the fact that practically every ox team in Cuba is in excellent physical condition.

Likewise in Porto Rico a determined effort has been made
to improve the native cattle by crossing with zebu blood. The
purpose of this work, as with similar work in Cuba, is to increase the working efficiency of the draft ox. Pure-bred
zebu sires were crossed upon Shorthorn, Hereford, and
Brahmin cows. The Shorthorn and Hereford blood appears
to broaden the frame of the hybrid somewhat and give more

depth of body. The Porto Rico Experiment Station has already obtained 300 head of progeny in these crossing experiments and has had opportunity to observe the habits and characters of the hybrid animals. In all cases the zebu appears to add constitutional vigor, active movement, strong bone, straight legs, and hard hoofs. The hybrids have been found to be almost completely immune to tick infestation and show a remarkable natural adaptation to tropical heat and short pasturage.

BUFFALO (*Bos Bubalus*)

The buffalo of India and the Oriental Tropics is now an important domesticated animal in Spain, Italy, southeastern Europe, Africa, India, Burma, the Philippine Islands, China, Formosa, Hawaii, and various Pacific Islands. The buffalo is a large powerful animal, weighing up to 2,000 pounds or more and standing about six feet high at the withers. The spread of the horns is often as much as six feet. The horns are flattened and curve upward and backward. The body is nearly hairless and of a bluish-black color. The buffalo, or carabao as they are called in the Philippines, are strong, slow, lazy, and willful. They do not endure cold weather or dry climate and must be maintained in the neighborhood of streams or standing water in which they may wallow. The buffalo is intimately associated with the rice industry. Horses and mules do not endure working in the mud as well as do the buffalo. In fact, the buffalo not only endures this sort of work, but appears to prefer working in the water and mud rather than on dry land The buffalo serves as a powerful work animal up to the age of 20 to 30 years.

Outside of the Buddhist and Brahmin communities, the buffalo meat is eaten, and while the meat of all buffalo oxen is reasonably tough, the flavor is not particularly unpleasant. The milk yield of the buffalo is larger than that of the zebu or other cattle under tropical conditions. The fat content of the milk is about 7½ per cent. and the casein nearly 6 per cent.

According to the most recent available statistics there are about 17,000,000 domesticated buffalo in British India. Many breeds have been developed in various localities, but none of these breeds varies in any pronounced manner from the wild form of the buffalo or from the general run of the domesticated forms. The buffalo was introduced from Italy into the Belgian Congo in 1911, but this importation was unfortunate on account of the prevalence of barbone, which disease carried off nearly all of the buffalo. In the Philippines and elsewhere, tremendous losses have been suffered from time to time from rinderpest. In 1902, for example, about 492,000 carabao died of rinderpest in the Philippine Islands. When it is remembered that this animal serves in the Philippines as the main source of power, meat, and milk, it may readily be understood that this outbreak of rinderpest was little less than a calamity.

The African buffalo (*Bos caffer*) has never been domesticated. The Indian buffalo, however, has been widely imported into Africa and has become a familiar work animal in that country. The gayal (*Bos frontalis*), a native of upland India and Indo-China, has been domesticated in the northeastern portions of India, Assam, and China. This animal is characterized by its short limbs, short horns, which stand almost straight out laterally, and extremely wide forehead between the horns. The milk yield is low but rich in fat. The milk has never been used very extensively but the meat is eaten, especially in Indo-China. The gayal is readily domesticated and makes a powerful ox but has not been widely used for work purposes. The color is usually brown but occasionally white. Crosses between the gayal and ordinary cattle are fertile. The gaur (*Bos gaurus*), a native of India, is perhaps the largest of all wild cattle. It is closely related to the gayal, which it somewhat resembles in appearance, but has never been domesticated. The banteng (*Bos sondaicus*) is a common work animal of Burma, Malaya, Borneo, Java, Sunda Islands, and neighboring countries. This ox is much like the gayal, but its horns are slenderer and rounder and are curved upward and back. The banteng is domesticated in largest numbers in Java, where it is extensively crossed with the zebu and other cattle. The banteng is an inferior draft animal but the meat is considered to be good.

HORSES AND MULES

The horse and mule industry has never in any tropical country attained the importance which it holds in temperate climates. This is due partly to the fact that horses and mules have been unable to resist some of the tropical diseases or the peculiar conditions of the tropical climate. On the other hand, in many parts of the Tropics, horses and mules are practically replaced for certain purposes by buffalo, zebu, camel, elephant, and more recently by the wide use of power machinery. In those parts of the Tropics, like Hawaii, where tropical animal diseases do not prevail, horses and mules may be reared and used under conditions practically identical with those which prevail on the mainland of the United States. On many of the sugar plantations, horse and mule power is extensively used where steam and gasoline power are not economically applied. The importance of the horse in the Tropics everywhere increases with the increasing control of the Tropics by the white man.

In the Belgian Congo, experiments with Senegal ponies indicate that this breed is well adapted for use in the Congo. The so-called Sandalwood pony of Java has also given a good account of itself in the Congo. Belgian horses have been used in the Belgian Congo for the production of mules but are considered too heavy for draft purposes. Russian horses, introduced into the Congo, have proved of great superiority for saddle purposes. In mule-breeding experiments in the Belgian Congo, it has been found that the Senegal jack is readily acclimatized, while with the Poitou and Italian jack, trouble was frequently experienced.

In the French colonies of western Africa, the horse is the most important animal for riding and driving. Arabian and Barb breeds are preferred. Horses are extensively bred throughout these French colonies, and a large percentage even of the natives in Senegal, Sudan, and Guinea are the proud owners of saddle horses. In Dahomey, on the other hand, the horse is not a common driving or riding animal. In the French West Africa colonies, the government has established studs and breeding stations at a number of convenient locations for the purpose of giving help and encouragement in the improvement of horses throughout the territory. Among the Sudanese, the ass is a symbol of captivity. The chiefs of these natives, therefore, never own jacks but many breeds of jacks are used by the common natives. Mules are generally popular and widely employed for work purposes throughout French Africa.

The thoroughbred horse originally came from the Arabian or Libyan native horse of northern Africa, and a similar type of horse prevails throughout Arabia, Turkey, Persia, and neighboring states. Not much success has been had with horses in southern India. In the native states further north, horses are a common sight, but are mostly of pony size and with Arabian blood. Ponies are extremely numerous in Bengal, the Federated Malay States, and Java. In Java, the favorite pony is the so-called Sandalwood pony. The horses of Borneo and the Philippine Islands are much like those in Java. In Madagascar, the horse apparently does not thrive well and the natives use oxen for the most part. In Mexico and Central America, the saddle type of horse is the one in greatest demand. In various parts of tropical South America, the horse is becoming a more and more important animal for work and pleasure uses, and in Brazil there is a quite unusual interest in horse breeding.

The African ass, the source of the domestic ass, still roams wild in various parts of Africa and quite generally in tropical countries it escapes and "goes wild" again. Mules are generally used in tropical America for work purposes but to a less extent in the African and Oriental Tropics. In the experience which has been had in the Tropics with mules, no reason has been developed for considering the mule more immune to diseases than is the horse.

Zebras have been tamed and bred in captivity and maintained as work animals in a number of tropical countries. Zebras are not susceptible to tsetse-fly disease and therefore give some promise of becoming work animals where the horse and mule are exterminated by tropical diseases. Zebroids, or the crosses between zebra stallions and mares, have been produced in a number of localities and have given good accounts of themselves. In making these crosses draft breeds of mares are used to produce work zebroids, and thoroughbred mares in the production of driving and riding zebroids. Thus far the most important breeding work in the production of zebroids has been done by Ewart in England and Baron de Parana in Brazil. The consensus of opinion of those who have had practical experience with zebroids is that these animals are very tractable, graceful, and of great endurance.

SWINE

Like the other familiar domestic animals of Europe and northern America, the hog in the Tropics shows an extremely irregular distribution, due to local conditions and customs. Throughout the Pacific and South Sea Islands, including Hawaii, and particularly in southern China and Brazil, the hog industry is an important one and pork constitutes a large feature of the diet. Elsewhere in the Tropics, the pig is a less familiar and less important animal. In Hawaii, the hog industry has been fairly well developed, particularly in the hands of the Chinese and Japanese who are extremely fond of pork. The breeds in most common use there are Berkshire, Duroc-Jersey, and Hampshire. Wild hogs are found in the islands and bring approximately as high a price as improved breeds. These wild hogs are, of course, merely the descendants of domesticated hogs which escaped and are taking care of themselves in the mountains. Pigs of Spanish breeds are found throughout French West Africa, but all hogs are, of course, taboo to all Semitic and Islamitic races in Africa or wherever they may occur.

The Chinese are constant pork eaters and the swine industry in China has been widely developed for ages. Certain breeds peculiar to China have been developed there, particularly in southern China, where a breed of white color is preferred. The hog industry has been extensively developed in the Island of Hainan, and Chinese pigs are also raised on a large scale in Sumatra, Java, and the Philippines. In Egypt, Tunis, and Algeria pigs are raised only by Europeans. In eastern Africa there is little development of the pig industry, except in Mozambique.

SHEEP

The sheep industry is far more important in some of the strictly tropical countries than is perhaps commonly supposed. In Hawaii, there are a number of ranches devoted chiefly to sheep, the most important breeds being Shropshire, Merino, and Tunis. On the Island of Molokai, considerable attention has been given to Tunis sheep on account of their adaptability to the local conditions and their somewhat unusual merit as mutton producers. On the Island of Lanai one or two types of Australian Merino have been tried with satisfactory results. The most serious disease from which sheep suffer in Hawaii is scab, and this is, of course, readily controlled by dipping. Horn flies and flesh flies give considerable trouble from their attacks upon wounds which sheep may receive.

The sheep industry of Brazil is an important part of the animal husbandry of that great country. There are now nearly 2,000,000 sheep in Brazil. The fat-rumped sheep are widely raised in the warmer parts of Asia Minor. In Turkestan and neighboring countries the broad-tailed sheep is a favorite breed. The caracul sheep is a race of broad-tailed sheep which is recently becoming popular in the United States for its mutton and for its fleece which resembles Persian lamb or Astrakhan wool. Mutton is the favorite meat of the Hindus and throughout India sheep are extensively raised. Most of them are small and resemble goats in appearance. Sheep are not important domestic animals in Indo-China, Malaya, Formosa, or the Philippines. In Egypt, on the other hand, the sheep industry is well developed. It has been found in Egypt that sheep furnish much help in keeping down weeds and grass along irrigation ditches, and in many localities they are raised primarily for this purpose and secondarily for their meat. Maned and broad-tailed sheep are quite commonly raised in Abyssinia and East Africa, while the Mauritanian and Macina breeds are found in considerable abundance in the French African colonies. In Central America and the West Indies, sheep are yielding their position to cattle and the sheep industry is therefore on the wane.

GOATS

Man has made use of goats since the dawn of history. They have constituted an important source of meat, milk, and hair for the production of certain fabrics in both tropical and subtropical countries. Hawaiian experiments with goats have been unfortunate. On account of their eminent ability to care for themselves in tropical countries they have escaped from domestication and run wild on most of the islands of the

Hawaiian group. On some of these islands, particularly Lanai and Kahoolawe, they have increased to such numbers as
to become a veritable pest, destroying grass and brush, and
greatly interfering with the growth of forests at higher altitudes. The destruction of vegetation by goats on these islands
has led to the development of semi-desert conditions under
which wind erosion takes place to an enormous extent. At
frequent intervals goat drives are organized by hunters for
the purpose of exterminating these wild goats. Some of the
drives have resulted in the capture and destruction of thousands of goats.

In the Philippines, there are but few goats and these are
raised for their milk. The goat is an important domestic
animal in almost all parts of Africa. Throughout Egypt the
goat is raised for both milk and fleece. The Angora goat
thrives excellently well in Algeria. The dwarf goat occurs in
the Sudan, and throughout Guinea, the Congo, Angola, and
East Africa the goat is a familiar domestic animal. The
goat is also an important animal in certain parts of Mexico
where it is raised both for milk and for fleece. In tropical
South America, the goat is of minor importance, except in
Brazil. Experiments with milch goats in the Belgian Congo
have thus far been rather unsatisfactory. They do not appear
to become acclimatized readily or to endure the heat of that
country.

CAMEL

The dromedary, one-humped, or Arabian camel is referred
by zoölogists to *Camelus dromedarius* and the Bactrian or
two-humped camel to *C. bactrianus*. The two forms, however, have repeatedly crossed and some authorities consider
them races of a single species. The camel will readily find
a living on brush, leaves, spiny salt bushes, and other coarse
plants of little use to other domestic animals. The camel does
not well endure a humid atmosphere but will endure excel-

lently well both extreme heat and the cold nights of the desert. As is well known, camels are chiefly used for riding and packing, the two-humped camel being used mostly for packing. A good riding camel will make a speed of five or six miles an hour with a reasonable rest at mid-day and will travel 16 out of the 24 hours, thus making 80 miles a day. In Egypt, it is customary to begin working the camel at the age of three years. He reaches full strength, however, only at six years when he may have attained a weight of 900 to 1,400 pounds. A mature camel will carry a pack of 200 to 400 pounds or even more.

The color of the Egyptian breeds of camel is brown, black, black and brown, or white. In the Cairo abattoir, camels are slaughtered in large numbers for human food. In the experience of this abattoir, it has been found that the dressed weight of camels is about 55 per cent. of the live weight. In Syria, the packload of camels is commonly 500 to 650 pounds. The ability of camels to go without water has been somewhat exaggerated. It has been found best to water them once a day and not to keep them continuously at hard work in hot weather for more than 48 hours at a stretch. In Arabia, camels are said to travel sometimes for five days without water.

The Bactrian camel is not used in Arabia, Syria, Palestine, or North Africa. In these countries, the dromedary or Arabian camel is the only breed to be seen. Statistics regarding the number of camels used for economic purposes are rather meager and incomplete. There are said to be about 2,000,000 camels in Somaliland. The camel is used extensively as a pack animal in the Island of Malta and in West Australia. In British India there are about 450,000 camels used for riding and packing.

An experiment was begun in 1856 in the use of camels in Texas and elsewhere in the southwestern part of the United States. The results were in every respect satisfactory but during the Civil War the camels were neglected and the experiment was allowed to lapse.

LLAMA AND ALPACA

These interesting cameloid ruminants of South America are commonly supposed to be domesticated races of the wild guanaco and vicuña. The alpaca is of more compact build and has a heavier coat of hair. The alpaca is mostly black in color, while the llama is commonly white with brown or black markings. The alpaca is considered decidedly of the more value and its long, fine, silky wool of metallic luster is much prized for use in certain fabrics. In 1914, the United States imported about 1,000,000 pounds of alpaca wool. The alpaca extends from the Equator to Cape Horn and the total production of alpaca hair amounts to several million pounds annually. Thus far all attempts to acclimatize the alpaca in Europe or Australia have failed. This animal is also used to some extent for meat.

The llama is the only native work animal of South America. The males are used as pack animals and are commonly made to carry from 80 to 90 pounds in the pack. The females are shorn for their wool which is decidedly inferior to that of the alpaca. Like the latter the llama is also used as a food animal.

ELEPHANT

Zoölogists distinguish between the African and Asiatic elephant. The male African elephant stands about 10 feet high at the withers at maturity and weighs 4 or 5 tons. The female is smaller than in the Asiatic species. The male Asiatic elephant is about 8 or 9 feet in height at the withers and weighs 2 or 3 tons.

The elephant becomes fully mature at about 25 years of age and lives to be 125 to 150 years old. He may be bred in captivity without great difficulty but most domesticated elephants have been caught young and tamed and trained. They have been used since the earliest times in war, in state processions, and for all kinds of labor. The elephant is an exceedingly clever and tractable work animal and his great strength makes him a very valuable source of power in lumbering and heavy freight operations.

The African elephant formerly existed in immense numbers but is now much reduced, largely for the reason that both males and females possess tusks and are killed for their ivory. In the Belgian Congo an elephant training station has been established at Api. The African elephant appears to be as easy to train as the Asiatic species. In domestication the African elephant stands about 7½ feet at the withers at the age of 15 years. No trouble has been experienced in the Congo in training them and they have proved eminently satisfactory for all kinds of work. In the Congo, elephants have been extensively used for carrying bunches of fruit of the oil palm to oil mills and for miscellaneous work. The exportation of ivory from the Ivory Coast, Sudan, Senegal, Guinea, and elsewhere is still of considerable proportions. Statistics on the number of elephants used for economic purposes are extremely fragmentary, but in Siam there are reported to be more than 3,000 elephants in domestication.

POULTRY

The jungle fowl, the wild ancestor of our chickens, occurs abundantly throughout India, Burma, Malaya, Indo-China, Java, the Philippine Islands, and neighboring tropical countries. Some or all of the various kinds of domestic poultry are raised in all tropical countries and most of the different kinds of poultry thrive fairly well in tropical climates.

In Hawaii, no unusual difficulties have been met with in raising chickens, ducks, geese, turkeys, guinea fowls, pea fowls, and pigeons. All of these kinds of poultry may and do escape from domestication into the woods. In this wild condition, they readily maintain themselves in considerable numbers and thus furnish sport in hunting. Wild turkeys, wild chickens, and wild pea fowls are quite commonly met with at the higher elevations on the Hawaiian Islands.

The so-called native breeds of chickens are small in most tropical countries, weighing up to about three pounds. Moreover, they are commonly of poor flavor, and the white settlers have everywhere carried with them into the Tropics improved breeds of poultry and with considerable success. All domestic ducks seem to have descended from the wild Mallard and musk ducks and are now found everywhere in the Tropics. Domestic geese came from the wild graylag goose of Europe and the Asiatic goose, and descendants of these two types are found in domestication in all parts of the Tropics. Apparent hybrids between these two types have been met with in India and Africa.

The guinea fowl is a native of Africa and readily makes itself at home in any part of the Tropics. The pea fowl is a native of Eastern Asia, particularly India, China, and the adjacent islands. It readily adapts itself to tropical conditions in all parts of the world and occurs in both a wild and domestic form in nearly all tropical countries. The turkey is a native of the United States, Mexico, and Central America, but has now been quite generally introduced into tropical countries, where it thrives excellently well.

OSTRICHES

There are at least three common species of ostriches in Africa, one characteristic of North Africa, a second of South Africa, and a third of Somaliland. The ostrich reaches a height of 6 to 7½ feet. In the wild state the female lays about 24 eggs. The ostrich industry is now carried on in the Transvaal, Cape Colony, Natal, Southwest Africa, Algeria, Tunis,

Egypt, Sudan, Madagascar, Australia, New Zealand, South America, and the United States.

Commercial ostrich farming began in Oudtshoorn, South Africa, in 1860. From this date on the industry increased rather rapidly, and at present Cape Colony has over 1,000,000 ostriches, Australia, 2,000, and the United States about 10,000 ostriches. The industry is important in the various other countries named above, but statistics on their numbers are wanting or unreliable.

South Africa in 1913 exported 1,023,000 pounds of ostrich feathers at a value of $14,000,000. In England, a campaign was started against ostrich farming on the ground that the plucking of the feathers was an act of cruelty. Ultimately, an antiplumage bill was passed in 1913 and at about the same time ostrich feathers began to go out of style in the United States. This country imported $6,250,000 worth of ostrich feathers in 1913, while the importation fell to the value of only $3,900,000 in 1914.

In the United States ostrich eggs are hatched almost entirely by artificial incubation, the incubation period being six weeks. About 95 per cent. of the eggs are fertile. In South Africa, the eggs are hatched chiefly by the parent birds, but also by incubators. The domestic habits of an ostrich family are quite interesting. Sometimes the hen ostrich sits on the eggs by day and the cock by night, while occasionally the cock does nearly all of the incubating. The cock ostrich is extremely pugnacious, even dangerously so, during the hatching season.

Ostriches begin breeding at the age of three or four years and continue to the age of 20 years or more. In Oudtshoorn, the common practice is to pull the first feathers at the age of 8 or 9 months. Six months later the primary feathers are cut off and two months later the quills of the cut feathers are pulled, thus giving three plumages in about 6 months and about one pound of feathers per bird.

Ostriches live to an age of 50 to 60 years. A great amount of breeding and selection work has been done with ostriches, especially in Cape Colony where fine breeding birds have brought as high as $4,000 a pair. An investigation of factors which influence quality of plumage has been carried on for many years in South Africa and a similar study is now under way in Arizona.

Alfalfa pasture or alfalfa hay has everywhere proved to be the best form of roughage for ostriches. A good ostrich ration contains about three pounds of alfalfa hay and five pounds of corn or barley per day. As is commonly known also, ostriches will eat all kinds of waste material. The egg yield under domestication varies from 30 to 100 eggs per year and the eggs weigh from 2½ to 4 pounds apiece. In South Africa, caponizing of ostriches has been practiced to some extent with the idea that capons would fight less and would thus not be so likely to injure their feathers. The meat of ostrich capons is frequently eaten and is said to be somewhat of a delicacy. Incidentally in connection with the study of domesticated ostriches, some of them have been trained for riding or driving, hitched to a sulky.

The South American ostrich, also called nandu or rhea, was at one time killed in large numbers and its feathers sent to the United States. Recently a beginning has been made in domesticating this bird as a source of valuable feathers. Among the other tropical birds which furnish articles of commerce, mention should be made of the marabou stork and the aigret heron, both of which may be readily domesticated but which for the most part have been hunted in the wild condition. In parts of western Africa, the aigret heron was hunted almost to extermination, while no effort was being put forth to raise them in domestication. The French are beginning to protect the aigret in their African colonies with the result that the numbers of these birds are rapidly increasing.

SILK

Among the useful insects which occur in tropical countries it may be worth while briefly to consider the silkworm, bees, the lac insect, and the cochineal insect. According to Chinese records, the silk industry originated in China about 2600 B. C. From China it passed over to Korea, Japan, Constantinople (550 A. D.), and then throughout the countries where silkworms are now raised. Both Chinese and Japanese use enormous quantities of silk and statistics on total production are not very reliable. In 1908, China produced 29,000,000 pounds of silk, Japan 25,000,000, India 10,000,000, the Levant, 5,-600,000, and Indo-China 2,400,000. The total world production for that year was about 77,000,000 pounds.

The total exports of silk from the producing countries is now about 60,000,000 pounds, of which Japan exports 26,-000,000, China 19,000,000, Italy 7,800,000, the Levant 5,000,-000, British India 220,000 and Indo-China, 33,000.

The United States imports about 25,000,000 pounds of silk annually. There is no likelihood, however, of the establishment of a commercial silk industry in the United States for the reason that hand labor is too expensive. The immense amount of hand work in silk culture makes cheap labor a necessity. Commercial silk production must therefore apparently be confined to regions where cheap labor is available, particularly China, Japan, Italy, and the Levant.

The silk moth lays 300 to 700 eggs and the life cycle occupies about 65 days for each generation. About 2,200 pounds of mulberry leaves are required for the growth of the worms which hatch from one ounce of eggs. This of itself indicates the enormous amount of hand work connected with the industry. Silk cocoons are gathered about 7 to 10 days after the beginning of the spinning. The length of the silk thread in a cocoon varies from 900 to 1,600 yards and cocoons commonly weigh at the rate of 155 to 320 to the pound. The

French, Belgians and Italians are introducing silk culture intó their tropical colonies in a serious manner, and it is to be expected that the production of raw silk will be greatly increased as the result of their efforts.

BEES

The Giant East Indian bee (*Apis dorsata*) occurs generally on the continent of Asia and the adjacent tropical islands, including the Philippines. This bee builds huge combs often four feet thick and six feet long attached to ledges of rocks or to the branches of trees. Perhaps the smallest species of honey bee is *A. florea,* a native of the East Indies. This species builds a comb only three or four inches across. The common bee of southern Asia is *A. indica.* It is kept for commercial purposes in crude hives in various parts of the East Indies. The brood comb of this species is much smaller than is that of our familiar honey bee.

· The common honey bee, *A. mellifica,* including the common German, Italian, Cyprian, Egyptian, Carniolan, Tunisian, and other breeds, is found everywhere in the Tropics and escapes by swarming to form nests in trees in other locations. The honey produced in tropical countries is largely used locally, while the wax goes into the world's commerce. Beeswax is an important industry in many parts of the Tropics, as is apparent from the fact that French Guinea and Senegal exports about 200,000 pounds of beeswax annually. The United States imports about 1,500,000 pounds of beeswax per year.

In Hawaii, a considerable development of the bee industry has taken place in recent years. The most important honey plant of the Territory is the algaroba which furnishes two crops of flowers annually. In all of the large forests of algaroba apiaries have been established at intervals so as to utilize the flowers most effectively. From Hawaii about 1,000 tons of honey are exported annually and also an excellent, very light colored beeswax in constantly increasing amounts. A similar development in apiculture has taken place in Porto Rico, where the industry began in 1900 and increased to such an extent that the exportation of beeswax was 18,000 pounds in 1914, while honey was exported to the value of $70,000.

SHELLAC

Shellac is a resinous secretion of scale insects (*Tachardia lacca* and related species), and is formed as a continuous incrustation on twigs infested with these insects. The material comes into commerce under a number of trade names. The term stick-lac is used in referring to the incrusted twigs removed from the tree without disturbing the incrustation of lac. Seed-lac is the term used for the granular lac scraped off from the twigs, while the term shellac is reserved for the pure lac melted and poured out on a cool surface in sheets.

The best lac is obtained from lac insects when living on *Schleichera trijuga* or on *Butea frondosa*. The latter tree is so familiarly known in this connection that in India it is called the lac tree.

The demand for lac is rapidly increasing. India produces about 15,000 tons annually, of which the United States uses about 6,000 tons. Shellac is used for a multitude of purposes, including electric insulation, gramophone records, sealing wax, polish for wood and metal, stiffening for hats, lithographic ink, in connection with the manufacture of painted pottery, and in innumerable other ways, especially in India. The industry is still largely in the hands of the natives of India and rights are sold to collect lac in government forests. The lac trees mentioned above are not the only ones upon which lac insects live. There is, in fact, a great variety of other trees upon which lac insects may produce a good quality of lac. The Department of Agriculture of India now gives instruction in the cultivation of lac, including the planting of special trees, the establishment of insect colonies on them, methods of pruning and scraping the lac, and other operations connected with the industry. At present there is a tendency, therefore, to make shellac production an agricultural industry rather than the mere haphazard collection of a wild by-product. The total output of shellac from India has an annual value of about $3,500,000 and a small shellac industry has been established in Ceylon. The average yield is about four to six pounds of stick-lac per tree.

COCHINEAL

The trade term cochineal signifies the bodies of a female scale insect known as *Pseudococcus cacti* which feeds on certain species of cactus. These insects were originally cultivated or cared for by the Indians of Mexico and Central America and were later introduced into the Canary Islands, Algeria, Java, Australia, and elsewhere. About 70,000 cochineal insects are required to make a pound of crude cochineal which yields 10 per cent. of pure dye. A few years ago the annual importation of cochineal into England from the Canary Islands amounted to 260,000 pounds, and in the eighties the United States imported 500,000 pounds of cochineal annually. The natural cochineal industry, however, like that of madder and indigo has been practically destroyed by the cheap aniline dyes manufactured in Germany. There is still quite an industry in cochineal, however, in Oaxaca, Mexico, among the Indians who maintain plantations of the Nopal cactus for this purpose. These Indians carefully preserve colonies of the cochineal insect and distribute them upon the cactus. In Teneriffe the insects are cultivated on *Opuntia ficus-indica.*

In harvesting this product the insects are scraped off, killed by plunging into hot water, and then dried. Cochineal is used not only as a pure dye but in the preparation of extremely valuable pigments other than the pure cochineal. For example, cochineal mixed with gelatinous alumina forms the pigment known as lake. Carmine is a brilliant scarlet pigment precipitated from cochineal decoction by acids or animal gelatin.

'APPENDIX

BOOKS AND PERIODICALS DEALING WITH TROPICAL AGRICULTURE

THERE is a large mass of literature dealing with the general field of tropical agriculture or with special phases of this subject. It is perhaps desirable to give a brief list containing some of the more important of these books, particularly for reference purposes on the general subjects, or on particular countries or special phases of tropical agriculture. As will appear in consulting the lists of books and periodicals given below, the English, French, and Dutch have contributed most largely to this subject.

REFERENCE BOOKS RELATING TO TROPICAL AGRICULTURE

Adams, F. U.—

> *Conquest of the Tropics.* Under this title the author has presented a general treatise on the banana industry, with especial reference to the part which the United Fruit Company has played in the development of the banana business. (New York: Doubleday, Page & Co., 1914.)

Belfort, R., and Hoyer, A. J.—

> *All about Coconuts.* The authors have presented perhaps the best general account of the coconut, with particular reference to the increasing and new industrial uses of coconuts. (London: St. Catherine Press, 1914.)

Boery, P.—

> *Les plantes oléagineuses.* The author gives an account of the oils obtained from coconut, olive, palm, peanut, castor bean, sesame, poppy, and other oil plants, particularly from the viewpoint of the technical utilization of these products. (Paris: Petite bibliotheque scientifique, 1888.)

Brannt, W. T.—

> *India Rubber, Gutta-percha, and Balata.* The volume is essentially a treatise on the botany, cultivation, and importance of these products, and deals with their industrial

349

treatment and uses. (Philadelphia: Henry, Carey, Baird & Co., 1900.)

Brown, E., and Hunter, H H.—

Planting in Uganda. On the basis of practical experience and study of agricultural conditions in Uganda, the authors give general advice to planters in this region and discuss particularly rubber, coffee, and cacao. (London: Longmans, Green & Co., 1913.)

Brown, H.—

Rubber: Its Sources, Cultivation, and Preparation. The various trees and other plants which yield rubber are thoroughly discussed in much detail. Particular attention is also given to an account of rubber latex and of the technical utilization of rubber. (London: J. Murray, 1914.)

Cameron, J.—

Firminger's Manual of Gardening for India. This volume contains much practical information on methods, especially adapted for gardening and fruit raising in India. (Calcutta: Thacker, Spink & Co., 1904.)

Capus, G., and Bois, D.—

Les produits coloniaux. The volume treats in particular detail of timbers, rubber, dyes, fibers, perfumes, drugs, and animal industry, especially ivory and feathers. (Paris: A. Colin, 1912.)

Chevalier, J. B. A.—

Les Vegétaux utiles de l'Afrique tropicale française; études scientifiques et agronomiques. A volume published in sections as material was accumulated by the researches of the author. It deals quite exhaustively with all the important vegetable products of the French tropical colonies. (Paris: Author, 1905-1913.)

Christy, C.—

African Rubber Industry. This is the best available discussion of the importance of the African rubber tree *Funtumia elastica.* The volume contains a thorough account of the botany, cultivation, yield, and uses of this tree. (London: J. Bale Sons and Danielson, 1911.)

Dudgeon, G. C.—

The Agricultural and Forest Products of British West Africa. This volume is arranged on a regional plan and contains summary accounts of agricultural conditions and important crops, such as cotton, other fiber plants, rubber, oil plants, etc., in the various regions of British West Africa. (London: J. Murray, 1911.)

Dybowski, J.—

Traité pratique de cultures tropicales. In this volume special emphasis is laid on tropical climate and methods of propagation of vegetables and fruits. Many details of particular use to tropical planters are included. (Paris: A. Challamel, 1902.)

Fawcett, W.—

The Banana: Its Cultivation, Distribution, and Commercial Uses. This book contains the most complete and authoritative account of the banana in all of its relations. It is particularly useful to the student in a study of the botany of the banana in its various forms and species. (London: Duckworth & Co., 1913.)

Foaden, G. P., and Fletcher, F.—

Text-book of Egyptian Agriculture. This two-volume treatise contains an account of the essential features of the agriculture of Egypt, with particular reference to soils, irrigation, cotton, and animal industry. (Cairo: National Printing Department, 1908-1910.)

Freeman, W. G., and Chandler, S. E.—

The World's Commercial Products. As indicated by the title, the authors have chosen to discuss in this form some of the chief products which enter into international commerce, including tropical products. Particular attention is given to sugar, coffee, tobacco, and oil plants. (Boston: Ginn & Co., 1907.)

Van Gorkom, K. W.—

Oost-Indische Cultures—edited by H. C. Prinsen-Geerligs. This is a large two-volume treatise on the important economic plants of Java and Sumatra. It is perhaps the most exhaustive and satisfactory account of the agricultural products of these islands. (Amsterdam: J. H. de Bussy, 1913.)

Haldane, R. C.—

Subtropical Cultivations and Climates. The author has brought together in this volume much information on tropical climate, starch foods, vegetable oils, fibers, drugs, tans, and dyes. These subjects are treated from the economic viewpoint of the utilization of the different products. (Edinburgh: W. Blackwood & Sons, 1886.)

Hanausek, E.—

Erdmann-Koenig's Grundriss der allgemeinen Warenkunde. This large volume deals in an encyclopedic manner with the chief agricultural products which have especial importance from an industrial viewpoint. (Leipzig: J. A. Barth, 1906.)

Heuze, G.—

Les plantes alimentaires des pays chauds. This is a small handy volume dealing largely with the essentials concerned in the production of cereals, legumes, fruits, and starchy foods in tropical countries. It is written chiefly from the viewpoint of the general reader. (Paris: Maison rustique, 1899.)

Johnson, W. H.—

The Cultivation and Preparation of Para Rubber. The author has presented a thorough and authoritative general account of the Para rubber tree, giving a detailed discussion of its distribution, method of planting, cultivation, and of methods of tapping and preparing the rubber. (London: C. Lockwood & Son, 1904.)

Jumelle, H.—

Les cultures coloniales. The author presents in this volume a rather elaborate account of starch foods, fruits, legumes, beverages, and spices, with particular reference to the extent of the cultivation of these crops in the French tropical colonies. (Paris: J. B. Baillière & Sons, 1913-1915.)

Kenny, J.—

Intensive Farming in India. In this book particular attention is devoted to fertilizers and the cultivation of rice, cotton, wheat, sugar cane, tobacco, tea, coffee, and coconuts. A discussion of agricultural associations is also given. (Madras: Higginbotham & Co., 1912.)

Lecomte, H.—

Le Vanillier. All the matters concerned with the cultivation, harvesting, fermentation, and sale of vanilla are here discussed in a thorough and authoritative manner with reference to the needs of both the planter and buyer. (Paris: C. Naud, 1902.)

Macmillan, H. F.—

A Handbook of Tropical Gardening and Planting. A general account of soils, climate, insect pests, fungous diseases, methods˅ of propagation and cultivation in Indian agriculture, particularly fruits, vegetables, windbreaks, cover crops and ornamentals. (Colombo: Cave & Co., 1914.)

Mukerji, N. G.—

Handbook of Indian Agriculture. The author has brought together a large mass of information, especially useful for the native planter and farmer in the cultivation, marketing, and economic utilization of all important crops in India. (Calcutta: Thacker, Spink & Co., 1907.)

Nicholls, H. A. A.— .

A Text-book of Tropical Agriculture. This is a small volume dealing in a general way with the more important tropical crops of international commerce. (London: Macmillan & Co., 1892.)

Olsson-Seffer, P.—

La agricoltura en varios paises tropicales y subtropicales. A two-volume treatise containing rather extensive accounts of important tropical crops with special reference to Mexico and Central America. (Mexico: Secretaria de Fomento, 1910.)

Reid, W. M.—

The Culture and Manufacture of Indigo. A thorough general account of the culture and utilization of indigo written at the time when this industry was of much greater importance than at present. (Calcutta: Thacker, Spink & Co., 1887.)

Ridley, H. N.—

Spices. In this volume the author has given the best available account of all the important tropical spices, including their botanical relationships, nature, culture, uses, and commercial importance. (London: Macmillan & Co., 1912.)

Rivière, C., and Lecq, H.—

Traité pratique d'agriculture pour le Nord de l'Afrique. The volume is devoted to the agriculture of northern Africa. It deals most exhaustively with soil, farm organization, forage plants, timbers, grapes, fibers, olives, and animal industry. The material is presented largely from the point of view of the tropical farmer. (Paris: A. Challamel, 1914.)

Sagot, P.—

Manuel pratique de cultures tropicales. In this volume the author has chosen for special emphasis a discussion of starch plants, cereals, forage plants, fruits, and animal industry, particularly camels and elephants. (Paris: A. Challamel, 1893-1897.)

Savariau, N.—

L'Agriculture au Dahomey. The volume treats particularly of starch foods, fruits, oil palm, fibers, and animal industry in Dahomey, particularly from the viewpoint of the prospective settler. (Paris: A. Challamel, 1906.)

Semler, H.—

Die tropische Agrikultur. A four-volume cyclopedia of tropical agriculture, dealing in a general way with the crops of all tropical countries. (Wismar: Hinstorff Hofbuchhandlung, 1886, 4 volumes.)

Simmonds, P. L.— .

Tropical Agriculture. A general descriptive account of the culture, preparation and use, and the commerce in more important tropical crops. The volume is written largely from the viewpoint of the general reader. (London: Spon, 1889.)

Torrey, J., and Manders, A. Staines.—

The Rubber Industry. This book contains the most important literary contributions to the rubber industry made at the London International Rubber Exhibition in 1911. Particular stress is laid upon the chemistry and utilization of rubber and upon rubber planting and the organization of plantations. (London: International Rubber Exhibition, 1911.)

Trabut, L., and Marés, R.—

L'Algerie Agricole en 1906. In this book the authors have discussed rather elaborately the cultivation and statistics of tobacco, fiber plants, garden crops, fruits, ornamentals, and animal industry in Algeria, particularly from the viewpoint of the prospective buyer of tropical products. (Algiers: Imprimerie algerienne, 1906.)

Wallace, R.—

Indian Agriculture. The author considered chiefly animal industry, native farm methods, rice, millets, forestry, and incidentally other less important agricultural crops. (Edinburgh: Oliver and Boyd, 1888.)

Watt, G.—

> *Dictionary of the Economic Plants of India.* An encyclopedic storehouse of information on the botany, importance, cultivation, and technical uses of all kinds of agricultural crops in India. (Calcutta: Govt. Printing Office, 1889-1896.)
>
> *The Commercial Products of India.* A condensed and revised form in one volume of the material contained in the dictionary of economic plants of India. (London: John Murray, 1908.)

de Wildeman, E.—

> *Les plantes tropicales de grande culture.* The author selected for thorough discussion coffee, cacao, kola nuts, vanilla, and bananas, giving in each case an account of cultural methods and an indication of the economic importance of the crop. (Brussels: A. Cartaigne, 1908.)

Willis, J. C.—

> *Agriculture in the Tropics.* This is a small handbook dealing chiefly with the peculiar agricultural conditions of India and the method of organizing agricultural operations on a large scale, with brief notes on some of the more important crops. (Cambridge: University Press, 1914.)

Woodrow, G. M.—

> *Gardening in the Tropics.* In this volume the garden crops, fruits, ornamentals, and incidentally other economic crops are treated from the viewpoint of the tropical farmer. The first edition considered only the conditions in India, but the revised edition is broadened in its point of view. (Paisley: A. Gardner, 1910.)

PERIODICALS RELATING TO TROPICAL AGRICULTURE

As will appear from the following list of periodicals, which deal for the most part exclusively with tropical agriculture, the number of such publications is quite large. It should be remembered that this list contains by no means all of such periodicals, but only those which may be of particular interest to students of the general subject. In addition to the periodicals listed below, one must remember that there are large numbers of journals in which tropical products are discussed along with other farm products. Such journals would include periodicals on paints, oils, perfumes, drugs, tans, dyes, fibers, etc.

Agricultural Bulletin of the Federated Malay States. Singapore. Monthly.

L'Agricoltura Coloniale. Florence, Italy. Bi-monthly.

Agricultural Journal of British East Africa. Nairobi and Mombasa. Quarterly.

Agricultural Journal of Egypt. Cairo. Irregular.

Agricultural Journal of India. Calcutta. Quarterly.

Agricultural Journal of the Companhia de Moçambique. Beira, Mozambique. Quarterly.

Agricultural Ledger. Calcutta. Irregular.

Agricultural News. Barbados. Semi-monthly.

L'Agriculture Pratique des Pays Chauds. Paris. Bi-monthly.

Agricultural Research Institute, Pusa, Bulletin. Calcutta. Irregular.

Agricultural Society of Trinidad and Tobago. Society paper. Irregular.

Agronomia. Boletin de la Estacion Agronomica de Puerto Bertoni. Puerto Bertoni, Paraguay. Monthly.

Annales du Jardin Botanique de Buitenzorg. Batavia and Leide, Java. Irregular.

Annual Report of the Agricultural Department. Sierra Leone.

Annual Report upon the Agricultural Department. Southern Nigeria.

Annual Report of the Agricultural Experimental Stations in Assam. Shillong.

Annual Report of Agricultural Stations in Charge of the Deputy Director of Agriculture, Bengal. Calcutta.

Annual Report on the Botanical, Forestry and Scientific Department, Uganda Protectorate. Entebbe.

Annual Report of the Camel Specialist (Punjab). Lahore, India.

Annual Report of the Cuban National Horticultural Society. Havana.

Annual Report of the Department of Agriculture, Bombay Presidency. Bombay.

Annual Report of the Department of Agriculture. Kingston, Jamaica.

Annual Report of the Department of Agriculture, Colony of Mauritius.

Annual Report of the Department of Agriculture, Uganda Protectorate. Entebbe.

Annual Report of the Director of Forestry of the Philippine Islands. Manila.

Annual Report on the Experimental Farms in the Bombay Presidency. Bombay.

Annual Progress Report on Forest Administration of the Lower Provinces of Bengal. Calcutta.

Annual Report of the Imperial Department of Agriculture (India). Calcutta.

Annual Report of the Superintendent of the Royal Botanic Gardens. Trinidad.

Annuaire Statistique de l'Egypte. Cairo.

Archief voor de Suiker-Industrie in Nederlandsch-Indië. Irregular.

Barbados Department of Agriculture. Report of the Sugar-Cane Experiments. Barbados. Irregular.

Board of Commissioners of Agriculture and Forestry, Territory of Hawaii. Biennial Report. Honolulu.

Boletín de Agricultura. San Salvador. Irregular.

Boletim da Agricultura. Sao Paulo, Brazil. Irregular.

Boletim da Directoria da Agricultura, Viaçao, Industria e Obras Publicas do Estado da Bahia. Bahia, Brazil. Monthly.

Boletín de la Direccion Fomento. Lima, Peru. Irregular.

Boletín de la Direccion General de Agricultura. Mexico City. Monthly.

Boletim do Instituto Agronomico. Sao Paulo. Irregular.

Boletin del Ministerio de Fomento. Caracas, Venezuela. Irregular.

Boletin Oficial de la Secretaria de Agricultura, Industria y Comercio. Habana, Cuba. Monthly.

Bulletin Agricole de l'Algérie, Tunisie, Maroc. Algiers. Semimonthly.

Bulletin de l'Association Cotonnière Coloniale. Paris. Irregular.

Bulletin of the Department of Agriculture. Kingston, Jamaica. Irregular.

Bulletin of the Department of Agriculture, Trinidad. Trinidad. Irregular.

Bulletin Economique de l'Indochine. Ha-Noi, Indo-China. Irregular.

Bulletin of the Imperial Institute (at South Kensington). London. Quarterly.

Bulletin de l'Institut Botanique de Buitenzorg. 'S Lands Plantentuin. Buitenzorg, Java. Irregular.

Bulletin van het Kolonial Museum te Haarlem. Amsterdam. Irregular.

Bulletin de l'Office Colonial. Melun, France. Monthly.

Bulletin Officiel de l'Etat Independant du Congo. Brussels. Irregular.

Bulletin of the Pan-American Union. Washington, D. C. Monthly.

Bulletin de la Société d' Horticulture de Tunisie. Tunis. Monthly.

Bulletin de la Station de Recherches Forestières du Nord de l'Afrique. Algiers. Irregular.

Cairo Scientific Journal. Alexandria. Monthly.

Cuba Agricola. Revista Mensual Organo de los Agricultores. Habana. Monthly.

The Cuba Magazine. Habana. Monthly.

Cuba Review. New York City. Monthly.

Cyprus Journal. Nicosia, Cyprus. Monthly.

Department of Agriculture, Bengal. Quarterly Journal.

Department of Agriculture, Bombay. Annual Reports.

Department of Agriculture, British East Africa. Annual Report. London.

Department of Agriculture. Federated Malay States Bulletin. Kuala Lumpur, F.M.S. Irregular.

Department of Agriculture, Fiji. Bulletin, Suva. Irregular.

Department of Agriculture in India. Bulletin. Bombay. Irregular.

Department of Agriculture. Mysore State Bulletin. Bangalore. Irregular.

Department of Agriculture, Punjab. Bulletin. Lahore. Irregular.

Department of Agriculture, Trinidad. Bulletin. Port-of-Spain. Irregular.

Estación Experimental Agronómica de Cuba. Boletin. Habana. Irregular.

Florida Agriculturist. DeLand, Fla. Weekly.

Florida Grower. Tampa, Fla. Weekly.

La Hacienda. Buffalo, N. Y. Monthly.

Hawaii Experiment Station Bulletin. Honolulu. Irregular.

Hawaiian Sugar Planters' Station. Bulletins. Honolulu. Irregular.

Imperial Department of Agriculture in India. Bulletin. Calcutta. Irregular.

Imperial Department of Agriculture for the West Indies. Reports. Barbados.

India Rubber World. New York City. Monthly.

Indian Forest Memoirs. Calcutta. Irregular.

Indian Tea Association. Pamphlets. Calcutta. Irregular.

Jaarboek van het Departement van Landbouw, Nijverheid en Handel in Nederlandsch-Indië. Batavia. Irregular.

Jaarverslag van het Proefstation voor de Java-Suikerindustrie. Soerabaia. Irregular.

Journal d'Agriculture Tropicale. Paris. Monthly.

Journal of the Board of Agriculture of British Guiana. Demerara. Quarterly.

Journal of the Jamaica Agricultural Society. Kingston, Jamaica. Monthly.

Journal of the Khedivial Agricultural Society and the School of Agriculture. Cairo, Egypt. Bi-monthly.

Liverpool University. Institute of Commercial Research in the Tropics. Quarterly Journal. Liverpool and London.

Louisiana Planter and Sugar Manufacturer. New Orleans, La. Weekly.

Mededeelingen uitgaande van het Departement van Landbouw. Batavia, Java. Irregular.

Mededeelingen van het Proefstation voor de Java-Suikerindustrie. Surabaya. Irregular.

Memoirs of the Department of Agriculture in India. Calcutta. Irregular.

Mémoirs Scientifique publiés par le Service de l'Agriculture du Ministère des Colonies. Royaume de Belgique. Brussels. Irregular.

Memoria presentada por el Director de Fomento. Lima, Peru. Irregular.

Moçambique Department of Agriculture, Lourenço Marques, Moçambique. Bulletin. Lourenço Marques. Irregular.

Nyasaland Department of Agriculture, Annual Report. Zomba.

Perfumery and Essential Oil Record. London. Monthly.

Philippine Agriculturist and Forester. Los Banos, P. I. Monthly.

Philippine Bureau of Agriculture. Bulletin. Department of the Interior. Manila. Irregular.

Philippine Journal of Science. Manila. Irregular.

Planting Opinion. Bangalore, India. Weekly.

Porto Rico Experiment Station Bulletin. Mayaguez. Irregular.

Porto Rico Progress. San Juan, P. R. Weekly.
Rapport Annual Station Agronomique, Mauritius. Mauritius.
Rapport Géneral de la Commission du Coton. Cairo, Egypt. Irregular.
Revista de Agricultura. Santo Domingo, W. I. Monthly.
Revista Industrial y Agricola de Tucumán. Tucumán, Argentina. Monthly.
Revue des Cultures Coloniales. Paris. Semi-monthly.
Rice Industry. Houston, Tex. Monthly.
Report of the Agricultural Department, Assam. Shillong.
Report of the Agricultural Department, Bengal. Calcutta.
Report of the Agricultural Work, Barbados. Barbados.
Report on the Aligarh Agricultural Station of the United Provinces of Agra and Oudh. Allahabad.
Report on the Cawnpore Agricultural Station in the United Provinces. Allahabad, India.
Report on the Experimental Work of the Sugar Experiment Station. Jamaica Board of Agriculture. Kingston, Jamaica.
Report of the Forest Surveys in India. Calcutta.
Spice Mill. New York City. Monthly.
Sugar Journal and Tropical Cultivator. Mackay, Queensland. Monthly.
Le Tabac. Paris. Monthly.
Tea and Coffee Trade Journal. New York City. Monthly.
Der Tropenpflanzer. Berlin. Monthly.
Tropical Agriculturist. Ceylon. Monthly.
Tropical Life. London. Monthly.
West Indian Bulletin. Barbados. Quarterly.

INDEX

Printed in Great Britain by
Amazon.co.uk, Ltd.,
Marston Gate.